Sorrow's Company

Also edited by DEWITT HENRY

The Ploughshares Reader: New Fiction for the Eighties
Other Sides of Silence: New Fiction from Ploughshares
Fathering Daughters: Reflections by Men (with James Alan McPherson)
Breaking into Print: Early Stories and Insights into Getting Published
   —A Ploughshares Anthology

Sorrow's Company

WRITERS ON LOSS AND GRIEF

Edited by
DeWitt Henry

BEACON PRESS, BOSTON

To my wife, Connie,
and to my children, Ruth and David

Beacon Press
25 Beacon Street
Boston, Massachusetts 02108-2892
www.beacon.org

Beacon Press books
are published under the auspices of
the Unitarian Universalist Association of Congregations.

05 04 03 02 01 00 8 7 6 5 4 3 2 1

This book is printed on acid-free paper that meets the uncoated paper
ANSI/NISO specifications for permanence as revised in 1992.

Text design by Preston Thomas
Composition by Wilsted & Taylor Publishing Services

LIBRARY OF CONGRESS CATALOGING-IN-PUBLICATION DATA
Sorrow's company : writers on loss and grief / edited by DeWitt Henry.
     p. cm.
   ISBN 0-8070-6236-7 (acid-free paper)
     1. Death—Literary collections.   2. Grief—Literary collections.   3. Loss
(Psychology)—Literary collections.   4. American literature.   5. English literature.
I. Henry, DeWitt.
PS595.D42 S67 2001
810.8'0355—dc21   00-057899

CONTENTS

How do we honor life? How do we love? How do we relate in sorrow?

Whether we are consciously grieving the loss of a loved one, being affected by the grief of loved ones, or confronting and contemplating our own mortality, the writers in this anthology speak for us all, expressing thoughts that lie too deep for tears. Writing at this level serves as a powerful ritual, which, if not taking the place of other rituals, then augments them and summons and creates kinship, as literature always has, across culture, space, and time. In dramatizing the act of the mind and heart in searching for value; in resisting denial, forgetfulness, and oblivion; and in honoring our common humanity, each essay adds to the vocabulary through which we may speak more truly to each other: "speak what we feel, not what we ought to say," as we are charged at the end of *King Lear.*

Too often we find ourselves at a loss for words in the face of death.

I think of those miscellaneous extras stricken dead and taken for granted, passing in a blur in that last action movie (did I even keep tally?), fictional deaths that flow by like lives and homes and towns from my subjective vantage on a speeding train, or in a car on the interstate. In motion, I am fixed and passive. Those lives out there for some moment are glimpsed, then blur, forgotten. And with no grief, memorials, or markers, I am myself, also, passing, gone. My train itself is speeding out of sight for those who have, perhaps, glimpsed me from their own subjective vantage points.

As in Robert Frost's poem "West-Running Brook," the current of our lives is unresisted, "save by some strange resistance in itself," protesting the very nature of flux, transcience, and loss. That resistance is "that in which we most see ourselves."

The America of my lifetime is a secular society. We have, in a pluralistic, relativistic world of different backgrounds, homogenized ourselves in terms of mass communications, commodities, and markets. In terms of families or communities, however, we are not as Americans have been and have imagined themselves to be historically.

We are not supported by our backgrounds. Our families are nuclear, at best; statistics tell us that most are broken by divorce or separation. Few of us stay, as adults, in the communities in which we have grown up. Throughout our lives we are on the move, displaced and replaced for education and for jobs, but also, in some deep pattern of deracination, seeking to escape our pasts and assert our independence, and only rarely seeking to create new worlds greater than the self.

In the process of reinventing lives, we are nonetheless riven with spritual longing. We experience the inevitable passages of living, each of us, as if for the first time, unsupported and unprepared. We may have abandoned community, family relations, and organized religion. We have forgone the rituals that somehow make public the private, and collective the personal.

Though her life as written seems exotic to me, Jamaica Kincaid's personal epic of leaving her impoverished island background in Antigua and reinventing herself as a writer in New York, and then as a wife and mother in Vermont, expresses that isolation with biblical finality.

In her memoir *My Brother,* Kincaid recounts being called back from her American life to Antigua and to her mother's house to attend her younger brother dying from AIDS. "What to make of it?" she asks, over and over. Kincaid is surprised and obsessed by her grief:

> death is like that (I can see); it happens every day, but when you see the mourners, they behave as if it were so new, this event, dying— someone you love dies—it has never happened before; it is so unexpected, so unfair, unique to you. . . . Why can't everybody just get used to it? People are born and they can't just go on and on, and if they can't go on and on, then they must go, but it is hard, so hard for the people left behind; it's so hard to see them go, as if it had never happened before, and so hard it could not happen to anyone else, no one but you can survive this kind of loss, seeing someone go, seeing them leave you behind; you don't want to go with them, you only don't want them to go.

Despite advances in medicine and science, both cancer and AIDS seem suddenly epidemic, striking down friends, colleagues, and family members, as children, as young adults, as adults in their prime, as randomly and unnaturally as if they were the civilian casualties of war. The death of his lover from AIDS occasions Mark Doty's powerful memoir *Heaven's Coast,* a contemporary chronicle of grief in the tradition of Tennyson's "In Memoriam." Doty alludes to the Book of Job and Job's refusal to submit: "Job's humanity lies in his no-saying. NO easy answer, no humble acceptance, NO—*I rage* against the excoriating process of loss in my life, I will not be silent in the face of it, I refuse to be quiet. . . . Silence is submission to the implacable order. For Job, silence equals the death of the self."

Poet Tess Gallagher speculates that American society in the millennium, beginning with the baby boom generations, is at last learning to grieve. Perhaps our national sentimentality was a collective denial of the abysses of World War II, the Holocaust and Hiroshima and the Cold War threats of nuclear annihilation. As Richard Yates wrote in his classic novel about the "good life" in the 1950s, *Revolutionary Road,* "It was invinceably cheerful, a toyland of white and pastel houses whose bright, uncurtained windows winked blandly through a dappling of green and yellow leaves. . . . A man running down these streets in desperate grief was indecently out of place." In my lifetime that sentimentality has been challenged by future shock, social and technological revolutions, ambigious war, and new and unforeseen plagues, as if these are the very perils of material power and privilege. Writes Gallagher, "America is, perhaps, a country almost ready to grieve, for the serious considerations and admissions, recognitions and healings of grief. I see the public and private reassessments of the Vietnam War as one of the recent signs of this new willingness and capacity" ("The Poem as a Reservoir for Grief," *American Poetry Review,* July–August 1984).

Certainly there is a remarkable preoccupation in recent literature, poetry, fiction, and nonfiction with confronting loss. Perhaps this is inevitable, given our preoccupation with memoir as literature, a preoccupation that is driven, I believe, by our search for a new sense of community—a community something like the "*Ukiyo*" envisioned by James Alan McPherson.

Deaths in My Life: A Personal Vocabulary

My first felt death was that of my father, when he was seventy and I was thirty-five. His death occurred at a physical and emotional distance from my adult life, without real warning, and no real goodbye, other than the cumulative good-byes, in health, of glad escapes from his closed horizons in suburban Philadelphia—the world of his own father, his boyhood, and his working and family life—and returns to my life in Boston, college, graduate school, and finally marriage and a teaching job. One day my mother called, with a strained, shaken voice, and told me he had gone into the hospital (where I had seen him only once, years before, after he had had a gall bladder attack, and he had laughed at my saucer eyes, as if I were seeing him on his deathbed). He had jaundice. My older brother Chuck, a surgeon in nearby New Jersey, was stopping by every day to look in on him. No need to be alarmed, no need to visit. You have your busy life, your teaching. He will be fine. And then she called again; he had to have an operation. And then, again: my oldest brother, Jack, was visiting from Colorado, and then Jack had gotten on the phone to say hello, and Dad was fine; he'd seen him and he was sallow skinned, but in good spirits. Jack returned to Colorado. Another call: Dad had come through the operation on his liver, but he was in a coma. No, don't come down. She was at his side, wanted to be there when he woke up. Some trouble now with his kidneys. The doctors said he was unconscious and couldn't feel pain, but he was crying out so loudly, the other patients were asking, "can't they give that man something?" And then the call: he'd died. Urine had gotten into his bloodstream and poisoned his brain. All within a week or ten days from the first call.

My wife, Connie, and I drove down for the funeral. There was no viewing. My mother said we wouldn't want to see him, the way his body was at the end. We filled their house—their retirement house—in Villanova, my next oldest sister, Judy, from Arizona, Jack (the oldest) from Colorado, Chuck (the middle oldest) from New Jersey, along with our spouses. My mother wanted only us, our nuclear family, not my aunts on my father's side. A limosine picked us up, a silent, stoic company, confused in loss as we had been in life between love and guilt, each of us somehow having wished him out of our lives, and out of our mother's. She had chosen the most expensive coffin and arranged for a graveside service with the Presbyterian minister because "he would have wanted it that way." No tears, at least on the outside. What I recall is silence and inexorability.

The grave was in a family plot, purchased originally by my father's father in West Laurel Hill, a fashionable Main Line cemetery.

We had been dragged here repeatedly as children and teenagers to put Easter flowers on my grandfather's broad stone at the head of the plot, which was engraved with my name (as the last of four children, and against my mother's wishes, I had been named after him). He had died in 1948, when I was seven; then in 1969 my grandmother had joined him, having spent her last years in a posh nursing home; and most recently my uncle John Spaeth, a spouse, had been buried in 1974. The plot was laid out with spaces reserved for descendants: first the head grave, then those for each of three children and their spouses, my father and his two younger sisters; then under those plots, graves for their children and their children's spouses.

What ritual there was felt foreign and offensive, a mockery, words by the minister about the Kingdom of Heaven, about dad as a loving husband and father, and then the coffin slowly cranked down. I remember, for all my irony, my disbelief, amounting almost to panic, that my father, so vivid to me always, was somehow in that casket. Alive, loved, troublesome, powerful; and that was him in there and being lowered into the earth. I couldn't believe that was him even though I knew it was.

I remember our returning home and eating, eating, eating ravenously. Halloween was only a day or so away, and perhaps our most genuine gesture, as bizarre and true as we felt we were, was while on some errand, on impulse to go into the local toy store, Halligans—a mecca at least of my own childhood—and buy clear plastic masks, the kind that eerily distort your features into Nixon's, say. We wore them driving back to Villanova, and laughed and laughed together as we tried on different faces for each other, my mother too.

Eight years later we gathered again at West Laurel Hill for my mother's funeral, on September 9, 1985. I was forty-four and my daughter, Ruth, conceived just months after my father's death, was seven.

My mother had lived a widow's life, alone all this time in the Villanova house. She had visited us two or three times in our Boston apartment after Ruth was born; then later we visited her with Ruth for several Christmases. "I know you know what loneliness is," she said to me once. She hadn't the energy to move or travel and make new friends. She did attend a Cornell class reunion and discover several classmates, with whom she corresponded.

We had nine months' warning, from her diagnosis with degenerative heart failure. The first episode had been on February 27. There had been a surprise midnight call from Chuck telling us she was okay—that she had gone into intensive care in the cardiac unit at Bryn Mawr Hospital. When we spoke to her, she said she had thought she had gone over, but she wasn't good enough. They'd thrown her back, like an undersized fish.

Connie and Ruth stayed with her for some nine weeks, while I came and went back to Boston and my job. My sister came and left. Jack came and left. Chuck came up from New Jersey as often as he could. But there were stretches, too, covered only by a live-in nurse (who smoked and otherwise got on Mom's nerves). We were there with Chuck, when he showed her the cardiologist's letter. She read the letter, then asked Chuck directly:

"How long do I have? Three months? Three years?"

He looked at her steadily: "Yes."

"Which?"

"Yes," he repeated.

Over spring and summer, we lived her decline and closure. As the disease progressed, as there were other episodes of hospitalization, a portable bottle of oxygen became a fixture, to be refilled from full-sized tanks as tall as she was, which were delivered by a medical service (all on Medicaid) and which stood like sentinels in a corner by her bed. She lived now in oxygen, with plastic nose clips.

She woke one morning I was there, feeling, she said, "like a girl, ready to get up and chase and spank babies. . . . "

One of the last last times (there were five or six), I drove back to Boston on the New York parkways, two in the morning, filled with the sense of losing her. I had the overpowering sense of her spiritual presence, that at this moment, this, as I drove, she had died; and feeling that so utterly, this was my time of weeping and farewell.

Chuck called at 5 A.M., first dawn, September 6, 1985, and said that she was gone.

She had asked to be cremated, a first in our family. Again we gathered at the West Laurel Hill plot. Judy and her husband, Hans, and the grandchildren John, Lucia, Bonnie; Jack and his wife, June, and the granddaughter Terry; Chuck and his wife, Nancy, and sons, Chuckie, Bob, and Scott; Connie, Ruth, and I; her sister, Janice, and Uncle Lloyd from New Hampshire. We each laid a yellow rose on the casket, which held the urn. Again the minister, a stranger to us; and again the graveside service: words so empty that they seemed like an offense.

She was Ruth's first death.

David Jung Min Henry, my adopted son, only an idea or hope at the time, which we had talked about with Mom, would be born some twelve thousand miles away in Korea one week later, September 15.

More deaths followed in my life, in Connie's, and in our children's. I think of a painting by my nephew John Friedericy, Judy's oldest son. There are in four rows, some sixteen heads, "the people in my life," he called it. His mother; his father; my mother; my father; his two sisters; his lover, Bruce; one of his older teachers; other best friends. Most of the faces look out at the viewer. But three, eyes closed and ashen, face left: they were the dead in his life at the time of his painting, including my father. John himself died of AIDS at age thirty-four, in 1990, after two years of treatment and decline. My sister and Hans had divorced shortly after Mom's death, and purportedly Hans had not condoned John's homosexual lifestyle. I saw John on my first visit ever to San Francisco, for a writer's convention, before he knew he had AIDS. Later, after he was ill, while visiting Judy in Los Angeles, their home for years, Connie flew out with David and

Ruth to see him. In one snapshot from that visit, John, mustached and balding, poses typically in my sister's backyard with a suction-tipped arrow dangling from his forehead, hamming the pose of either El Greco's crucifixation or the Temptation of St. Anthony or both, flanked by his mother in blue sunglasses and his lover, Bruce; Connie; and my children on the other side. He would in the two years to come be hospitalized repeatedly with pneumonia and be surrounded by his sisters, his mother, and his friends, as he grew weaker.

I did send him a good-bye letter, near the end, but before he was ready to accept it. I wrote him that I was grateful he and I had had our visit in San Francisco, "to catch up and rerelate and to be family and friends. I don't know how to say good-bye, or quite how to be normal under the shadow of good-bye, though I have lived it once, with your grandmother. . . . In your grammy's case, I felt she'd given me me, that I had her love to live up to. In yours, at this distance, you've given us your work, which is what you have been given to give, and says you. Your exuberance is there, your relish of life, your wit, as well as your puzzlement, anger, pain, and steady strength. . . . Our gain is having known you, and continuing to love and feel that essence that is you; our loss is missing you and missing your continued growing and experience and all that you would have given still, but have not been given to give. . . . In missing, or in getting ready to miss you, what I feel, John, is a debt."

He wrote back, thanking me for the letter, explaining that his doctor thought by the time John's tolerance for AZT wore off, that "there will surely be a new legalized treatment for me. . . . This combined with my strength makes me confident that I can stay ahead of the game. . . . They hope that AIDS will become something to be lived with, not cured, rather like diabetes." He was confident that "there are years (and maybe decades) left." Meanwhile he had his drawing, painting, and sculpture. "I don't think people die until their life's purpose is taken away from them—and I'm not ready to retire yet." He also described a collaboration with his oldest sister,

Lucia, making collector dolls. "The dolls are one of a kind, made of porcelain, and covered in beeswax. I sculpt the hands, feet, and heads, hollow and fire them, and then Lucia paints faces, dips them in beeswax, and creates the characters."

Four years after John died, I flew to Los Angeles to see Judy for the third time since our mother's funeral. She was fifty-nine; I was just turning fifty-three. I knew from phone conversations that she had continued in John's place to collaborate with Lucia and that Friedericy Dolls was now an established, thriving business. Also that she had dedicated herself for the past two years as a volunteer in a "buddy" relationship with a young girl, Jessica, who had been born with AIDS, and who would die before much longer. She wouldn't be in her Pasadena cottage to greet me when I arrived, but she told me the key would be in the mailbox. How strange to enter her intimate world, the shell of her living with the opening of that door.

Paintings filled nearly every available portion of wall, foyer, living room, dining room, bedroom. Mostly the paintings were John's, some original canvases I had seen in his San Francisco apartment, some I had seen only in slides and now was startled by in full size and richness of color. Other paintings I recognized as my mother's and Judy's. John's sculptures, too, occupied every available surface. Nudes, primarily female, were everywhere. Papier-mâché stylized birds of John's hung on wires from the ceiling. Startling dolls peered from tables, corners, chairs, in sizes ranging from twelve inches high to some thirty-six (a Don Quixote seated on a horse, Quixote's face resembling my brother Jack's, stood before the fireplace). As I waited for Judy, I told her later, I didn't feel alone. The house and its art told her silence over time, and told John's. The walls talked, the corners, every table, every square and cubic inch. John's art merged with my mother's, with Judy's, and with the dolls and sculptures that were Judy's and Lucia's. I felt as if death were no more than a continuum of absence in space and in time, like physical distances between the living.

Judy had a meeting of her "buddies" hospice group the next

night and took me along. After John's death, his lover, Bruce, who had infected him, attempted suicide by jumping off a roof, only to end up maimed. Judy had taken care of Bruce until his own death from AIDS. It seemed to me that out of her love for John, her mission was to immerse herself in the problems of the gay community, especially the AIDS community. Not to flinch, as Hans had done, and turn away, but to immerse herself. And in the Buddies meeting this night, she tried to comfort another Buddy, a librarian, who had just been told by the social worker in front of us that her buddy/girl had taken a turn for the worse and that the doctor had told her, the social worker, in medical confidence, that the girl would not recover and would die soon. The librarian had broken down in tears.

A spare bedroom was cluttered with archives of John's work as well as some incompleted mosaics and canvasses of her own. Within the creation of the house and its shown art, there was the so-called studio, where an archive of all John's sketches, notebooks, letters, and other papers were stored in flat art drawers. Also where unhung canvasses of his leaned against one wall, and where the entire original of a series of lithographs called "Heron Dance" was leaning on an easel ("I put up a new panel each week"). There were two mosaics messily in progress and abandoned on cluttered work tables. Of her own painting and sketching, the canvas propped on one of those tables that gripped me was indeed a self-portrait. "I did that after John died," she said. It was stark, all brown and white, a face contemplating suicide. Angry, empty, devastated, blank. The stunned, helpless, beyond howls and tears face of a Hiroshima survivor, or victim waiting for execution.

There was a nine- or twelve-inch doll on her dresser, in front of her mirror (a mirror stuffed with snapshots of family and friends and her buddy, Jessica) that I took for another self-portrait, though she said it was not. This was a life-worn woman lifted young and shining, if those are the words, arched somehow, all alive, enthralled, as if in exaltation out of her aging body and mortality, as if to greet the lost love found, the dead reborn.

I felt proud of my sister, who seemed to know more about the mysteries of grief than anyone in my life; and who, for me, embodied the triumph of love.

This book represents that spirit, in all of its complexity, and offers the best words of resistance I have found.

Essays as Ritual

The essays I have chosen for the opening section, "Leave-takings," commemorate in different ways last words to, from, and with the dying, while the essays themselves become in the fuller, public sense, words for the living. Debra Spark's farewell to a sister dying too young, as yet unmarried, childless. William Gibson's farewell to a mother at the close of a full life. Tess Gallagher's farewell to Raymond Carver, her husband, himself a writer, where writing and the living words of the long dead Chekhov become the medium of love. Rebecca McClanahan's farewell to an "other mother," who is not a blood relation. Ann Hood's farewell to an aged father, where the quest for a miracle to cure his cancer is itself the miracle, the rehearsal, and the enactment of love.

The essays in the second section, "Bereft," immerse us in the wound of loss. The survivors struggle with injustice, and with their powerlessness, as they contemplate the unbearable. Jamaica Kincaid fixes her blank and seemingly pitiless stare on the body of her brother. Similarly, Mark Doty insists on accuracy, on the physical evidence of death, as he describes the fading warmth in his dead lover's body: "[Language,] the instrument through which I look at that night . . . holds me at enough distance that I can describe what I see, that I can bear to look and to render, and yet it preserves the intimacy of those hours. That quality, their intimacy, is perhaps more firmly unassailable than any feeling I've ever known. I have never felt so far inside my life, and Wally's." In Jane Brox's "At Sea," the author waits in the hospital on deathwatch for her father with strangers facing similar calamities: "we were one family of the eleven waiting there . . . all on the same journey. . . . How strange it was to have lived day and night for a week with those people, and now to hug them one last time and leave them forever to their fates." Her larger embrace, of course, is in the writing now, including us as readers. Cheryl Strayed's grief takes the form of self-abuse, as she mimicks with her heroine addiction the cancer that has taken her mother. Gordon Livingston's diary entries chart his day-by-day "journey" of enduring, and surviving the hardest of injustices, the death of his six-year-old son, Lucas, from leukemia. Elsewhere in his book *Only Spring* (from which these entries are excerpted), he questions the very act of writing. "What will people think of my agony spread over these pages? How can other families of sick children take heart from what must seem like a hopeless story?" One such family tells him then that his writing "helped to recall us to the humanity of the world." Another father tells him "that his first reaction was to hug his healthy young son." He concludes: "If a few hearts can resonate with mine, perhaps we can share an understanding of what it means to love, to grieve, to be human. . . . Lucas evoked in me a capacity for love that I did not know I had."

Finally, in the last section, "Legacies," physical objects, ritual acts, memory, and imagination connect the living and the dead through passing time. Andre Dubus writes about investing his present-day act of making sandwiches for his two young daughters with a "sacramental" meaning, comparable to the remembered gestures of love between himself and his father, specifically the act of lighting a last cigarette for his father on his deathbed: "His eyes watching me light his cigarette were tender, and they were saying good-bye." At the hour of his distant father's death, Scott Russell Sanders uses woodworking tools inherited from his grandfather and father in carefully paneling a wall of his own family's house, an act that affirms the continuity of love. James Alan McPherson discovers reconnection to family, friends, and a still greater community of spirit at a time of his own life-threatening illness. Margot Livesey, displaced and cosmopolitan in her adulthood, revisits the literal landscape in which she was raised, seeking in memory the legacies of her Scottish childhood and in imagination the love of a mother who died when she was two and a half. Finally, literary critic Anatole Broyard, suffering from terminal cancer, draws strength from the legacies of the literature of illness, and in writing affirms his own legacy: "I want to write [my book]—to make sure I'll be alive when I die."

"Creative expression is healing," Beth Baker observes ("Mourning in America," *Common Boundary,* May/June 1999). "When we lose someone, we lose what they give us . . . taking on these functions ourselves or being open to new ways of finding them can . . . bring a new appreciation for life."

Similarly, Barbara M. Sourkes, a grief psychologist, writes, "Through words, the pain of loss is preserved. . . . Individuals who are facing their own death, and those who are bereaved, go through a process of converting presence into absence, actuality into memory. The dying patient hopes to leave his or her life intact and complete unto itself, while the bereaved gather shattered fragments into a fabric of wholeness. Both psychotherapy and poetry express, hold, preserve, and ultimately transform experience. The imprint of evidence endures through time" ("Witness Through Time," *Journal of Palliative Care,* 6:1 [1990]).

Each of these fifteen essays offer recognitions, for me, and I trust for readers like me. The writing, the act of attention so fairly, intently, and lovingly paid, reminds me to value the living, to rehearse the miracle of love, and never, never, ever to take a person, friend, lover, daughter, son, neighbor, colleague, student, for granted, though in living I must. Of course, Rebecca McClanahan in her essay reminds me that, too, there is "plenty not to love, and plenty left besides."

I am grateful to these writers for their eloquence, tenacity, and largeness of heart. This is a book radiant with life.

Leave-takings

REMEMBER

Remember me when I am gone away;

   Gone far away into the silent land;

   When you can no more hold me by the hand,

Nor I half turn to go, yet turning stay.

Remember me when no more day by day

   You tell me of our future that you plann'd:

   Only remember me; you understand

It will be late to counsel then or pray.

Yet if you should forget me for a while

   And afterwards remember, do not grieve:

   For if the darkness and corruption leave

   A vestige of the thoughts that once I had,

Better by far you should forget and smile

   Than that you should remember and be sad.

         —CHRISTINA GEORGINA ROSSETTI, 1830–1894

Last Things

My sister and I step briskly out of the greengrocer to get away from the men behind us in line who have told us, in great detail, what they'd like to do to us, where they intend to put certain parts of their bodies. The clerk, kindly, rings their purchases up slowly, so Cyndy and I have a chance to hurry across the street, almost bumping into two men who are breaking raw eggs in their hands and leaning over to slip the viscous mess into their mouths.

One of those Manhattan nights, I think.

Earlier today, as Cyndy and I were taxiing away from Grand Central to her apartment in Chelsea, we were thrilled, saying: "New York. It's so great. Look at the dirt! Look at the guy peeing in the alley! I love it!" A joke, sure, but only partially. We'd just spent a claustrophobic weekend with our parents and other two siblings in the Berkshires. The occasion, I guess, was Cyndy's mastectomy last week.

Cyndy's nerves are pretty much gone in the right side of her body, so the operation didn't hurt as much as the lumpectomy she had two years ago, when she was twenty-one. Still, I can't help thinking, Wound, especially now that we're out with the crazies. And also, I'm thinking of my own toes, which are so black and blue with cold (a circulatory problem, I will learn later in the month) that I am having trouble walking. Indeed, at the moment, I feel more damaged than Cyndy appears to. We shuffle by the guys with the eggs, and I put my right arm around Cyndy's back—companionably, I think, because I want to restore the playful order that has reigned most of today, that was operative when we were at New York City Opera, and I was meeting Cyndy's coworkers and admiring the Mr. Potato Head doll she had placed over her desk, presumably to supervise her efforts as rehearsals coordinator. My arm has barely touched Cyndy's black coat (the coat I will someday wear) when she says, vicious as possible, "Don't you *dare* try to protect me."

I am quiet—my throat, for a minute, as pained as my toes— and then I say, my voice strangulated, half the words swallowed, ". . . not trying . . . protect you."

Cyndy is dead, of course. That is why I wear her black coat now. She died of breast cancer at age twenty-six, a fact which I find unbelievable, a fact that is (virtually) statistically impossible. When she was twenty-one, she was in the shower in her dorm room at the University of Pennsylvania. She was washing under her arm when she found the lump. She was not checking for breast cancer. What college girl does monthly exams on her own breasts? Laura, my twin sister, says that I was the first person Cyndy called about the cancer. I don't think this is true, though Laura insists. I'm certain Cyndy called my father, the doctor, and that he told her to fly home to Boston. He demanded her return even though the doctors at Penn's health service pooh-poohed her concern. Finally, after a long conversation, I realize why Laura thinks Cyndy called me first and I tell her: "I think you're thinking about the rape."

"Oh, yeah," Laura says. "That's probably right."

———

When my father called me in Wisconsin to tell me about Cyndy, I said, "Oh, well, I'm sure, she's okay. Lots of women have fibrous breasts."

"No, Debra," my father said, sternly. "That's not what this is about."

"Do you think she'll have to have a biopsy?"

He was quiet.

"A mastectomy?"

"That's the least of my concerns."

I guess I wasn't quite able to hear him right then. I hung up the phone and pulled out my copy of *Our Bodies, Ourselves* to look at that book's photograph of a jubilant naked woman—out in the sun, with one breast gone, the stitches running up her chest like a sideways zipper. I remember wailing, literally wailing, at the image and at the prospect of my sister losing her breast.

I didn't know yet that my father had examined my sister when she came home from college. My father is an endocrinologist, a fertility specialist. He examines women every day in his office, but to feel your adult daughter's breast—breaking *that* taboo, because medical care is shoddy and you *do* love your daughter desperately and *appropriately*—and to know, right away, what it is you are feeling . . . I have to stop myself from imagining it. And I think my father has to disremember it, too, because even though he knew, right then, she had cancer, he tells this story about himself: When the x-ray of Cyndy's chest was up on the lightboard, my father pulled the x-ray off the board and turned it over to look at the name. "Spark, C." He looked back at the picture. Turned the x-ray over again to check the name. "Spark, C." He did the whole thing again. And again.

Later, two weeks before she did die, I remember seeing her x-ray up on a lightboard. Not something I was supposed to see, I know, but Cyndy's treatment all took place at the same hospital my father has worked for twenty-five years. I knew my way about and I knew how to take silent advantage when I needed to. I looked, but from a distance. I was out in the hall, standing over Cyndy in her gurney, as orderlies were about to move her out of the emergency ward and up to a floor. My view was oblique and once I knew there was nothing happy to see there, I said, Don't look. Though later, all I would do was say, Look, Debra. Look, this is a person dying. Look, this is Cyndy going away.

My mother was always the most pessimistic of all of us, and I used to hate her for it. "She'll be okay," I'd say. And, "We can't read the future." My mother said we were lucky we *couldn't* read the future or we'd never get through it. Which is probably true. That night in Manhattan, things seemed tragic but manageable. In the past was the lumpectomy and the radiation. Now, the mastectomy was completed. The chemo was to come. Cyndy had cut her hair short so the loss of it wouldn't be too upsetting. Back in Boston, she'd gone with my mother to buy a wig. Now, she was trying to wear it over her hair. That was the advice she had been given: to start wearing it so it would be like a new haircut and no one would notice. I thought, Who cares who notices? I was for announcing the illness as just another fact, among many, about Cyndy. To keep it secret was to imply that it was either shameful, like a sin, or special, like a surprise gift, and it was neither.

The wig bothered Cyndy. It was itchy and, though we'd tell her otherwise, it had a dowdy look, a look that owed nothing to the haircuts Cyndy had always had—the funky asymmetrical do she'd sported when she'd gone to London for a year or the long red mane she'd had as a child. One day, while I was still visiting with her in New York, we went out to lunch with some friends of mine who had never met Cyndy. In the middle of lunch, Cyndy, impatient and in the midst of a story (she was a magnificent and voluble talker), pulled off her hair—to my friends' surprise, especially since there was another head of hair under the one she'd pulled off.

After all the preparation for baldness, however, Cyndy's hair didn't fall out. At least, not that year. The first round of chemo was bad, but, again, in the realm of the get-overable. Every three or four weekends, my mother would come into New York and take Cyndy to the hospital and then out to my grandmother's house for a weekend of puking. Cyndy handled it well. The biggest long-term effect was that she wouldn't let anyone say the words "pot roast" when they were around her. And she couldn't stand the smell of toast for years to come.

Some time later, after Cyndy had finished up the chemo, she decided to go to business school, to get a degree in arts administration at UCLA. She loved school. She had never been too happy as an undergraduate, but UCLA was right for her. Her goal had been to make opera, which she adored, accessible to people who ordinarily wouldn't go. She had a special column in the school newspaper called "Kulture, Kulture, Kulture"; she was proud of her ability to drag business students (a surprise! stiff business students!) to the opera. I imagine Cyndy as the life of the party in those days. Cyndy going to the graduate-student beer bashes; Cyndy leading the talk at the business-school study sessions; Cyndy still earning her nickname "Symphony."

I know she slimmed down in those years, too. She had an intermittent problem with her weight, and it was probably the real clue that Cyndy—handle-everything-Cyndy—sometimes had her unhealthy way of handling things. When I visited Cyndy in Chelsea, after her mastectomy, we were toying with the idea of living together. At the time, I was profoundly (read "clinically") depressed. I had left the man I had been living with for four years and had been unenthusiastically debating what I should do next. Cyndy was moving up to Inwood, and we had found a small apartment that would accommodate the two of us should I decide to move with her. I remember that one of her real enthusiasms about the two of us living together had to do with food. She was convinced that I'd have her eating large green salads for dinner, that my own good habits would rub off on her, and she would no longer find herself in the middle of secret, ruinously upsetting food binges.

Cyndy had been a chubby kid, but never really fat, even when she weighed a lot. When she was older, her figure was sensual if robust. Still her weight was an occasional issue: my father telling her, at dinner, not to be a *chazar,* my mother spinning her own anxiety about weight onto Cyndy. At Cyndy's college graduation, Cyndy said "No, thank you" to the dessert tray that a waiter was offering our table. We were all too full. My mother said, "Oh, I'm so proud of you," to Cyndy. Cyndy said, "I'll have that chocolate cake," to the waiter. And the rest of the children—Laura, David, and I—hooted with laughter. It was our turn to be proud. After all, the request for cake was her version of "Oh, stop it, Mom."

Still, toward the end of Cyndy's stay in Chelsea, I got my first glimpse of how painful the problem with food could be. Like many women, I had my own issues, and Cyndy and I would often have long talks about what all this meant. Once, she told me about how she used to have a secret way of slipping cookies silently out of the cookie jar and hiding under a dining-room table to eat. This might have struck me as funny—so often our childhood stories charmed me—but I wanted to sob when she told me. I felt stricken but stricken by our—her, my, everybody's—desires. How easily they became desperate or grotesque or hateful, especially to the person who did all that desiring.

Her desires must have been met in L. A., however, because she looked so good. At the end of her first year there, she organized a student show, a big, campy celebration that everyone dressed for. She brought a videotape of the show back to Boston for the rest of us to see. Now, we fast-forward through the tape so we can see the intermission. Someone has filmed her—happy her—backstage exuberantly organizing things. Then we fast-forward again and there is Cyndy in a gorgeous, retro, off-the-shoulder dress. Her hair is long, just above her shoulders. She needs to flip it out of her eyes. She has long dangling earrings. She is glamorous by anyone's account and quite sexy. By this point, she's had reconstructive surgery. The new breast is lumpy and disappointing—not that anyone says this. It's just clear that when my uncle, the surgeon, said, "Sometimes they do such a good job you can't tell the difference," he wasn't one hundred percent correct. Part of the problem is that Cyndy, like all the women in the family, has large breasts. They couldn't reconstruct her breast so it would be as big as the original one, so she had a smaller breast made, and she wore a partial prosthesis. The doctors had asked her if she wanted the other breast reduced—for balance's sake. But she decided no. After all, she didn't want to run the risk of not having feeling in either breast.

In the videotape, when Cyndy starts to sing, the audience is clearly amazed. And they should be: her voice is stunning. She could have had an operatic career if she had wanted it. Months before her death, a singing instructor made it clear to Cyndy that she not only could, but she had to, have a singing career. Her voice was that beautiful.

Now, when I listen to the tape, I watch Cyndy's mannerisms. Each time, I am surprised by the fact that she seems a little nervous about performing. Cyndy nervous? Cyndy is never nervous, as she herself will admit. (Except about men. That's the one exception.) But she gets comfortable as she proceeds, as the audience's approval is clear. She sings, beautifully, the Carol King song "Way Over Yonder." *Way over yonder, that's where I'm bound.*

Even before she died, I knew the irony would always break my heart, once she was gone.

In the summer after Cyndy's first two semesters in L. A., I was living in Lincoln, Nebraska. I was teaching a summer class, and late at night, I'd get tearful calls from Cyndy. Mostly about men, for I was, in many things, Cyndy's confidante. Sometimes, now, I think that I am wrong about this. I *was* Cyndy's confidante, wasn't I? She *was* the person who I was closest to, wasn't she? When we were young, I always thought that Cyndy and I belonged together, and David and Laura belonged together. Laura always had a special way with David. Laura and I were close (the twins, after all), and Cyndy and David (the youngest) were playmates. Still, I felt Cyndy and I were a pair. When they met Cyndy, people used to say, "Oh, so she's your twin?" And I'd shake my head no. "Your older sister?" No, I'd say again. Cyndy loved being mistaken for my older sister. "I really am the smartest one in the family," she'd say, even when she was in her twenties. I'd have to disagree; it was a distinction I thought I deserved if by smart you meant (and Cyndy did) commonsensical.

Our closeness was somewhat competitive. We delighted in being competent—more competent than the one in the family who was spacey, the one who was overemotional. We just had things together, and we understood the world. The one fight I remember us having (I'm sure we had many when we were young, but I can't remember them) is about driving the car. She snapped at me for correcting her driving. She hated it when I played older sister.

When Cyndy first started making her tearful phone calls to me, I was proud. I took a secret pleasure in the fact that she confided in me, that she came to me first. I'd even felt a slight pleasure—mixed with my horror—when she called to tell me, and, at first, only me, that she'd been raped. It was during her first year at college. I was in my senior year at Yale. It was a date rape, I suppose, although that term doesn't fit exactly. The man was someone she met in a bar—a sailor, good God—and Cyndy got drunk and later, after some flirting, he didn't understand that no meant no. I honestly don't think he knew he raped her. I think for a while Cyndy was bewildered, too. Her previous sexual encounters had not amounted to much, and, later in college, her experiences remained disappointing.

Given her history, Cyndy's tears on the phone made sense to me. I thought she was finally addressing the issue that had always so frightened her. She spoke, with uncharacteristic frustration, of the way her women friends were always talking about *their* relationships, and she didn't have any relationships, and how upset it made her. With the encouragement of the family, Cyndy started talking to a therapist. I was all for this, I would tell Cyndy, as I sat late at night in my small rental in Nebraska. After all, I had been helped, enormously, by a psychiatrist. My parents agreed with my assessment,

I think, although Cyndy spent less of her time on the phone with them talking about men and more time talking about her headaches, her terrible headaches, that stopped her from getting any work done.

So, it's clear where this goes, no? We hope it's not, we hope it's not—as with each test or checkup we have hoped—but it is. Cyndy has cancer in her brain. When they do the initial radiation on her brain, and later when they do an experimental treatment that *does* shrink the tumor, it becomes clear that all that crying had a physiological base. Her tumor shrunk, her headaches go away. She stops crying or talking about men.

But, of course, she does cry, though only once, when she learns about the brain tumor. When I find out, I am standing in my kitchen and kneading bread. I get the call, and then I phone MIT to tell a friend of Laura's not to let her go to lunch. I want to come get her and take her to the hospital. I feel like a rock when I do all this, like a cold rock. I throw the dough in the trash and hear the *thump-swish* of it hitting the plastic bag. Then, I go and get Laura, who screams—as in bad movies, screams—and I drive to the hospital. Laura, instantly feeling everything, spins out of control with grief. She's sharp with nurses who seem to be blocking her way to Cyndy. She won't allow what my father says when he says it. She just tells him, No, no, you're wrong. She turns to me and says, Why aren't you acting like anything? And I think, Because I am so very competent.

In the fall, Cyndy comes and lives with me in my big apartment in North Cambridge. This is so clearly better than staying with my parents in their suburban home. She is immensely disappointed about having to take time off from UCLA. But it is only time off, we reassure her. She will get back there. And she does. After a year with me, she goes back for a semester. But she is too sick and has to come back to live with me for good. She lives with me for two years. This is the part that I'm glad I didn't get to see when I was in my Wisconsin apartment and worrying about the possibility of my sister having a mastectomy. I think now, A mastectomy! A lousy mastectomy! Who cares? I remember once, not long after I'd moved to Cambridge and before Cyndy moved in with me, I was in bed with a temporary lover. He was an old college friend, a doctor, in town to do some work for the year. Cyndy and I had been talking, earlier that day, over the phone, about men. I was encouraging her to approach a young man she was interested in, in L. A. She'd said, "But, it's so complicated. Like at what point do I say, 'Hey, buddy. One of these isn't real.'" I knew she'd be gesturing, even though we were on the phone, to her chest, pointing to first one, then the other. ("I can always tell," she'd said, "when someone knows and they're trying to figure out which one it is.") That night, in bed, I'd said to my friend, "Well, if you loved someone, it wouldn't make a difference . . . say, before you were involved . . . if you found out they had a mastectomy, would it?" He looked at me. "Yeah," he said. "I don't mean to be horrible, but of course it would."

"But," I said, as if he'd change his mind because I needed him to, "*I* said it wouldn't. That's what *I* said."

Cyndy and I had fun in the apartment where we lived. My boyfriend, Jim, would come by in the evenings, and they would talk music or we'd go out for dinner. Nights when Jim was working, we'd get George, a musician friend from around the corner, to come over. Cyndy took classes at Boston University. She worked for the Boston Opera Theatre. She got involved with a project involving musicians in Prague. Related to that, Vaclav Havel's press secretary and her son came to live with us for a while. And during all this, cancer would pop up in one place or another—her knees, the back of her tongue. Still, it always honestly seemed to me that we could make her better. Healthy denial, I suppose. Certainly, Cyndy had a lot of it. She was always willing to be cheered up, to imagine her future.

Some things stand out, but I can't (I won't) put them in order. Like: the number of times I would be in bed, making love with Jim, and hear Cyndy hacking away in the next room. That would be the cancer in her lungs.

Or the way she would call out to me each morning that Jim wasn't there: "Derba, Derba, Derba," she'd say, in a high-pitched silly voice. And I'd call back, "Der-ba Bird," because that was what she was, chirping out the family nickname for me. Then, I'd go crawl into her bed and rub her back. There was cancer in the spine by then, and she could never get comfortable. Sometimes, she'd wail at her pillows. She couldn't get them in the right position.

Or the way, one night, when I was making dinner, she said, "Oh, God," and I said, "What is it?" and she snapped, angry as could be, "You *know* what it is!"

There was an odd stretch when I felt her oncologist was trying to convince her that her symptoms were psychosomatic. Like when she couldn't get enough energy to move, and we'd spend days inside, only making an occasional trek to the back porch. Perhaps, he seemed to be suggesting, she was only depressed?

The few times Cyndy did snap at me, I felt like I would dissolve. My mother said, "Well, I guess you're getting a sense, before your time, of what it's like to have an adolescent." In truth, my mother got the brunt of it. When Cyndy was in the most pain, she would leave the apartment for a stay with my parents. When she was well enough, she would come back to stay with me. Wherever she was, though— my house, my parents' house—we were all there, all the time.

And even when she was doing relatively well, there were lots of visits back and forth. One day, in the beginning of her stay with me, Cyndy and I were driving out to our parents' house for dinner. We were talking about death, and Cyndy said, "Oh, well, you know, sometimes I think about death. And I try to force myself to imagine what it would be like but then I'm like . . . whoa . . . you know, I just can't do it."

"Yes," I said, for I knew exactly what she meant. "I'm like that, too."

Now I'm even more "like that." For if a parent's job is to protect his or her child, a sister's is to identify with her sibling. Which means, of course, that the whole family gets, in the case of a terminal illness, to fail in what they most want to do for one another. So I push my imagination to death, make myself think "no consciousness." I have, regretfully, no belief in heaven, an afterlife, reincarnation. I believe in nothingness. I try not to let myself pull back, try not to say, "Whoa, that's too much." But my brain—its gift to me— is that it won't let me do what I want.

I think, in this regard, of the time ten-year-old Cyndy came home from school in a snit. She'd learned about black holes in science class. She'd stomped up to her room and flopped on her bed. As she went, she ordered the family never to talk to her about black holes. I thought she was joking. So, I opened the door to her bedroom, stuck my head in—cartoon-fashion, the accordion player poking his head through the stage curtain to get a peek at the crowd—and I said, rapidly, "Black hole, black hole, black hole." Cyndy, already lying on her bed, threw herself against the mattress so that she bounced on it like a just-captured fish hitting land. She started to sob. "I'm sorry," I said. "I was kidding. I thought *you* were kidding." But why should she have been? What's more terrible than everything going out?

Once, during one of her final stays in the hospital, Cyndy said to my mother, "I'm going to be good now," as if that would make her healthy, as if a planet could blame itself for being in the wrong part of the universe.

"Oh, honey," my mother had said. "You *are* good. You are so *good.*"

One trip out to my parents that stands in my mind: Cyndy had the shingles, an enormously painful viral infection that runs along the nerve path on one side of the body. Just getting her down the staircase into my car was horrible. Cyndy was sobbing and sobbing, and ordinarily she didn't cry. I put her in the passenger's seat and cursed myself for having the kind of life that made me buy such an inexpensive and uncomfortable car. The requirement of bending was too much, and Cyndy wept and wept. I drove as fast as I could and neither of us talked. I thought, I'll just get her home and it will be all right. My father, the doctor, would know what to do. My mother would be, as she could be, the most comforting person in the world. When we got there, I said, "It's okay, it's going to be okay," as Cyndy walked, with tiny paces, from the car to the front steps. My parents were at the front door and it was night. My mother brought a kitchen chair to the front hall so as soon as Cyndy got up the stairs, she could sit down. I stood behind her, and my parents stood at the top of the six stairs that lead to our front door. My mother (blue turtleneck and jeans); my father (stooped). Both of them had their hands out and were reaching for Cyndy but they couldn't get her up the stairs. She had to do that herself. And I thought, looking at them in the light, and Cyndy still forcing herself up through the night— *Oh, my God. All this love, all this love can't do a thing.*

But that wasn't completely true. The love did do something. It just didn't save her.

Laura, my twin sister, gave Cyndy foot rubs and Cyndy loved them. Laura would give foot rubs, literally, for hours. I gave back rubs but I never liked giving them, would wait for Cyndy to say I could stop. When Cyndy told Laura she could stop if she wanted to, Laura would ask for permission to keep going—as if Cyndy were doing her a favor by putting her feet in the vicinity of Laura's hands. One day, Cyndy was lying on her bed in our apartment and Laura was on a chair at the end of the bed and she was rubbing Cyndy's feet. I was "spooning" Cyndy and occasionally rubbing up and down her spine where the cancer was. We were talking about masturbation. "I can't believe you guys," Laura was saying, telling us again about how amazing it was that, of the three of us, she had discovered masturbation first. We were giggling. This conversation wasn't unfamiliar. We'd had it before, but we could always find something new to tell each other.

"What was that bathtub thing you were talking about?" Cyndy said.

Years earlier, I'd instructed both of my sisters about the virtues of masturbating in the bathtub. Something I'd learned from my freshman-year roommate at college. "Got to try it," I said now.

"Exactly how do you do it again?" asked Cyndy.

"Lie in the tub. Scoot your butt under the waterspout and put your legs up on the wall and let the water run into you. Guaranteed orgasm."

"De-bra," Cyndy said, hitting me, as if I'd gone too far in this being-open-with-sisters conversation.

"Sor-ry," I said. "Still, you've got to try it, but wait till this thing gets better." I pointed at her head. There was a new problem these days, something that caused Cyndy to get, on occasions, dizzy. She had some new medicine, so I talked as if the problem would be solved in a matter of weeks. (Aside from the dizziness, Cyndy had occasional aphasia. One night when I was on the phone, Cyndy screamed from her bedroom. I ran in. She'd forgotten a word, couldn't produce it, and felt her head go weirdly blank. The word, she realized, five minutes later, was cancer.)

We decided to leave the topic of sex behind for something else. But not before I insisted, once again, that Cyndy try this bathtub thing. I was rubbing her back and Laura was still rubbing her feet, and I was thinking, as I stroked her skin. Yes, an orgasm. Let this body give her some pleasure.

You *do* get inappropriately intimate with a body when the body is ill. Sometimes there's something nice about it. Cyndy used to sit on the toilet in our bathroom and I'd take a soapy washcloth and wash her bald head. I'd say, "Stamp out dry scalpy skin." This struck us, for some reason, as terribly funny. We'd soak our feet in the bathtub and talk about our favorite Gogol stories. We'd walk arm-in-arm. Say: "This is what we'll be like when we are old ladies."

When Cyndy's symptoms were at their worst, my own body struck me, especially my legs, which stretched—it seemed amazing—from my torso to the ground. The miracle of walking. I still feel it. The air behind my legs is creepily light as I move. Who would have ever suspected that you can feel grief behind your kneecaps?

One very bad night: Cyndy was upset about everything, but especially men, relationships, never having had a boyfriend. According to her, I didn't, *couldn't* understand because I had had a boyfriend. This was a point of connection between Cyndy and a few of her intimates, an absence they could discuss and from which I was excluded. It didn't matter that I felt, for the sadness of my own relationships, included. I had had sex. Many times even—enough to have had a sexually transmitted disease which I (paranoid, irrational) thought I could pass on to Cyndy through ordinary contact. It didn't matter that I was cured of the problem. Her immune system was down. Anything I did might hurt her. My own desires might kill her.

This one night, Cyndy was crying, so I went into her room to put my arm around her, and she said, "Don't. Don't you touch me." Fierce, again. Vicious. I retreated to my bedroom. Cried softly, but still felt I had to do something. I stepped back to her bedroom, and she started to scream, waving me away, but saying, "It's just that I realize that nobody but my family or a doctor has touched me in the past five years."

It'll change, it'll change, it'll change. That was always my mantra for these relationship conversations. But it didn't. She died before it could change.

After that terrible night when Cyndy had the shingles and had to struggle out of our apartment to the car, she spent six weeks at my parents' house. Those were miserable times. She couldn't move from her bed. We'd all climb onto the double bed, a ship in the ocean of her room, and play word games or watch TV or be quiet because a lot of the time she couldn't stand for anything to be going on. As she started to feel a bit better, she worked on the course that she was going to teach in January of 1992. It was going to be called "Opera—What's All the Screaming About?" and it was going to be for high school girls, for kids who, presumably, could care less about opera. We rented opera videos and watched them with her. Then, she decided she was ready to come back to our apartment to work on her course syllabus. I cleaned the kitchen while she worked. At one point, she started to faint, but she grabbed the doorjamb, and I came in and caught her, wrapped my arms around her waist—big now, she was bloated with steroids—and set her down on the ground. She was okay, so she started to work at her computer, and I made us some cocoa. She handed me her syllabus to proofread. She sipped, while I read it, and she said, in a sort of campy voice, "Mmmm . . . this is love-ly." I laughed, still reading. She made a funny gurgling noise. I thought it was a joke but when I looked up from the syllabus, Cyndy was slipping out of her chair. I ran the few feet to her. She was crumpled on the ground. I rolled her onto her back and saw blood. There was water on the floor—her urine. "Are you okay? Are you okay?" I screamed. Her wig had rolled off her head and she looked like a gigantic toppled mannequin. She was gasping, breathing oddly. A seizure, I knew. I am, after all, a doctor's daughter. When the convulsive breathing stopped, she said, "What happened? What just happened?" She was as purely frightened as I'd ever seen her.

"Close your eyes," I said. "You just fainted. Close your eyes." I didn't want her to see her own blood. I thought that would scare her. I ran to the bathroom to get a towel and wipe her up. I tried to see where the blood was coming from.

"It's okay, you bit your tongue."

I felt—I have to say this, only because it's so horrible—a slight pleasure. It was the old thing; I would be competent, take care of this trouble. I was good in an emergency. But, there was also part of me—small, I promise myself now, very small—that thought, with some relief, It's over.

The ambulance came. We rode over to the hospital. My parents were there before us. When they rolled Cyndy away, I cried to my mother, "Oh, Mommy. I thought she was dying. I thought she was dying."

Inside, Cyndy was saying the same to my father, "I thought I was dying. I thought I was going to die."

And about two weeks later she did. But not before her body put her through enormous suffering. Not before she had a little more fun with the family. So, last things. The last thing she ever produced was a picture from a coloring book. She had asked for the book and some crayons, and we all earnestly filled in Mickey Mouse's ears and then signed our names and ages. Debra, twenty-nine. Laura, twenty-nine. David, twenty-four. Mommy, fifty-three. Daddy, fifty-five. Cyndy signed hers, "The Queen." (A joke from our two years together. When she was queen, Boston drivers were not going to be allowed to be obnoxious.) Under "age," Cyndy wrote, "None of your damn business." Last meal: gray fish from the kosher kitchen, but she didn't eat it. Last thing she *did* eat: Jell-O. I know, I spooned it into her mouth. Last thing I said to her: I told her that the man she was interested in was in love with her, that I knew because of what he'd said when I called to tell him she was in the hospital. (I was making this up, but who cares?) Last thing Cyndy ever said to me: "Oh, good. Well, tell him we'll get together when I get out of here." Last thing she ever said: I didn't hear this because I wasn't in the room, but she woke up, delusional and panicked and worried because she was going on a long trip and she hadn't packed her suitcase.

As my fiction-writer friends always say, You can't make this stuff up. No one would believe you if you tried.

And I have to agree: real life is just too heavy-handed.

Very last thing: her body still desiring life, she takes every third breath, though her fingers are dusky, though her kidneys have already shut down. We give the funeral director the pretty purple dress she bought for special occasions. We put her in the ground.

Our desires, I sometimes think now, as I'm walking down the street. Today, outside a bakery, I stop myself and say, "Yes, Debra?

What about them?" And I realize I don't know. "What? What?" I stand for a while feeling disgusted with the world—those horrible leering men in the greengrocer's; that stupid sailor in the bar; foolish me, making love with my sister dying in the next room. *Our desires, our desires, our desires.* I know what the refrain is; I just don't know what to do about it. It's a reproach for me, an always unfulfilled wish for my family, and a sad song—it's a dirge—for Cyndy. Still, since I am here, stuck among the living, I have to remind myself that the song owes nothing to the beautiful ones that Cyndy sang. So I go into the bakery and get a shortbread cookie, dipped in chocolate. It is so delicious I start to cry.

WILLIAM GIBSON

An Exaltation of Larks

I could not see her as I saw other women; she was a limb from the same hardwood as her own mother, and I never believed her capable of a weakness like death. I led her and the boys one October on a hike to a waterfall in a woodland gorge, sliding and slipping on a footloose trail that pitched down under great hemlocks among fallen rock, and below the falls we waded in the riverbed, scrambled along the lip of the ravine above it, risky enough, she helped me herd the boys to safety every third minute, and two hours later, tired and bruised, we trekked up the trail with the younger on my shoulders; my mother had not been in virgin forest before and said it was "beautiful, like no one was ever there." Only that evening she confessed she had felt so exhausted she doubted she could make it, and I realized she was a woman past seventy with a variety of ailments, including congestive heart failure, and a son who was a fool.

So I heard the little cough in her which commenced when my

second play was in rehearsal, and forgot it. Throughout the autumn it was persistent, and troubled my sister, but she could not prevail upon our mother to "bother" a doctor, nor could I; first the painters were redoing her kitchen, next she was in a bustle of her fall cleaning, next she must prepare a Thanksgiving feast for my sister's family, then she was embarked upon her Christmas baking and shopping; "always rushing, always breathless," she had no time for physicians. By midwinter the cough was a nag, in seizures of a minute, and since my mother insisted on "talking and coughing at the same time" her daughter told her it was "annoying to everybody." Somewhat hurt, my mother made an appointment with a doctor in her neighborhood, and was informed she had "walking" pneumonia. With a low fever, she retired to my sister's house for a week in bed, on antibiotics; the fever subsided, the cough disappeared, and when she went back to the doctor he pronounced her cured.

Once more in her three rooms, my mother was not too worried about a pain in her chest, sharper when she breathed deeply; she understood it was a normal remnant of pneumonia. In any case, between goiter and heart, she was accustomed to a shortness of breath. Until spring I spoke with her dutifully on the phone—she would "go to sleep happy" after an I-love-you-I-love-you-too ritual which I was reluctant to mouth, but managed—and in our commonplace chats, to which I half listened, I heard nothing ominous of what the year was to unfold; I was hardly alarmed by her mention of a date with the hospital for "some tests," which were habitual. The cough had reappeared, a minor symptom, my mother was taking it to the doctors who never failed her.

Indecisive, they asked her to come back time and again. Several mornings a week she travelled two hours to the hospital benches, waited among the outpatients for a couple of hours, went in to this brief lab test or that, and travelled two hours home; it was her routine day. She was depleted by these trips, she no longer had the "pep" of her late sixties. Two years earlier, when in her sitz bath she had discovered a lump in her groin, the doctors said it was a hernia, not ma-

lignant, but told her to stay off her feet, a waste of breath; still, my sister and I had argued enough with her career as a houseworker that after ten or twelve months of assent—"I can't keep doing this forever"—my mother let the work peter out. She was grown thinner, so bony in a dress with a scooped neck that my sister advised her "not to wear such bare dresses anymore," and now was losing weight on the hospital benches in a round which left her not only worn out, but irritated with the doctors. I urged her to go to a private physician without fretting about the money, but she would not hear of it, and in June a staff doctor looked into her face as well as her hemoglobin; the clinic suggested that she enter the women's ward for further study. It was the thirteenth of the month when she took her suitcase in, and my sister noted it as an unlucky day.

I came into the city next week to see her in the ward. Out of the elevator, I walked into a spacious room with a bleak odor of medicines and disinfectants, a dozen beds, a busy nurse or two, and relatives at every other bedside; at my mother's I joined my sister, there with a couple of her in-laws, and for two hours we took turns on a single chair, making conversation. Wan, on her hip in a hospital gown, my mother felt better than she looked. The chest x-rays had shown a right pleural effusion, and on her fourth day a thoracentesis had been done—a syringe impaled via her back to withdraw a few hundred c.c.'s of "yellow foamy fluid"—which was painful, but freed her breathing. Of the tests in progress she said most were repeats of those done in her weeks of outpatient visits; she thought it odd but "very thorough" and said, "I hope they find something," meaning a muscle impairment or perhaps emphysema; a young doctor on the floor had told my sister that an x-ray shadow might be tuberculosis. Often summoned to the tests at mealtimes, my mother had small appetite for hospital cooking to begin with, and was underfed, drawn and weakly. Yet she was in good spirits, chatty with the wardmates to whom she introduced me, and confided that one of them who was skin and bones made her realize "how fortunate I am." It was almost incidentally that on my visit the next day she said if the tests revealed a cancer she wanted me to tell her, and I promised I would, neither of us—certainly not I—expecting it.

I drove home again, and a week passed. The tests went on, of her liver, colon, urethra, intestinal x-rays, another biopsy of her thyroid, a bone series for spine and pelvis; all were so remote from my mother's complaint that she was perplexed. I talked with her once on a public phone in the corridor, and her daughter visited her each afternoon or evening. Still not eating, she was weaker by loss of a few pounds, and weary of her imprisonment in the ward; my sister was anxious to bring her home to some tempting food.

Late in the month, on a night made hectic by a tornado warning, our phone rang; my wife had hurried the boys into the cellar with blankets, and on my way down I picked up the receiver in hope of a word on the weather. Instead it was my sister from the hospital, her voice shaky, telling me the floor doctor had just led her aside with "bad news," our mother had cancer of the lung. From the cellar my wife was shouting up at me to hurry and I shouted down at her in a rage to shut up, and my sister said it was inoperable, the doctors gave her less than a year. Instantly, after twenty years like a day, I felt upon us the monstrous weight of my father's dying, and I said it would be a long year, and we talked on until my wife came upstairs to hear; I told my sister I would drive to the city, and hung up. The tornado blew itself out somewhere, forgotten, my wife and I were numb. In bed that night, speaking of my wish to be truthful with my mother, I tried to say I didn't "want her to be lonely" but could not get the word out; some floe of pity in me, unsuspected, was breaking up in tears, the first I ever cried for her.

In the next few days my wife was on the phone to influential colleagues in the city. I learned the floor doctor was a resident, unauthorized to speak for the staff, and the diagnosis was not final; a possibility of error like a fool's light flickered before us. Leaving a housekeeper with the boys, my wife and I drove down in our convertible to meet my sister, and confer in the hospital with a "big doctor" not usually seen by clinic relatives.

An elderly surgeon, he received the three of us in a rich wood-panelled wing of offices, together with a young doctor who was in attendance on my mother; with a patient factuality born of a lifetime in the presence of death, he told us what they knew. Cells in the fluid withdrawn from my mother's lung were malignant. The tests were a search not only into the extent of metastases, but for a primary site; they assumed the lung cells themselves were metastatic, and were pursuing the tests. I asked why, and he said the determination of a primary site would influence the therapy. Yet his voice, kindly enough, suggested no hope in treatment by irradiation or chemotherapy, nor in surgery, which he judged would be fatal. To our inevitable question, how long would my mother live, he replied that a doctor who predicted would be a fool; he could only say that it was "not a matter of weeks."

From his office, the three of us in silence descended by elevator into the poorer reaches of the hospital. In a basement hall we kept an appointment with an empty desk; awaiting its occupant, we sat on a strip of wooden chairs and debated my promise to tell my mother. To me it was catching at a straw, I had withheld most of my life from her, to be honest now would open us to each other at last. It meant an hourly commitment to her while she was looking the spectre in the eye, and was conceivable if she lived in our house; my wife said my mother's ease of mind was more to be desired than mine and was likelier if, ignorant of the facts, she spent her days with a daughter she was already close to; agreeing, my sister doubted she herself could see it through if our mother knew she was dying. The occupant of the desk, a young woman, returned to greet us. For a quarter-hour we talked with her of aftercare, nurses for hire, readmission— a doctor had advised my sister they took no terminal cases but "if your mother ever wants to come back we'll find a place for her"— until we had no questions; we thanked her, and looked again for the elevator. I saw by now that my sister must carry the load of our mother's death, as my mother twenty years ago had carried our other, and with the same smile of false cheer, it was her legacy. At the elevator I said I would not keep my promise, but do as she wished.

Upstairs, in the ward past the beds astir with patients we came to our mother in hers, inert, her eyes closed. We settled to wait in a sun room beyond, but on my way back to the corridor I gazed again at her bed as I passed, and stopped; in a sleep of exhaustion, the woman who had borne us lay on her back with her head fallen to one side, hair limp with summer sweat, her face starved and without make-up, mouth half open, and I saw her as dead. For a minute I stared, experimenting with the sensation. In the past when a rare image of my mother's dying had crossed my eye I foresaw myself as calm to it, if not indifferent, I thought even it would simplify my life; rid of my duties to her, I would have less guilt and more money, a notion not in me now. I was on the brink of a loss and a liberation of a different order, but it eluded me, the figure was only that of my mother sleeping. I knew the corpse I had recognized must be, but like my emergence out of her vulva it was not believable, the most elementary realities of birth and death are untenable in the mind. And in that minute, with my promise forgone, some expectation in me was already turning from her; it is the last image I keep of her face in the ward.

Once she awoke we sat with her until nightfall, but of all we said I recall only our lie that the tests showed a "chronic inflammation" of her lung. Otherwise it was small talk, unreal even then; what I remember is irrelevancies—my plateful of chicken cacciatore in a restaurant nearby, the ballpark with a nightgame where we dropped off my sister to join her husband and sons, a movie my wife and I walked to from our hotel in midtown—like intermissions of fact in a bad dream. Sometime that evening we arranged for a consultation the next noon with an internist known to my wife. Listening to us over lunch in the cafeteria of another hospital, the one place he could fit us into his day, he judged that to subject my mother to such dubious therapy as nitrogen mustard would only turn the remnant of her life into a misery; the chief aim must be to "make mother comfortable," and at my wife's request he agreed to find us a humane doctor on the staff of a hospital near my sister's house. Grateful for a small solace, we spent the afternoon at my mother's bedside in further chitchat, but of that visit too I retain nothing; my wife remembers how my mother introduced her to a woman in the next bed as Jewish also, spoke proudly of our careers, and played hostess with her sprightly talk and smile until, quite suddenly, she paled out in fatigue. By early evening we were driving home again, and from a phone booth on a parkway I called the dressing room of the star of my play to say that if she could visit my mother in the ward it would enliven her face, and so she did.

In the mirage of those two days I cannot pin it down, but for an hour I was alone in the convertible and drove it into the past; the distances of the city, so vast and alien in my boyhood, had shrunk, and the throng of buildings in which my mother lay was hardly more than a mile across the Harlem River from the tar road where I had been born. Parking the car, I walked among pedestrians and delivery trucks from one streetcorner to another that bounded the old neighborhood of my innocence, heartbroken at how forty years had changed it for the worse. So lovely in memory, the road was now an asphalt street, empty of the poplars, and the charm of the shady sidewalk with its slabs of slate, on which the smallfry of the block had scratched with stones a history of who loved whom, was gone under a merciless flow of cement; the field of vegetable gardens had grown into a parochial school in concrete behind an iron fence, and the rollicking hill with its ballfield and sled runs, the communal oak in the dell, the ledgy corner which hid my father on his way to work, had been levelled to make way for a huge apartment house; others with stores crowded around me in all directions, and everywhere the green of the earth, grass and trees and even the primal rock, was no more. In this hive and pavement litter, the band of narrow three-family houses with bay windows still stood, preserved in tarpaper of simulated brick, mean and ugly. Passing a porchlet once fashioned of wood—on it had hung a black tin mailbox bearing our name in my father's large clear hand—but now also cement, I stared up at the second floor with its trio of windows, unforgettable, where lurked in the gaslight of my childhood the ghosts among furniture made of dreams in the five unheated rooms which had warmed all my life, and eyed the same window in vain, my young mother would not again be half out of it to wave and cry her "I, L, Y!" after the jaunty figure who long ago had disappeared around the corner and out of the world, for here was no continuing city, and I walked on back to the convertible, homeless, in the midst of a thousand families who had made strange the place of our past.

Homeless I hardly was, for my mother invoking "the old days in Highbridge when we were all so happy" meant a household lively with her small children, and it was to ours that my wife and I drove back; next week we were to take possession of a second house for summers, a Cape Cod cottage in a pine woods overlooking the ocean. I thought my mother might convalesce with us there, but when I invited her via the phone in the hospital corridor she said it was "so far, dear," and she looked forward to the familiar room at my sister's. In July the staff came to the end of their tests for a primary site, fruitless, and discharged her "to be treated symptomatically." Called for by her daughter in the ward, my mother said goodbye to the other patients, and took her last leave of the great clinic which in the infirmities of her flesh had for thirty years kept her alive; my sister drove her and her suitcase out of the city, across the river and past the cemetery where whatever was left of her husband lay, to the trim and pretty dwelling in the suburbs twenty miles beyond. I was in touch with it by phone from our cottage three hundred miles farther on. Here along the stretches of solitary sandbars the boys and I broadjumped as naked as born, my wife in the salt foam arose feeling "tall and beautiful," and we scrambled up to the headland dunes for a gull's view of dipping moors and long beach and green ocean in its lace of breakers, the four of us tan and lucky; only my stomach, never free of its tie to my mother, was digesting itself in a new ulcer. I was loth to let a month now go by without a visit, and one morning in August I set out on a day's drive to my sister's.

I found my mother in a housedress sitting under a little apple tree in the backyard. It was a moment to put me in mind of my father in his last summer, and indeed the neighborhood was not unlike that to which he had raised us, the houses more prosperous and varied, but inhabited by clerks like him who commuted to the city; my sister's was white, two-storied, with two redbrick steps and an iron handrail to a screen door of aluminum scrollwork, and the six rooms within were spick-and-span, as smartly furnished as the alcoves on display in stores; my mother was always at home in this household born of her own. For a time each day she sat in a corner of the backyard under the apple tree, peeling vegetables, and was content, if less than brisk.

She had been taken by my sister to the doctor found for us by the internist. In his hands for a month, our mother had regained a half-dozen pounds, and felt she was on the mend; she was invigorated perhaps by his injections of a vitamin complex, and certainly by her daughter's cooking. My sister coaxed her appetite back with favorite foods, and regularly in the backyard served her a thick "cocktail" made of fortified milk, raw egg, malt, and other nutrients, which my mother swallowed dutifully. Not entirely a docile patient, she resisted the young doctor's instruction to take what she called "pain pills" every six hours, nor could she be kept from helping in the light chores of the household; they also fed her. The pain had put her in a hospital nearby, the week preceding, for withdrawal of another syringeful of pleural fluid. Again it relieved her difficulty in breathing, but the true bill of her health was in the abstract which described her as a "small cachectic woman"; no one had ever thought her small before.

Never fleshy, she had lost eighteen pounds since the onset of her cough, and when my sister fetched some of her clothes from the apartment "nothing fit her"; as we sat my mother spoke with much interest of a dress worn by one of her friends. It had been bought in a town a few miles out, and late in the afternoon I drove her there in the convertible. We spent an hour or two in the stores searching for it, my mother picking others from racks, putting them on and off in booths, thanking the saleswomen who at the mirrors urged them upon her, and she would let me buy none; all looked identical to me, and I knew she would not live to wear whatever she chose, but her heart was set on a particular dress. It was a joy to both of us that finally in a long rowful of sleeves she discovered it, the very print and style, in her size. She tried it on, I saw its distinction was a flounce of bosom ruffles, and when my seventy-two-year-old mother with a flutter of fingers at her flat chest said rather shyly, "It fills me out here," I could have wept.

The bright face of my sister was commencing to be etched—she too would lose twenty pounds by winter—but nothing in the house was out of the ordinary. I was host at dinner in a restaurant dear to my mother, one of a chain throughout the city that she said served "clean food," after which we returned to sit in the living room over gossip and small jokes until yawning time. Lights clicked off at ten o'clock, for my brother-in-law arose at six to commute; all went upstairs, and I went down to a couch in the basement. I was undressing when my older nephew in pajamas appeared on the steps. Seventeen, tall, about to matriculate next month at Princeton, he had remembered or been reminded to thank me for helping pay his tuition, the favor my mother had asked of me, and in a moment of awkward duty we played out again the scene in which I thanked my affluent uncle Ben for maneuvering me into a brainier high school; a reticent boy with intellectual interests of whom my sister said, "I don't know what he's thinking or even feeling about things," he then withdrew to take up his original life. I retired to ponder mine, and overhead my mother, who had not finished elementary school but taught him to read on her lap and me to spell in a highchair, lay ignorant that her own life—so unintellectual I thought it empty until I learned that love was the substance, and could rise to fill every crevice in her as amply as in me—had come to its end.

I drove back next day to the Cape, and the mirage of her improvement grew; in September she was strong enough that my sister, by way of a deep breath, spent a week alone with her husband in a resort not too far away. My mother stayed in the house with the boys.

To help out, their father's mother also arrived with a suitcase, a jolly woman who a year earlier had undergone a breast removal for cancer. Sympathetic when this in-law passed the days on the sofa with a back pain, my mother cooked, served, kept house for her and their grandsons; my sister came home to a neighbor's tale of "your skinny mother waiting on your fat mother-in-law," but in fact she had enjoyed one of her best weeks, "useful and happy." She then insisted on moving back to her three rooms in the redbrick building on the avenue, she had "so much to do." For two weeks I heard some of it by phone, how our mother shopped and housecleaned and walked a mile to lead her half-blind spinster pal out of a furnished room home to the kitchen couch for a stay as in former days, and "did everything" for her too; she could not sustain it. Tenants in the front soon told my sister that after church she "could barely make the stairs." Driving down for her and her toothbrush, my sister escorted her out of the streetdoor of the building, and my mother never again opened it to climb to the three rooms on the second floor rear in which she had lived out her widowhood, independent of us; the mirage was over.

I think something in her was coming to know that leavetakings now were for keeps. The last snapshot I have of her is on our lawn in early October after my wife and I had driven her up from the city for what we, and perhaps she, suspected would be her final visit. Glinty with eyeglasses, she stands in the sunlight in a gray housedress too loose upon her, and beside her is our four-year-old, fondling a toy she has brought him; her right palm, cupped around his cheek, draws his head to her hip. She admires his big brother—amused, she has told my sister how at this age over crayons he would say, "Go away, Nana, you bother me in my work"—but it is the younger who always runs to her hands; together they have been under every bed in the house playing "squealy pig," and a year ago at a theater rehearsal it was her lap he climbed into, content in her arms for two hours, and on this visit, when floor play is beyond her strength, they share a table over his favorite game of "merry milkman" with its toy truck and toy milk bottles; on her deathbed ten weeks later she will sigh of "my boys, my two boys," and mumble to my sister's question the names of her first grandson, at college, and of this boy, her last. Behind them is the dark green house with its white windows whose host of small diamond panes is an aggravation to her, some flaw in the old glass has survived all her scourings, and she never arrives without a new brand of cleanser to "get them," but this time is unequal to the challenge. She wears her "hiking" shoes—flat low-cuts I bought her for country use, which between visits she keeps in the guest closet—and around them the grass is still green, with a few autumn leaves; in her left hand she carries a basketful of zinnias, red, yellow, white, gathered for her in the garden by my wife's father. If I lay a thumb over her head I see a body straight and slim, thirtyish, stiffnecked as ever, but in her scraggy throat and sunken face, unsmiling, despite lipstick, brown hair, pearl earrings, her brow and nose and jaw so bony now, is the coming of a death's head. And on this lawn she says to me, lightly, "I think I must be dying, everyone is so good to me." It is windy weather, and she will sit in it for a few days before she hugs our boys whom she is not to see again, goodbye dear, goodbye dear, while I put her suitcase and shopping bag in the convertible; and with the top down I drove her for the last time out of our amber hills, back to the city.

Two days later on the phone my sister reported her face was "all windburned." I said in pain I could as well have put the top up, and so my sister had observed, telling her it was silly not to ask me; my mother said, "Oh no, dear, Billy likes it down."

Later in the fall she undertook one more journey. The summer gone was the first in fourteen years she had not vacationed in the seashore nest of widows, and now, though she "looked so dreadful," she made plans to go; unable to dissuade her, my sister and her husband drove her through Jersey to the deserted town with its boardwalk and surf, and left her in the hands of her friend, the landlady. For a week she lived in her old room, and sat solitary with her thoughts on the boardwalk, looking out at the sea. Because her son-in-law could not come back for her—his own mother was in a hospital with her lumbar pain—the landlady kept her company on the long bus ride to the city, where my sister met her; she was haggard. It was a shock to all when next month the other mother, as plump as when she so recently had come to oversee mine, died in the hospital of the cancer which had sprung up anew in her liver and bones. Fond of her, my mother by then was too fragile to travel even into Brooklyn for the wake; she consoled their tearful twelve-year-old grandson, and out of his earshot said, "One down and one to go."

I was alone with her an evening of the wake. I undid the orderliness of my sister's living room by pulling a chair to the sofa where she lay with a pillow under her head, and we talked of old days—she said, "Where there's dying there's fighting," but it would not be true—until I saw it was an effort for her, now that I had time she lacked breath; by nine-thirty she was in need of bed. I bent to kiss her goodnight, and with her thin arms around my neck, clinging, her lips at my face three or four times, I felt something almost amorous in her, I think it was another goodbye. But she said nothing again to suggest the imminence of her death.

She passed most of each day on the sofa; she was so fatigued even by the auto ride to the doctor's that he was now calling on her. Once more he had arranged for a thoracentesis in the nearby hospital, a stay of two nights made unhappy by a blunder about her "pain pills." On the second evening my sister discovered our mother was suffering rather than complain that the pills were not on the tray of medicines the nurse bore on her rounds; my sister went to inform the nurse a pill was due every six hours, the nurse refused it because she had "no order," and my sister in a rare loss of temper said, "It's all you're doing for her and it's the least you can do," and marched back to dig a bottle out of her own purse, but our mother would not take it without the doctor's knowledge, whereupon my sister phoned me; from two states away I phoned the doctor and reached a colleague on call, the colleague got word to the doctor, and the doctor called the hospital; it had taken all of us two hours and more than three hundred miles of telephoning to move a pill a distance of twenty steps to a dying woman. My sister brought her home the next morning—the third lung tap, less of a relief, showed "clusters of malignant tumor cells"—and a week later escorted her on a last outing. It was to an endocrinologist who, after testing her for thyroid activity, administered a dose of radioactive iodine. Leaving his office, my mother was so exhausted her daughter with difficulty seated her in the car; she rode with her head lolling back, and had to be helped into the house to the sofa.

Thanksgiving came, and with it her grandson home from college; my mother said, "I'll cook a dinner," and made the pot roast he loved. It was her last family act—and of a kind I never knew mattered to me until after her death I awakened from a weeping dream of the recipes I had typed for her in my teens, there was nobody left to feed me—but of that feast she herself ate only a mouthful, at my sister's urging. She was emaciated, her weight unknown because the news on the bathroom scale was worse each week and my sister hardly encouraged its use; if our mother weighed herself when alone, she was silent afterwards. Without hunger, she sat at the table with the family each evening but soon asked to be "excused," too tired to be up, and made her way back to the sofa. In the afternoons she dozed a good deal. When neighbors and friends visited to chat she made an effort to sit up, but the conversations sapped her; she no longer wrote her letters or travelled to the basement to watch television, and the one entertainment in her day was the tabloid her daughter went out to buy for her. Yet she continued to put on her lipstick and rouge with a deft touch—she never liked to be seen "without my face on"—and when I visited she took pains to be at her perkiest.

I heard her testy once when she said, "I can't *do* anything." It was not literally so, she made up her bed until the last and on her knees she scoured the tub with cleanser after her bath, to my sister's despair, but over the episode of her Christmas cards she lost heart. To mail out two hundred or more was her habit; working from an address book which in her inkscript contained the name of every acquaintance in her life, our mother by three envelopes at a sitting, with rests between, reached the C's and was helpless to finish; my sister took over the task. Glum, she kept to the sofa in a mood so alien to her that my sister spoke to the doctor, who prescribed "some potassium medicine," and antidepressant. Its effect was a worse humiliation, my mother lost control of her bowels; hurrying to the lavatory off the kitchen, she refused to let her daughter in to help, and scrubbed out her soiled clothes in her hands. Thereafter she spread pads on the sofa to protect it from the treacheries of her body.

Unaccepting of them, she made it a daily rite to walk three times around the table, for "exercise." She was no less stubborn about the analgesic pills; my sister and I argued with her to forestall the pain, but she resisted until it was unbearable. She was of old "not a medicine taker," and when the doctor to circumvent her wrote out a more potent prescription it so nauseated her he cancelled it. The worst time in her day was when she first awoke and sat on the edge of the bed endeavoring, mutely, by cough, wheeze, gasp, to loosen the clotting in her lungs; each morning it was thirty minutes before she could breathe enough to walk. My sister could not watch that effort, and went about her housekeeping with ears alert until our mother, clutching the banister, came downstairs to a sip of breakfast. It was an expenditure in vain; the next week when I visited she was not on the sofa, nor would she be again.

Upstairs I found her in the bedroom which had been vacated for her by the younger boy. It spoke of him in the gay pennants on the wall, a cozy room perhaps twelve feet by nine, with bookcase, desk, chair, but his narrow bed with a night table filled most of it; the table held a small crucifix my wife had sent. Here my mother lay, too enfeebled now to manage the stairs or even to dress herself. She no longer ventured to the bathroom after bedtime. To get to it meant traversing a landing where the stairhead opened, and my sister, worried about a misstep, had furnished her with a hand bell to summon aid in the night; she refused to ring it. My sister then set at the bedside a "potty" of enamelled metal—an heirloom, we had both used it in childhood and been succeeded on it by her own offspring—but it proved too low for our mother to squat upon in comfort. My sister substituted a bucket made of plastic. Deceptively apt, it had no weight or stability, and in the small hours my mother in urinating on it fell to the floor, and sat in its spill unable to get up; in the next bedroom her daughter awoke to hear a weak voice calling, "Please help me," and with her husband ran in to lift our mother back into bed. The work machine of her body was at last abandoned by its demon of energy.

Not of will: the next day she stood under the shower to shampoo her hair. It was a weekly ritual—she would accept no help, never permitted her daughter to see her undressed, and with her own hands put her hair up in curlers afterwards—and although my sister now argued that someone be called in from a beauty parlor my mother said no, they "wouldn't wash it clean enough," and closed the bathroom door on her. My sister waited outside it in dread of a fall. None occurred, but she came back to encounter our mother on her knees mopping the floor, and with a touch of hysteria screamed at her, "Don't do my work!" Unoffended, my mother let herself be tucked back in bed; she had confided to her daughter, bearing meals upstairs on a tray, that a "good thing that came out of this sickness is I know how much you love me." The meals were liquids, she had no appetite but thirst.

She was also wasted in interest. I sat with her off and on throughout two days, our talk desultory; she asked after my family, I said all were well, she said good, but my news no longer engaged her. So wan now, without cosmetics, the skin on her bonework of face had a clarity almost girlish, only her lips were cracked and dry, and when I kissed her I was surprised at how unfouled her breath was. She was dying rather sweetly, not in much pain—the doctor was injecting morphine into her—except for difficulty in swallowing; the bloody death of my father was not to be hers, but the grief of it was sufficient.

I was at her bedside when the doctor came up the stairs, a man several years younger than I, and she introduced me to him as "a good boy." Shy for a moment, the doctor murmured some mercy about "a famous man now," and my mother, to whom that fact was bread in her last seven years, said with indifference, "Well, famous," and more firmly said, "But he was always a good boy." I left the room while he ministered to her; later he joined me downstairs to discuss the necessary matters of terminal care, from medication to undertaker. Getting his overcoat on, he asked me where she "came from," I said the city, and in some surprise he said, "I see mostly weak people, she's like a pioneer." And he informed me how in receiving him yesterday my mother, too tired to reach, had said, "I'll give you the left hand, it's nearer the heart"; he thought it "beautiful."

I had arrived in the wake of a talk between him and my sister; she was of a mind to sleep in a beach chair at the door, the doctor recommended a night nurse, and my sister was worried about the expense. I said of course we could afford it, but the choice implied was one of where our mother should die. I hoped not in a hospital. My sister was mulling it over with her husband, and was troubled; our mother had detested the hospital nearby, the city was too distant, yet they wished to spare their twelve-year-old the memory of his grandmother's corpse in his bed. In mentioning it to the doctor I was struck by his saying offhand, "If it's done right it's done right forever," and quoted it to my sister without further effort to impose my sentiment on her bedding. She and I had a more immediate decision, whether to protract a life become so unsatisfactory to our mother; the doctor judged he could "take her through Christmas" with blood transfusions if the holiday mattered to us, and we said no. I was content to see, when my sister phoned the agency for a night nurse, that the other choice too was in the making.

I told my mother I would be down again soon, and drove home with her last greeting and gifts to my wife and sons; it was a week and a day before Christmas. Seven and four, the boys were in a simmer of expectations, as innocent of my pain in the loss of their grandmother as I had been of hers in the loss of Mary Dore, and next morning in our woods we cut the young pine they were to hang with ornaments. In the night a blizzard whipped in, and by afternoon the county was deep in snow, still falling; outside our windows all was whiteness and wind when I answered the phone. It was my sister to say our mother was weak and incoherent, had rambled on for a day and a night in a monologue like a caricature of her talk, and now, quieted by sedation, might or might not be in her dying hours. The roads were undriveable, so I took a suitcase to the only train out, and after six hours of glancing at my wristwatch every fifteen minutes I was picked up sometime before midnight by my brother-in-law at his depot. I was set to hear of a death; he said there had been no change. My mother was still in a drugged sleep when I stood with my sister in the dark bedroom.

In the morning she awoke clear of mind, but feeble, and in the kitchen my sister and I talked over the matter of a priest. The two of us were alone in the house with the patient—with her males away at work and at school my sister had been so for four months, durably cheerful, but in fear of the hour when she would sit with the face of death—and now were at the edge of the unknowable, it lurked under our practical talk of arrangements, and the reality of the kitchen was less solid; I knew how easily we were in tears when unseen of each other, but in me a fluttering had opened, as of a small eager bird. It was not a question of whether our mother would wish a priest, but of when, and not to alarm her too soon with the ritual of the last sacrament we put it off for a day.

Yet my mother, in touch again with the world of her room, saw she was on her deathbed and was without fear. Complaining only that her mouth was dry, she moistened it often at a tumbler of water in her daughter's fingers or mine; more than that she could not drink, and the bedpan now at hand was not to be used, the workings of her body were done. To care for her in her dying, as in her living, was no task. My sister bathed her skin with alcohol, and I took my turn on the chair at the bed, held her left hand, conversed in mur-

murs, watched her doze off; sleep was a surcease from the drought on her tongue. And in the enigma of whoever in past weeks was pretending for whom, my mother came first to the end of it. In my attendance on her bony face with its large eyes awake, I bent to catch her low voice, "Billy, was it cancer?" and was ashamed to hear my quick word, "No."

The day passed without event—the doctor came, a neighbor stopped in, I phoned my wife, the twelve-year-old ran in from school, the afternoon darkened—except that I notified a mortuary. My sister said our mother had always spoken with approval of the looks of a funeral home a few blocks from her apartment, and when in a heavy sleep of morphine she could not hear I phoned it; they recorded her name, and said they would come for the body at whatever hour I called again. It was a simple evening, supper in the kitchen, dishwashing, the boy and his father with us at the bedside for two words and a squeeze of my mother's hand, until the nurse rang the doorbell and took charge of the sickroom for the night.

With breakfast, my sister and I sat again to our vigil, and saw our mother was aware both of us and of other presences in the room, but so was I; if her eye detected a perturbation of butterflies in a corner, mine was widening on an iridescence in me. For the most part, she spoke to us intelligibly. Of her money in the bank, she said each of her grandsons was to have five hundred dollars for college; that year I had declined three-quarters of a million for my play from a movie star I did not want, and put aside a trust fund for my mother of some thirty thousand, and her legacy—twice she told us, five hundred for each boy, the rest for my sister and me—was insignificant until with a lift of her starveling head she said, "I scrubbed and cleaned for seventeen years to keep it there." Yet her eyelids were feebler, and at times her talk sidled off to unseen listeners in a mutter I could not follow, other than to hurt when she said with a sigh, "All my flowers died. They were so pretty." I held the fingers that had worked so long, and earlier throttled in me the capacity to give myself into the hands of a woman, but escape at last—surely it was there—was not all the quickening in me.

Late in the wintry morning I walked several blocks to the parish house, to find the priest gone; I wrote out my sister's number for his housekeeper, and walked back between the heaps of snow past fifty dwellings that also could not hold in life, but the misery in me was strangely eager as spring. I took turns again with my sister at the bedside. Despite the dreamlike fragments of talk my mother was in touch with each of our small attentions to her, remarking idly, as my sister washed her limbs, "Your Daddy always said I had pretty legs." While she dozed I picked up a book of common prayer on the night table, and read in it; at once it was like food, a voice from heaven saying unto me, Write, blessed are the dead, I thought yes and no, but the burial service spoke to me more than as solace, it was the only truth, and I knew that in the valley of the shadow of death was no evil. I heard it too in the voice of my mother when, in the twilight, her uses in the world done, she said to no one, "Why doesn't the Lord take me?" It was a puzzlement her tongue was to wander back to, twice, like a child thirsty and fretful, and at her ear I said as a promise, "Be patient." The fact is that half of the fluttering in me was of the dead, darkling, near, live, I almost did not doubt they were live, a mingling of faces and hands waiting to receive and comfort her, and me, and all of us; the distinction between life and death was dissolving in the grave, and at its edge I saw I could invent immortality, but others had been before me. At nightfall the priest phoned, and on my judgment that my mother would be rational said he would come in the morning.

Soon after daylight the nurse took her leave, and our mother was rational enough that in mentioning the priest's visit we said it was for confession, not extreme unction. By her head the night table was dressed with a white napkin, two candles, a crucifix, holy water, a spoon—brought in a communion box by a devout girl, on hand to guide us in the sacrament—but my mother was without curiosity in the preparations; she lay with her eyes big in a stare at the ceiling, her cracked lips parted to each breath, and to speak or swallow was an effort. When the doorbell rang, the girl covered her hair with a handkerchief, asked my sister to cover hers, told me not to talk to the priest while he was carrying the host, and bore a lighted candle down the stairs to usher him in.

It commenced like a comedy, she could not unlock the door; I hurried down after her, and both of us worked at the knob in vain under the gaze of the shivery priest just beyond the glass, to whom we could utter not a word, and by candle we conducted a search of the lock for its release until my sister too ran down, losing her handkerchief, and the three of us let the priest in. Silent, he followed the girl and her candle up the stairs. Last in to my mother, I saw her eyes were brighter and attentive upon the priest, and I knelt on the floor with him, my sister, the girl, while he adored the crucifix; muttering in Latin, he sprinkled holy water on my mother and on us, and presently sent us out. The door shut on her last confession.

Of what pale sins she had to unburden herself I could not imagine, but after the priest reopened to us she told him she must not be a good mother because—uncertain of eye, not of charity, she asked if my wife was in the room—both her children had married out of the faith; she had it in her head for twenty years, and we never knew. The priest consoled her that God had his reasons, and the four of us went again to our knees around the narrow bed. Murmuring after the others the confiteor which came back to my lips, I confessed that I had sinned exceedingly in thought, word, and deed, and the priest stood to the crucifix; in his fingers he elevated the wafer which was the body of the hanging Saviour, and showing it to my mother—I supported her while she sat upright—he intoned three times the *non sum dignus,* I am not worthy, and laid it upon her tongue. My mother could not swallow it. Twice she tried, gasping, but the wafer, which I knew disintegrated at the touch of salivation, reappeared entire in her parched mouth. Retrieving it, the priest fed her a spoonful of the holy water, and soon she tried again, hungering for it, but gagged, coughing in such a shortness of breath that my sister hurried to the window, raised it, struggled with the storm window to no effect until I joined her to pound, and loosened it to the winter air. My mother with her eyes closed said, "Oh, God, let me take it."

Disturbed, the priest said it was not necessary, he could give her a spiritual communion, but my mother shook her head, and we waited; after a moment of inward summoning she once more offered her tongue to the wafer, it was the last chore she set herself in this world, I knew she would manage, and she swallowed it whole. For a few intakes of breath she sat, resting, seventy-two years of workaday bones, and then she said clearly, "I thank you, God, for everything."

It was a sentence that shattered me. She lay back on her pillow, and we knelt around her while the priest with a hand above her head invoked the archangels against the power of the devil over her, but I heard and still hear the voice of my mother dying with thanks on her tongue for everything she had seen, blessings and afflictions, toil, love, tears, pleasures, the pinching, the plenty, the ills of her body, the births and the burials too; she meant the gift of her life. More, she meant even the gift of her death, and with her affirming of it the fluttering in me rose, I was filled with a joyous taste of my-self as I watched the priest at the candles moisten his thumb in holy oil. In the sign of the cross he anointed her eyelids, praying aloud for forgiveness of the wrong she had done by the use of her sight, dipped his thumb and anointed her ears, praying for forgiveness of the wrong she had done by the use of her hearing, dipped his thumb to anoint her nostrils, and I saw he was purging her body of the deeds of its senses, it was a rite that for a thousand years had made peace with the defects of the human material, and the thumb of the priest anointed her mouth, for the wrongs of its taste and speech, and her open palms, for touch, and lastly her feet, for the wrong done by her power to walk. Mute, our mother lay in exhaustion, all her strength had gone out in the offering of her little gloria. At last the priest joined us on our knees, and we muttered with him the prayers to keep her from the enemy, the eleison, the paternoster, others ancient and wise, but none that opened the gates of my being like her words, always known, in my ear from my birth to I hope the day of my own death; with them my tale began, and is almost done.

I led the priest down the stairs to the door, where I gave him ten dollars, and not long after my sister unlocked it again to the doctor. She and I hovered near while he sat beside our mother, taking her pulse and temperature, and only his shot of morphine put her thirst to sleep; I asked him to leave some. It was a busier day, the older son was back from college for the holidays, and later the half-blind Nelie was brought to the door by a crony. Sole survivor of their schooldays when my mother had befriended her as a stricken girl, she sat at the bed through the afternoon until the daylight failed and the lamps in the house went on; they spoke seldom, but old ghosts were in the room. My mother dozed, or flopped a hand, or mumbled; once she said, but to no one, "Let me look pretty." To me at her flank with alcohol and needle she sighed, "Oh Billy, you have to see everything"—with reason, my glimpse of the lean groin wherein I was conceived was not innocent of a flicker of the erotic—and I thumbed the morphine in. After a time she murmured, "My husband, my husband, no one could play piano like my husband," and drifted into sleep. I was to drive Nelie home for supper but she lingered, would neither eat with us nor go, sat, could not be budged, and I was impatient but suddenly knew what she knew, to rise from the bedside was to take leave of my mother forever.

Next day she died. In the hours before dawn she awoke and attempted to crawl out of bed; the nurse restrained her, but she babbled of a trip, she must get dressed and pack for a trip; reporting this at breakfast the nurse said it was not uncommon in the dying. When I sat to my mother's hand it was too cool, and at the blanket's edge her foot was gross, purpling around the heel. With her jaw hanging and eyes adroop she was conscious half of the morning, breathing over her caked tongue in a distress neither my sister nor I could suffer. I injected her thigh with morphine, and once again—often, in those four days—said in her ear, "I love you"; I had said it many times in the years preceding, that dutiful lie in my mouth, and it turned out to be true. She slept until after lunch, with my sister at the bedside, and when she awoke to more distress I emptied a second needle into her thigh. It may have been the load she could not carry into another day; she fell into a sleep like a coma.

Late in the afternoon, no change obvious, I buttoned my over-coat and went for an hour's walk; it was the shortest day of the year, cold, the light gray on ice in the streets, and somewhere unseen the sun had reached its furthest point, would creep back now through all of the winter that lay ahead; when I returned it was almost dark. I recognized a station wagon at the curb, and upstairs found my wife seated with my mother. Caressing her knuckles, my wife, who would always pay a price for their scourings in me, told her over and over she was "a good girl"; she thought the gaunt face, its eyelids closed, smiled. After a family supper we rejoined my sister—she kept watch alone while we ate her cooking—to share her vigil in twos or threes, sat, gazed, waited, the talk subdued and fragmentary, and pondered what our lives meant. Still no change was seen, and we vacated the bedroom when the nurse returned to duty; in the midst of her ministerings, she found a moment to tell me she doubted our mother would survive the night.

I was on my couch in the basement with a letter my wife had brought—from my young worldling, middle-aged, divorced, un-employed, asking for five thousand dollars so he might write a play—when my sister called that the nurse wanted me. I ran up the two flights of stairs to the bedside where the nurse made way from the pillow; I saw my mother's face had come to life, her eyeballs wide and bulging, her mouth open as in a despairing cry, mute, and out of that cavity I then heard an exhalation which was not human breath, low, even, long, it was air leaving a crypt. The others had fol-lowed my run, and before our eyes the miracle went out of my mother. Something altered less than a shadow, the eyeballs simply died, her dropped mouth was the gaping of death; she had aban-doned her body to us. All that had kept it flesh was soul, and within a minute of the stilling of the blood it was a corruption, yellowing, a great haggard doll of evil in the bed, unclean and sickening. I could not take my eyes from it. My sister, I, the others stood in si-lence for some minutes over a carcass of which we must be rid, once our good mother, who had made us the last gift a parent owes to chil-dren, a good death; and for what was in us speech had not been invented. Yet from this moment a spacious quiet was in the house, and in me too, as I went downstairs to phone the doctor and the mortuary.

It was almost midnight when the drivers rang the doorbell, two men in black like ministers, and I showed them up to the waiting nurse. Downstairs, my sister was boiling water in a kettle and setting out tea cups, and we all took refuge in the kitchen, out of sight and hearing; I thought better of it, and moved into the dining room where I sat at the table in the dark, the stairway in view. Down it the two men soon came with a stretcher. It was of black canvas which, overlapping its contents, was strapped and buckled, although what rode within was of such negligible bulk it seemed the canvas held nothing but itself; and in that airless bag, too ugly for eyes, the thing of bones, skin, hair which had been my mother was carried out of the house.

I watched the door shut, and suddenly my sister thinking of rigor mortis remembered her mother's plate of false teeth. I ran upstairs while she hurried to call to the men, and in the small bedroom—the bare mattress was a shock—I located the teeth in the drawer of the night table; I ran down with them, the driver stood at the door with my sister, and I put this relic of our mother into his hand so that, her last wish granted, she might look pretty.

Tess Gallagher

Soul-Making

Last things, we learn, have rights of their own. They don't need us, but in our need of them we commemorate and make more real that finality which encircles, and draws us again into that central question of any death: What is life for? Raymond Carver lived and wrote his answers: "I've always squandered," he told an interviewer, steering a hard course away from the lofty and noble. It was Carver's law not to save up for some longed-for future, but to use up the best in him each day and to trust more would come. Even the packaging of the cigarettes he smoked carried the imprint of his oath in the imperative: NOW.

This injunction would bear down on us with increasing intensity in the final months of his life. In an episode eerily like that preceding the death of Chekhov, to whom he had paid tribute in his story "Errand," Ray had been diagnosed with lung cancer after spitting up blood in September 1987. There would follow several months of struggle after which the cancer would reoccur as a brain tumor in early March 1988. After twice swerving off recommendations for brain surgery by several doctors, he would undergo seven weeks of intense, full-brain radiation. The respite was short, however, for by early June tumors would again be found in his lungs.

These are the facts of that time, enough to have made realists of us if we hadn't been realists already. Nonetheless, much as Chekhov had kept reading the train schedules *away* from the town in which he would die, Ray kept working, planning, believing in the importance of the time he had left, and also believing that he might, through some loop in fate, even get out of it. An errand list I found in a shirt pocket after his death read "eggs, peanut butter, hot choc" and then, after a space, "Australia? Antarctica??" Ray's insistent belief in his own capacity to recover from reversals during the course of his illness gave us both strength. In his journal he wrote: "When hope is gone, the ultimate sanity is to grasp at straws." In this way he lived hope as a function of gesture, a reaching *for* or *toward,* while the object of promise stayed rightly illusory. The alternative was acceptance of death, which at age fifty was, for him, impossible. Another journal entry revealed his anguish as the pace of the disease quickened: "I wish I had a while. Not five years—or even three years—I couldn't ask for that long, but if I had even a year. If I knew I had a year."

In January 1988 Ray began keeping a journal under the inspiration of Stephen Spender's *Journals 1939–1983,* but with the discovery of his brain tumor it broke off suddenly in March, though he would start again later in another notebook. Our attentions turned instead to the drafting of a short essay to appear in the commencement booklet for the University of Hartford, where Ray was to accept a Doctorate of Letters in May.

During much of this time I had been clinging to the stories of Chekhov, reading one after the other of the Ecco Press volumes, and now I offered two passages to Ray from *Ward No. 6* to illustrate the epigraph from Saint Teresa ("Words lead to deeds . . . they prepare the soul, make it ready, and move it to tenderness."), which he'd taken from my book of poems, *Amplitude,* to begin his essay. Ray incorporated the passages from Chekhov into his piece, and this was the beginning of an important spiritual accompaniment which began to run through our days, and which eventually would play an important part in the writing of *A New Path to the Waterfall,* his last book.

The fervor with which we both seized on these particular moments in *Ward No. 6* came, I think, directly out of the ordeal we were undergoing with Ray's health, and this was particularly true of the second passage in which two characters, a disaffected doctor and an imperious postmaster, his elder, suddenly find themselves discussing the human soul.

> "And you do not believe in the immortality of the soul?"
>
> "No, honored Mihail Averyanitch; I do not believe it, and, have no grounds for believing it."
>
> "I must own I doubt it too," Mihail Averyanitch admits. "And yet I have a feeling as though I should never die myself: 'Old fogey, it's time you were dead!' but there is a little voice in my soul that says: 'Don't believe it; you won't die.'"

In his framing of the passage Ray underscored the power of "words which linger as deeds" and out of which "a little voice in the soul" is born. He seemed almost grateful to observe how, in the Chekhov story, "the way we have dismissed certain concepts about life, about death, suddenly gives over unexpectedly to belief of an admittedly fragile but insistent nature."

I continued to bring Chekhov into our days, reading a story first thing in the morning, then telling it to Ray when I came down for breakfast. I would give the story in as true a fashion as I could, and Ray would inevitably become engaged by it and have to read it for himself that afternoon. By evening we could discuss it.

Another of Ray's influences came from one of the books he'd been reading early in the year, Czeslaw Milosz's *Unattainable Earth.*

In the interest of what he called "a more spacious form," Milosz had incorporated prose quotes from Casanova's *Memoirs,* snippets from Baudelaire, from his uncle Oscar Milosz, Pascal, Goethe and other thinkers and writers who'd affected him as he was writing his poems. He also includes his own musings, which take the form of confessions, questionings and insights. Ray was attracted to the inclusiveness of Milosz's approach. His own reading at the time included Federico Garcia Lorca, Jaroslav Seifert, Tomas Tranströmer, Robert Lowell, *The Selected Poems* of Milosz and a rereading of Tolstoy's *The Death of Ivan Ilych.*

In early June, when we were given the devastating news that tumors had again shown up on xrays of his lungs, it was to Chekhov, our literary companion, to whom we instinctively turned in order to restore our steadfastness. One night I looked at certain passages I had bracketed in the stories and realized that they seemed to be speaking toward poems of Ray's I'd been helping revise. On impulse I went to the computer, shaped some of these excerpts into lines and gave them titles. When I showed the results to Ray, it was as if we'd discovered another Chekhov inside Chekhov. But because I'd been looking at the passages with Ray's poems in mind, there was the sense that Chekhov had stepped toward us, and that while he remained in his own time, he seemed also to have become our contemporary. The world of headlong carriage races through snowstorms, of herring-head soup, of a dish made of bulls' eyes, of cooks picking sorrel for vegetable soup, of peasant children raised not to flinch at the crude language of their drunken parents—his world was at home with the world of Raymond Carver.

It was a bewildering time for us, but instead of giving over to visitors and a parade of sorrowful goodbyes, we made the decision not to tell anyone about the cancer's recurrence in Ray's lungs. This allowed us to keep our attention on the things we wanted and needed to do. One important thing we decided was to celebrate our eleven years together by getting married in Reno, Nevada, on June 17. The wedding was what Ray called a "high tacky affair" and it took place across from the courthouse in the Heart of Reno Chapel, which had a huge heart in the window spiked with small golden light bulbs and a sign that read SE HABLA ESPANOL. Afterwards we went gambling in the casinos and I headed into a phenomenal three-day winning streak at roulette.

When we returned home Ray wrote "Proposal," which carries the urgency of that time, the raw sense of life lived without guile, or that cushion of hope we count on to extend life past the provisional.

> *Back home we held on to each other and, without*
> *embarrassment or caginess, let it all reach full meaning. This*
> *was it, so any holding back had to be stupid, had to be*
> *insane and meager. How many ever get to this? I thought*
> *at the time. It's not far from here to needing*
> *a celebration, a joining, a bringing of friends into it,*
> *a handing out of champagne and*
> *Perrier. "Reno," I said. "Let's go to Reno and get married."*
> (from "Proposal," p. 116, *A New Path to the Waterfall*)

Our having married anchored us in a new way and it seemed we had knowingly saved this occasion to give ourselves solace, and perhaps also to allow us to toss back our heads once more in a rippling cosmic laugh, as from that "gay and empty journey" of which Kafka writes.

This was also the time during which Ray wrote "Gravy." The idea for the poem had come from a conversation we'd had while sitting on the deck at Sky House, facing the Strait of Juan de Fuca, taking stock. "You remember telling me how you almost died before you met me?" I asked him. "It could've ended back then and we'd never even have met. None of this would have happened." We sat there quietly, just marveling at what we'd been allowed.

> *No other word will do. For that's what it was. Gravy.*
> *Gravy, these past ten years.*
> *Alive, sober, working, loving and*
> *being loved by a good woman. Eleven years*

ago he was told he had six months to live
at the rate he was going. And he was going
nowhere but down. So he changed his ways
somehow. He quit drinking! And the rest?
After that it was all gravy, every minute
of it, up to and including when he was told about,
well, some things that were breaking down and
building up inside his head. "Don't weep for me,"
he said to his friends. "I'm a lucky man."
I've had ten years longer than I or anyone
expected. Pure gravy. And don't forget it.

("Gravy," p. 118, *A New Path to the Waterfall*)

Here Ray displaces the devastating significance of impending death by recalling memory of a prior death, one narrowly avoided, when in 1976 he nearly died of alcoholism. In effect, he used his oncoming death as proof of a former escape; and death, he realized, once displaced by such an excess of living during the ten productive years he'd been allowed, could never be quite as unrelenting. For Ray, of course, in facing his death, there was the question of whether the memory of his life would persist importantly through the survival of his writings. At the same time, his poems suggest that an artist's obsessions and signs, fragmentary and intermittent as they may be, belong to a world of necessity that transcends anyone else's need of them.

Shortly after our wedding, we had been given a gift. Our painter friend Alfredo Arreguin had been working on a large canvas about which mysterious, tantalizing hints had been leaked at intervals to us by his wife, Susan Lytle, also a painter. The day before our wedding reception, Alfredo and Susan arrived at Ridge House with the painting strapped to the top of their car. The painting, once hung in our living room, proved to be of several salmon leaping midair toward a stylized waterfall. In the sky, what Ray would call "the ghost fish" were patterned into clouds heading in the opposite direction.

The rocks in the background were inhabited as well, studded with prehistoric eyes.

Each morning we took our coffee in front of the painting where Ray could sometimes be seen sitting alone during the day, meditating. When I look at it now, Ray's vitality seems embedded in the pageantry of a cycle we had seen played out year after year in the river below our house. In the painting the salmon are heading upstream, bowed eternally to the light in a fierce, determined leap above water, and above them the ghost fish float back unimpeded in an opposing current, relieved of their struggle.

Three weeks after Ray's death, as I entered into the computer the last corrections Ray had made to his poems, I realized I had perfectly, though unwittingly, enacted the instructions of his poem "No Need" the night before his death.

> *I see an empty place at the table.*
> *Whose? Who else's? Who am I kidding?*
> *The boat's waiting. No need for oars*
> *or a wind. I've left the key*
> *In the same place. You know where.*
> *Remember me and all we did together.*
> *Now, hold me tight. That's it. Kiss me*
> *hard on the lips. There. Now*
> *let me go, my dearest. Let me go.*
> *We shall not meet again in this life,*
> *so kiss me goodbye now. Here, kiss me again.*
> *Once more. There. That's enough.*
> *Now, my dearest, let me go.*
> *It's time to be on the way.*
>
> ("No Need," p. 119, *A New Path to the Waterfall*)

The three kisses which had been meant as "Good night" had, at the time, carried the possibility that Ray would not wake again. "Don't be afraid," I'd said. "Just go into your sleep now" and, finally, "I love you"—to which he had answered. "I love you too. You get some sleep now." He never opened his eyes again, and at 6:20 the next morning he stopped breathing.

In "Late Fragment," the final poem of his last book, his voice has earned its coda.

> And did you get what
> you wanted from this life, even so?
> I did.
> And what did you want?
> To call myself beloved, to feel myself
> beloved on the earth.

("Late Fragment," p. 122, *A New Path to the Waterfall*)

There is the sense that the need to be beloved has been central to the effort of the life and, therefore, to the writing, and that one's own willingness to award that to the self—to "call myself beloved" and, beyond that, to "feel myself beloved on the earth"—has somehow been achieved. When I was thinking of what poem to put on his gravestone, this one claimed the right. And many who visit that wind blown bluff, I've come to know, carry the poem away with them to use for a wedding ceremony or to honor one of their own dead.

For a recovering alcoholic, the self-recognition Ray expresses in this poem, and the more generalized feeling of love he was allowing himself, was no small accomplishment. He knew he had been graced and blessed and that his writing had enabled him to reach far beyond the often mean circumstances from which he and those he wrote about had come, and also that through his writing those working-class lives had become a part of literature. On a piece of scrap paper near his typewriter he had written: "Forgive me if I'm thrilled with the idea, but just now I thought that every poem I write ought to be called 'Happiness.'" And he was happy, in spite of facing up to a much too early death. During those last, long summer evenings, we were both in the keeping of a grateful equanimity as we talked during those long summer evenings of our life together as writers, lovers and helpmates.

In Alaska, on one last fishing trip, we raised glasses of Perrier to toast having finished Ray's book, and to pay tribute to ourselves, for managing to complete it against so many odds. In the crucial last days of our work, guests had arrived for an extended stay and Ray's son had come from Germany. We'd kept working, parceling out the day. "Don't tell them we've finished," Ray said to me—"them" meaning the guests. "I need you here." So the book as pretext allowed us a few more precious mornings with each other before what would be the final onset of his illness.

After our guests had left, we began making calls, trying desperately to arrange a trip to Russia to see Chekhov's grave and to visit the houses of Dostoevsky and Tolstoy. I wanted to find certain places associated with Akhmatova. Even though this wasn't to be, our planning in those last days was, in itself, a kind of dream-visit that lifted our spirits. Later, when Ray entered the hospital, we talked about what a great trip it would have been. "I'll go there," I said, "I'll go for us." "I'll get there before you," he said, and grinned. "I'm traveling faster."

After Ray's death, at home in Port Angeles on August 2, 1988, the mail was heaped for weeks with letters and cards from people all over the world mourning his passing. Many sent moving accounts of their having met Ray even briefly, things he'd said, acts of kindness performed, stories of his life before I had known him. Copies of obituaries began to arrive from papers around the country, and one day I opened a packet from London with the obituary from the *Sunday Times*. The headline above the photograph of Ray with his hands in the pockets of his leather jacket reads simply: "The American Chekhov." From *The Guardian* there was the possessive "America's Chekhov." I seemed to be reading these *with* Ray, and to be carrying his knowing of it. Either headline would have been accolade enough to have made him humbly and deeply grateful.

To the end, Ray's poetry was a spiritual necessity. The truths Ray came to through his poems involved a dismantling of artifice to a degree not even William Carlos Williams, his early inspiration, might have anticipated. Ray had read Milosz's lines in *"Ars Poetica?"* and they'd confirmed his own poetics:

> *I have always aspired to a more spacious form*
> *that would be free from the claims of poetry or prose*
> *and would let us understand each other without exposing*
> *the author or reader to sublime agonies.*

> *In the very essence of poetry there is something indecent:*
> *a thing is brought forth which we didn't know we had in us,*
> *so we blink our eyes, as if a tiger had sprung out*
> *and stood in the light, lashing his tail.*

Ray used his poetry to flush the tiger from hiding. He did not look on his writing as the offering of commodities to a readership. He was purposefully disobedient when pressures were put on him to write stories because that's where his reputation was centered and where the largest reward in terms of publication and audience lay. He didn't care. He was not "building a career." He was living a vocation, and this meant that his writing, whether poetry or prose, was tied to inner mandates. These insisted more and more on an unmediated apprehension of his subjects, and poetry was the form that best allowed this.

In his own fashion, Ray did as much to challenge the idea of what poetry can be as he did to reinvigorate the short story. He wrote and lived his last ten years by his own design, and as his companion in that life, I'm glad to have helped him keep his poetry alive during the journey. I'm grateful for the comfort and soul-making he drew from it, and for the gifts he left us all, despite his own too-early going.

REBECCA McCLANAHAN

The Other Mother

"Who was she?" friends ask, seemingly bewildered by the extent of my grief. Sometimes I answer that she was my mother's closest friend. Sometimes I say she was *my* dear friend, but when I explain that we were a generation apart I feel the listener's sympathy deflating, as though a generation's "remove" distances the power of loss. What I want to say is, "She was my other mother." This seems the only vessel large enough and deep enough to contain all that she was.

"Now, who was she again? I forget." Had I buried my biological mother, people would not keep forgetting. Theodore Roethke's poem for his dead student, Jane, ends with this outpouring of grief: *I, with no rights in the matter, / Neither father nor lover.* What right do I have to mourn Carolyn's death? If I say I feel I've lost a mother, does this rob Carolyn's daughter of her rightful place on the ladder of mourning? Should I weep in private, wring my hands of her memory? Ours was an unregistered, unofficial relationship, the kind that can't be claimed on income taxes, the kind that engenders what death educators call "disenfranchised grief." (Disenfranchised mourners also include children, whose grief is often not valued; survivors of a friend or family member who died under conditions considered shameful; and anyone who mourns a relationship unsanctioned by society.)

It was not mother love I was seeking in Carolyn. From the first colostrum it was granted me—breast- and hand- and eye-love. Unlike those unfortunate infants who suffer from "failure to thrive," who literally die from lack of touch, I grew fat on mother's milk and attention. Call it happenstance, fate, something the stars tossed my way in the guise of a woman named Juanita, my biological mother.

Jung would have called Juanita my "accidental carrier," a term embedded in the idea that as daughters grow into womanhood, we "must come to recognize 'the human being who is our mother' as the 'accidental carrier' of the archetype." No wonder she gets so tired. Enough to carry *us* for nine months, then another few years, our bodies sleep-heavy, our arms linked Simian-style around her neck. But to carry the *idea* of mother, the whole ball of wax? The universe must have known this was too much for one woman to manage. So Mother Earth was born, and Mother Nature, and goddesses and grandmothers and plowed fields and caves and ovens and all manner of scooped-out vessels. At different times in my life, one or another face of the archetype has guided me. At one point, my biological mother; at another, my maternal grandmother; then her sister, Great Aunt Bessie. Lately, the face that swims up from my dreams is Carolyn's.

My mother is a down-to-earth, gentle woman, easy to be around and easy to love. She is also emotionally private. Though I am sure she has wept long and hard, I have never witnessed her tears. Her mother was also this way, as were my aunts and most of the significant women in my childhood. Carolyn, on the other hand, cried easily and often, at times seemingly unable to distinguish between joy or sorrow. Any occasion could bring on tears—a story, a photograph, a song played on her spinet. "No, no," she'd say when I'd take my place on the bench, cranking up Vivaldi, my foot tapping a military beat (Carolyn had no use for metronomes). "No baroque," she'd say. "Schumann, please. Or Brahms." But I knew none of the Romantics. My piano teachers frowned on them, as they did on my tendency to play by ear. "Well, then, make something up," Carolyn would say.

I'd been punished by teachers for not playing the notes on the page, and now here she was encouraging me. "Like this," she'd say, leaning forward, her hands resting lightly on the keys. Music theory held no interest for her; she lacked precision and formal technique. Nevertheless, the music came—haltingly at first, then infused with passion, her tears falling on the keys. If her husband Walt was home, he'd sit on the couch and listen, his hand stroking the back of some aging dog or cat.

To say that Carolyn cried easily is not to suggest that her life was an open book. Like my mother, Carolyn maintained her private places, and in some ways her boundaries were more staked off than my mother's. You entered at your own peril. The door to her study, which she called "my inner sanctum," was always closed, and only a few people "in God's entire world" as she put it, were allowed in. Inside were rows of books—and when the rows filled, *stacks* of books on the floor, against the window, on her desk. Though each room in her house contained items she'd collected in her travels with Walt, the inner sanctum was the repository of the most precious treasures. Every wall, file cabinet, closet, and window ledge was filled: beads, shells, feathers, pots, teacups, bracelets, scarves, handmade paper, hand painted eggshells, weavings. Hundreds of objects, and a story beneath each one. When I picked up a single bead or a shell or a shard of pottery, I was given the tale of its acquisition—the sounds and smells of the outdoor booth, the squint of the seller's dark eyes, the leathery feel of his hands as money was exchanged. And sometimes story layered upon story—the seller's tale, how he'd come to possess the treasure.

During the forty years I knew Carolyn I was allowed into the sanctum only twice. It was not enough to be a loved and trusted member of her inner circle. Your entrance key was also the promise that 1) you would not touch anything unless she gave permission, and 2) you would not pass judgment on the extent of the clutter. Carolyn made no apologies for her style of housekeeping, but she quickly grew defensive if she sensed a visitor's unspoken judgment. My father was such a visitor. A fastidious man, he found it difficult to ignore the stacks of magazines, newspaper clippings on the refrigerator, dog hairs on the sofa. Carolyn's casual attitude toward housekeeping extended to the kitchen table, where cats curled beside your coffee cup and the dog licked the plate you'd momentarily abandoned.

My parents' house—though comfortable and homey, the kind of place where friends and neighbors drop in unannounced, sprawl, and linger—is relatively clutter-free. Like me, my mother is married to a man more enamored of order and cleanliness than she is, and without the influence of our neatnik husbands, both of our homes would probably look more like Carolyn's. Our natural instincts run to collecting, reusing, holding on to objects of emotional value, but unlike Carolyn, we keep our clutter out of sight. Under the watchful eyes of our husbands, every few months we make a clean sweep, reorganize, file away our treasures, which we can retrieve at a moment's notice. For beneath the layers lies an order known only to our minds.

Carolyn was a master of such order. She knew not only the location of each feather and scarf, every letter sent to her, but she could put her hand on it. If something was out of place, she sensed the loss, the way God, in the parable recounted in Matthew, numbers every hair on your head and notes each sparrow's fall. Once while I was visiting during the last year of her life, we sat in the living room, my eyes surveying the small cocktail table. Beneath the glass cover, tiny shards of pottery were arranged on a velvet cloth. They all looked the same to me—nothing special, just broken pieces of clay and glass. Suddenly, in the middle of a sentence, Carolyn gasped, "My God!

The Israeli Blue, where is it?" She opened the case and began searching among the folds of velvet, where she found the piece her eye had
momentarily passed over. A broken fragment, no blue I have ever
seen. Blue, perhaps, only in memory, the color of the sea that washed
over her bare feet one morning thirty-five years ago as she waded
with her young daughter.

If the universe accidentally supplied me with a loving and fertile
mother (my mother gave birth to seven children), it also twisted this
complication: my other mothers, both Carolyn and Aunt Bessie,
were biologically childless, as I am. Thus the world names us. There
is no term for women-who-do-not-give-birth that does not emphasize the *without-ness*. Barren, childless, sterile, even the more modern (and supposedly upbeat) *childfree*. In *A Sense of the Morning*,
David Hopes writes, "Somewhere I picked up the notion that things
must be mine before I can love them." Yes, we pick up that notion
early on, never quite relinquishing it. We give lip service to other
possibilities *(she was like a mother to me)*, but finally, blood is thicker.
No matter whom we take into our homes, how hard we love them,
how fierce the extent of our delight and grief, it appears our bonds
cannot stack up against uterine ties, the blood that binds. "Step,"
my stepson repeated adamantly whenever he introduced me to his
friends during the many years he lived with us. "Yes," I'd think.
"Step." A step is a place between.

And nature is a mother. All else is measured against her stan-
dard. In my case, Nature and I were like those star-tossed lovers
whose paths keep crossing, yet never intertwine. The lovers approach one another, dance awhile, fall away, meet and marry others,
fall away, meet again, and so the dance continues, the timing always
a bit off. Like Aunt Bessie, I *miscarried*. Another unfortunate word,
as if we'd made some mistake, failed to carry not only the child but
the whole idea of mother. Neither of us tried again.

Carolyn carried two children full-term—that is, her daughter
and son survive as adults—though both were birthed by other

women. She and Walt adopted the children while they were stationed in Germany. (Like my father, Walt was a career military
man.) Many years later, Walt found himself once again en route to
Germany, this time with their daughter Karen, who was a teenager
at the time. "It was Carolyn's idea," Karen told me recently, though
that's not the version I remember Carolyn relating; she'd once told
me that Karen, in a fit of adolescent rebellion, had demanded to see
her "real mother."

"She wanted me to have the chance to meet my blood mother,"
Karen continued. "She needed to know that my loyalties were chosen, not compelled." So Walt and Karen set off on Eurail passes, visiting Barcelona, Paris, and finally Germany. It was a Monday when
they arrived in Frankfurt, and the orphanage, where they were to
obtain the birth mother's address, was closed. "We could have stayed
over another day," Karen told me. "But suddenly it didn't seem to
matter. I told my father it wasn't that important to me, that I was
ready to go back. He was touched, I think. We left for home that
day."

I can't know what the birth mother carried all those years, or
what the reunion might have meant to her. I'm too focused on Carolyn, on the difficult love her decision required. Carolyn, waiting at
home while her daughter embarked on a journey to the other side of
the world, half a universe away. The King Solomon story again: how
would the child be divided, which mother would win?

Early on, I'd toyed with the idea of a different mother, but any full-
fledged adolescent rebellion was short-circuited when, shortly before my eleventh birthday, my mother nearly died when my sister
was born. Carolyn and Aunt Bessie were both present during the
week of the difficult labor and birth, my mother's return home, the
bloodied sheets, the midnight dash to the hospital, three dark days
of waiting, no resurrection in sight. Terrified and helpless, certain
that my mother was dying, I begged answers from these women.
Neither, to my knowledge, had ever lied to me; both were incurably,

sometimes brutally honest. "Yes," both said. "She is very ill. No, I can't promise she will live."

Nights, unable to sleep, I walked to the upstairs window and stared down at the street, at the perforated line that divided it. I tried on one possibility, then another. If she died, which one would make the better mother? My choices, I remember thinking, were meager. Great Aunt Bessie was too old, too moody and emotionally unpredictable. I could imagine her, as I'd been told she'd often done when she was a newly married woman, suddenly getting fed up, strapping on her shoes in the middle of the night and lighting out for easier pastures. And Carolyn? Would she, like my mother, be waiting for me when I walked through the door?

More important, would she play with me? Sit on the floor, cut the deck or shake the dice, trade Park Place for two railroads? Carolyn had so many interests. What if my science project was due the next day and her study door was closed? Or what if she left in the middle of dinner for one of her classes—a grown woman going to school at night, taking religion and philosophy, what was the world coming to? I'd never seen Carolyn at a sewing machine—did she even own a needle? Carolyn was a good cook; I'd eaten many meals in her house. But was her cooking the kind I could depend on, day after day? Her menus, when she executed them, seemed European, inspired. What about those days when she wasn't inspired? My mother was like the trail cook on Wagon Train, capable of daily miracles. No matter what was or wasn't in the cupboard, there would always be a meal.

I also feared that Carolyn might be too hard a taskmaster. My mother granted me plenty of space, as she did all her children. Though she maintained adequate order, she was not strict, and I never felt pressured to pursue a certain track. Opportunities were offered, but not insisted upon. We all took piano lessons, but after a few years, no one was forced to continue; my younger brother and I kept on simply because we wanted to. As high school graduation approached and my friends were admitted into prestigious colleges, my mother did not berate me when I made noises about getting a job, maybe taking evening classes at the junior college. She encouraged my writing ability but did not push me into English or journalism, and for a few years I changed majors the way I changed clothes, trying on one, dropping it before the mirror, then scrambling for something to suit my present mood: piano, voice, theater, dental hygiene.

Poetry was a garment I tried on early and never totally discarded, though I kept my passion, and most of my early attempts, secret. Outside of English teachers, the first person to whom I showed a poem was Carolyn. I was sixteen, and there were three characters in the poem: the universe, my existential angst/joy, and me. The universe was portrayed first as a huge cosmic womb, then as a potter. I, in turn, was the infant being birthed, then the clay being formed into a vessel. (Looking back, I see the poem was not only sentimental and cloying; it was also technically inaccurate. Unaware of verbs for pottery-making, I'd resorted to the woodworker's *carved* to describe what the universe had done to me.)

I recopied the poem in my best handwriting, with my best cartridge pen, onto dimpled blue stationary. When I showed it to Carolyn she gave her full attention, reading it slowly, thoughtfully. She did not tell me it was bad; she did not ask me, as one university professor would a few years later, to "please remove this from my presence, it is fouling the air." She simply pointed to the last line, which read *I am intricately carved.* "I'd make one change," she said. "I'd insert 'being' right here, so that it reads 'I am *being* intricately carved.' We are never finished."

During Carolyn's last spring on this earth, she sent a letter saying that the cancer had metastasized to her liver, that she was trying to be hopeful but realistic, that she would like for me to visit. Soon. In the meantime, she was putting her things in order—what did I want? I wrote back that I wanted to have her around for a long time. She dashed back a postcard: "Don't get sentimental on me. Just tell me what you want." In answer, I phoned to say that I'd love to have some of her books, especially the mythology, poetry, and anthropology. "Wonderful!" she said. "Come when you can, we'll go through them together. But when you see me, you can't cry." To be with Carolyn, in the shadow of her death, and not cry? Carolyn, for whom tears were as natural as breathing? I paused. "Okay," she said. "You can cry a little, but not much. We don't have time."

During my preadolescence, the place in Carolyn's house that most intrigued me was her bedroom. I'd never known a married woman with a room of her own. My parents always slept together; in my mind, marriage was synonymous with their double bed, and the closed door meant *do not enter*. Once, when our family was visiting friends, my parents were offered twin beds in the guest room. The children of both families made pallets on the living room floor. After the midnight movie was over and I discovered my pajamas were still in the guest room, I knocked softly. When I got no answer, I tiptoed in. There they were, curled together in the twin bed by the window, the other bed undisturbed. I stared down at them—my father's face pressed into the back of my mother's neck, his arm flung across her waist. This is what it means, I thought, to be married.

So when I discovered that Carolyn and her husband had not only separate beds but separate rooms, I questioned my mother. "People are different," she said. Having failed to receive a satisfactory answer, I began probing, teasing out scenarios. Maybe they didn't like each other anymore—why else would married people sleep apart? What if they'd *never* slept together, not even when they were first married, and that's why they had to adopt? Maybe they'd had a fight a long time ago and one of them had slammed the door the way I did in my sister's face sometimes and they never got around to making up. Then how to account to obvious affection between them—the handholding, the pats, the occasional loving glances across the room? Did he knock on her door? Did they kiss each other goodnight—and what kind of kiss—before parting at the stairs? Was it like having a roommate?

Years passed and the riddle deepened. As I grew into adolescence and beyond, then into my own marriage, their sleeping arrangements came to signify a kind of sanity, a different brand of eroticism, perhaps, the polar opposite to the easy familiarity my parents shared. Does distance keep passion alive? Maybe I'd had it wrong all these years. Maybe there were other ways to love, ways I'd never imagined. The last day I saw Carolyn alive I was kneeling beside the bookshelf in her bedroom while she sat on a three-legged stool, supervising my selections. Her daughter had left for a moment to answer the phone, which rang incessantly those last few months. "Walt is the one I most worry about," Carolyn said. "He loves me so much."

The room suddenly emptied of all sound, as if a drain had been unstopped, all our words sucked away. I snatched at the first noise I could find, a cliché. "What's not to love?" She turned and faced me squarely, sternly, as if betrayed by my dishonesty, my inability to meet her on her chosen ground. "Plenty," she said. "Plenty."

She was right, of course. Dying people are almost always right —they have no time for insignificant babblings. There is plenty, in all of us, not to love. Yet plenty remains. In the last few weeks Carolyn's edges, always sharp, had become even sharper, honed by pain and knowledge. All was centered on the flame of her impending death. Though not yet finished, she was as close as she would get. I reached with one hand to touch her, my other hand on the books that had filled her shelves and would soon fill mine.

Carolyn and Aunt Bessie were both avid readers—selfish readers, as I am. My mother, who also loved to read, is only now catching up on all the books she denied herself during the years she was raising children. Carolyn not only read every book she could get her hands on, she also took them deeply into her mind—questioning, weighing, reconsidering. Though deeply religious (she taught Sunday School for forty years), Carolyn did not passively walk the party line. She tested every belief, each chapter and verse, her worn King

James laid side by side with concordances, the Greek originals, texts by Kierkegaard, William James, Aquinas. And she would argue—at the piano, in the garden, after one of her fine dinners, even before the dishes were cleared and stacked and washed. She'd push aside the platters, stroke the cat's back, and begin the debate with her son, her daughter, my father or me. Predestination. Proofs for the divinity of Christ. The nature of faith or forgiveness, and why Southern Baptists should ordain women.

At the time, already chafing against the church's restrictions and planning my escape to secular humanism, I failed to see why Carolyn remained loyal to the church. Was it her signature stubbornness? Perhaps it was simply a refusal to relinquish the fight. Though she'd preached from a Baptist pulpit, ordination was denied her; when she applied to be a missionary, she was refused. Her son would later leave the church, partly for this reason, to become a Methodist minister. He officiated at Carolyn's funeral, held in the Baptist church where she remained a member, and his words that day were part elegy, part diatribe against the denomination that had tried to force his mother into a subservient role.

I say *try,* for true to her nature, Carolyn managed to find a way. Though never sanctioned by the Southern Baptist Convention, her missionary work nevertheless thrived. Wherever she and Walt were stationed, she taught reading to children and adults, distributed books, lobbied for the opening of schools and libraries. She also employed maids and other domestic workers (at a more than substantial wage) as a way to help not only her family but theirs. Some of these maids were skilled needleworkers. Twenty-seven years ago Carolyn sent me the most beautiful wedding present I was to receive—a pair of embroidered pillow cases for which, I am certain, the maid was generously compensated.

When I think of Carolyn I think of beautiful things. Extravagant, even. "I love things too much," she'd say. "I am too attached to this world." Her bedroom, at the far end of the main floor, held a twin bed, one half of a matched set. The other half, her husband's bed, was in a small basement room furnished with dormlike simplicity. But while Walt's bed was anchored securely in the corner of the room—a bed for sleeping, plain and simple—hers floated like a small boat in a sea of exquisite clutter. Books, clothes, cards and letters, diaries, collections of hats and beads and jewelry from every continent on the globe. From her bed you could reach out and touch any part of her world, any treasure. And within sailing distance was a closet filled with lace blouses, silk dresses, matching gloves and purses and shoes.

Carolyn did not possess a casual wardrobe. She dressed in stockings and low-heeled pumps, accessorizing with jewelry and dramatically draped shawls or scarves. This suited her temperament and lifestyle, which I came to think of as "indoor," as opposed to my mother's more active "outdoor" life. Carolyn's daughter, Karen, refers to her mother's style as a "grand worldliness." My mother's beauty was—and still is—less intentional, something that happens accidentally on her way to something else. Though she often dresses up for weddings, parties, and other occasions, her inborn taste tends to the comfortable; when the occasion is over, she's hurrying upstairs to change into jeans or khakis, sweaters or soft plaid shirts. This leaves her free to bend, to plant, to saddle a horse, lift a grandchild, scramble beneath a blackberry bush, clean out a shed. "Can you use this?" she'll say, pushing a crate of dishes or a basket of linens in my direction. Apart from their sentimental attachment, material things mean little to my mother. She'll give me anything I ask for.

Carolyn, though equally generous, was more selective about her possessions. "Now you can't have this one," she'd say, pulling a silk scarf from an open drawer filled with them. "But any of these just take your pick." Even at the end of her life, she remained territorial. On our last afternoon together, we rummaged through bookshelves in her basement library. Each book was scrutinized individually. She'd hold it in her lap, hesitate, close her eyes as if recalling the book's place in her life. African folklore, myth and magic, folk tales from Thailand and India, feminist theory, the history of the Negro in America, gemology. "For now, these," she said, gesturing to the left side of the bottom shelf. Then a grand sweeping gesture that took in the whole room of books, her fringed shawl draping over the wooden crates. "When I'm gone, of course, they're all yours."

Through the years, Carolyn gave me many gifts; I never went home from a visit empty-handed. A string of seed pods from South Carolina, a turquoise ring, perfume bottles, the cameo pin that had belonged to her mother-in-law. The most frivolous yet intimate gift was a quilted lingerie case with pink tassels. It had belonged to her mother decades before, and it still held a pair of silk stockings in a pale, rosy shade. Though I'd never met Carolyn's mother, I felt as if I had. The portrait over the piano was a tall, stately woman with deeply expressive, hooded eyes and the full, slightly upturned lips that were Carolyn's. Once, while we were watching a Marlene Dietrich movie, Carolyn began to weep. "She looks like Mother," she said. A grown woman crying for her mother? The sight derailed me. "She was so lovely, I wish you could have known her. How can someone that beautiful suddenly not be here? How can that happen? Just like that—gone."

A few years before Carolyn's death, she and I were browsing in the gift shop of a Smithsonian museum, where she had been a volunteer docent. I was wearing garnet earrings, and when she saw a garnet necklace under the display glass she insisted on buying it for me despite my protests. "You worry too much about money," she said. "Besides, I get a discount." She hooked the clasp at my neck and stepped back to admire the purchase. "Garnet is the blood stone, you know," she said. "It signifies the deepest ties." Recently, when I looked up *garnet* in her gemology book, I learned that it derives from *pomegranate,* the "apple of many seeds." With its red juice and numerous offspring, the pomegranate is the traditional symbol for the womb and its lifegiving blood. The shrine of Our Lady of the Pomegranate shows the Madonna holding the fruit in one hand and the child in the other.

When did Carolyn become a mother? When she first saw her

daughter, her son? Did the pregnancy begin in her mind? Perhaps it occurred in the first tears—of joy or pain—that she wept for her children. The Archbishop of Syracuse once wrote, "A woman who weeps always becomes, in the very act, a mother." A few weeks ago I stood in the shower and cried for my niece, for all that awaits her. The violence of the weeping surprised me, wave after wave that gripped my belly and brought me to my knees; when my knees no longer held, I sat down hard, letting the water pour over me, a baptism. I'd chosen the shower, thinking that the sound of the water would muffle my tears, which always distress my husband. I imagine him outside the door, pacing, wringing his hands, frustrated at his inability to ease my "hysteria." But this is no medieval terror, no empty womb gone roaming. Emptiness does not contain the power to fill us. Or, as the Archbishop of Syracuse put it, "there has never been a sterile tear." In ancient matriarchal tribes, all females were called mothers, regardless of which woman gave birth to the child. Look around; they're still in our midst. Foster mothers, adoptive mothers, sisters, nannies, teachers, aunts, mentors, grandmothers, godmothers. Step-mothers, all. Steps between. They help complete the archetype, help bear the weight.

The last time I saw Carolyn she was wearing a bright red dress and a shawl of Russian design, red roses against a black background. Over the phone she had warned me—"I'm a very sick woman, and I look it"—but even so, I audibly gasped when she met me at the door. Carolyn had always been a tall, substantially built woman who carried herself well. This woman was smaller, thinner. Though her face and neck still retained their dignified, almost haughty lift, her chest and belly had caved in, leaving hollows where there had once been roundness. All afternoon the phone kept ringing—friends, doctors, ministers, neighbors. She was a loved woman, but I suspected that the love had become too much for her. She told me that she was craving quiet, solitude, and I took this to mean that my presence was wearing on her. I needed to go, to leave her to herself.

Quickly I finished packing my car—several boxes of books, a

sack of Winesap apples Walt had gathered from a nearby orchard, and two framed collages of African tribeswomen that had once hung in Carolyn's inner sanctum. But when it came time to say goodbye, I hesitated, my arm resting on the piano. As if she sensed my reluctance, her tone turned suddenly breezy. "Next time we'll do the rest," she said. "We'll finish that last shelf. How about after Christmas?" Was this some new game, some new place she was leading me? We both knew she would not be here Christmas. Was she trying to protect me? Or was this, finally, the way she had chosen to release me?

I thanked her again for the collages. "They're from the Ivory Coast," she said. "Crafted from torn bits of butterfly wings. Did you notice that?" I nodded. Yes, I'd been studying them carefully for many years—two tribal women in profile, each wearing an extravagant headdress. One woman is framed in gold leaf, the other in crude wood. The younger woman is tall, strong, a child bundled to her back. In her hand is a club-shaped pestle lifted above a mortar, as if about to grind grain for supper cakes. The other woman is smaller, older, hunched. The pestle has become a walking stick that supports her body, the only burden left to carry.

ANN HOOD

In Search of Miracles

The day my father was diagnosed with inoperable lung cancer, I decided to go and find him a miracle. My family had already spent a good part of that September chasing medical options, and what we discovered was not hopeful. Given the odds, a miracle cure was our best and most reasonable hope. A few weeks earlier, while I lay in a birthing center having my daughter, Grace, my father had been in a hospital across town undergoing biopsies to determine the cause of the spot that had appeared in his mediastinum, which connects the lungs. Eight years before, he'd given up smoking after forty years of two packs a day and had been diagnosed with emphysema. Despite yearly bouts of pneumonia and periodic shortness of breath, he was a robust sixty-seven-year-old, robust enough to take care of my son, Sam, to cook, and to clean the house he and my mother had lived in for their forty-seven years of marriage.

We are a superstitious family, skeptical of medicine and believers in omens, potions, and the power of prayer. The week that the first X ray showed a spot on my father's lung, three of us had dreams that could only be read as portents. I dreamed of my maternal grandmother, Mama Rose. My cousin, whose own father had died when she was only two and who had grown up next door to us with my father stepping in as a surrogate parent for her, dreamed of our great-uncle Rum. My father dreamed of his father for the first time since he'd died in 1957. All of these ghosts had one thing in common—they were happy. A few days later, my father developed a fever as the two of us ate souvlaki at the annual Greek Festival. The X ray they took that night in the emergency room was sent to his regular doctor. Nine months pregnant, I arrived at my parents' house the next morning with a bag of bagels. My father stood at the back door with his news. "The X ray showed something," he said dismissively. "They need to do a few more tests."

For the next month, he underwent CAT scans and -oscopies of all sorts, until, finally, a surgeon we hardly knew shouted across the hospital waiting room: "Where are the Woods?" I stood, cradling my newborn daughter. "Hood," I said. "Over here." He walked over to us and without any hesitation said, "He's got cancer. A fair-sized tumor that's inoperable. We can give him chemo, buy a little time. Your doctor will give you the details." He had taken the time to give my father the same information, even though as he was coming out of anesthesia it had seemed like a nightmare to him.

When someone died in our family, my father pulled out his extra-large bottle of Jack Daniels. It had gotten us through the news of the death of my cousin's young husband, my own brother's accidental death in 1982, and the recent deaths of two of my own forty-something cousins, one from melanoma and one from AIDS. That late September afternoon, my father pulled out the bottle for his own grim prognosis. As the day wore on, we'd gotten more news: only an aggressive course of chemotherapy and radiation could help, and even then the help would be short-lived, if it came at all. "Taxol," the pulmonary specialist had told us, "has given some people up to eighteen months." But the way he bowed his head after he said it made me realize that eighteen months was not only the best we could hope for, but a long shot. My sister-in-law, a doctor, too, was harsher. "Six months after diagnosis is the norm," she'd said.

Sitting in the kitchen that once held my mother and her ten siblings, their parents and grandparents, every day for supper, I did some quick math. Was it possible that the man sitting across from me sipping Jack Daniels would not be alive at Easter? A WASP from Indiana, he had married into a large, loud Italian family and somehow become more Italian than some of his in-laws. At Easter, he was the one who made the dozen loaves of sweetbread, the fresh cheese and frittatas. He shaped wine biscuits into crosses and made pizzeles that were lighter than any my aunts produced. At six-foot-one and over two hundred pounds, cracking jokes about the surgeon, he did not look like someone about to die. He was not someone I was going to let die. If medical science could only give him a year and a half tops, then there was only one real hope for a cure. "There's a place in New Mexico with miracle dirt," I announced. "I'm going to go and get you some." "Well," my father said with typical understatement, "I guess I can use all the help I can get."

A Leap of Faith

Perhaps for some people the notion of seeking a miracle cure is tomfoolery, futile, or even a sign of pathetic desperation. The simplest definition of a miracle that I know is the one that C. S. Lewis proposes in his book *Miracles:* an interference with nature by supernatural power. But even that definition implies something that many people do not believe—that there is something other than nature, the thing that Lewis calls the supernatural. Without that other power, there can be no miracles. For those who cannot buy into the notion of this other power, miracle healing belongs back in the Dark Ages, or at least in a time before the advent of modern medicine. To believe in miracles, and certainly to go and look for one, you must put aside science and rely only on faith.

For me, that leap was not a difficult one. My great-grandmother, who died when I was six, healed people of a variety of ailments with prayer and household items, such as silver dollars and Mazola oil. The source of a headache was always believed to be the evil eye and was treated by my great-grandmother by pouring water into a soup bowl, adding a few drops of oil, then making circles on the afflicted person's palm while muttering in Italian. Curing nosebleeds involved making the sign of the cross on the person's forehead. Around our hometown of West Warwick, Rhode Island, she was famous for her ability to cure sciatica. In order to do this, my great-grandmother had to go to the person's house on the night of a full moon and spend the night, so she could work her miracle at dawn the next day. There was a time when she had a wait list for her services.

Most miracles occur through the intercession of a saint. If one wants a favor, one prays to a particular saint to act on one's behalf. My great-grandmother was no different. She had prayers to various saints to help find lost objects, answer questions, heal. Her prayers to Saint Anthony could answer important questions, such as, Will I have a baby? Does he love me? Will my mother be all right? The prayer was in Italian. She would go into a room, alone, and ask the question. If she was able to repeat the prayer three times quickly and without hesitation or errors, the answer was a favorable one. But if the prayer "came slow" or she couldn't remember the words, the outlook was dire.

The legend goes that my great-grandmother learned all of these things as a young girl in Italy. She was a shepherdess on the hills of a town outside Naples, near a convent. The nuns took a liking to her and passed on their knowledge. Her faith was sealed years later when my grandmother, her only daughter, was three. On a vacation in Italy from the United States, where they had immigrated, my grandmother came down with scarlet fever. The doctors said she would not live through the night. My great-grandmother bundled up her daughter and walked all the miles to the convent. There, the nuns prayed in earnest to the Virgin Mary to spare this child. By morning, she was completely well except for one thing: her long dark curls fell off at the height of her fever. My great-grandmother took her daughter's hair and gave it as an offering of thanks to the Virgin Mary. When my grandmother's hair grew back, it was red, and it remained red until the day she died, seventy years later.

I grew up with this story, and others like it. I never questioned it. Like the story of the day I was born or the day my parents met, I accepted it as fact. But when I shared the story with a friend recently, he said at its conclusion, "But of course that's not true." Startled, I asked him what he meant. "Why, that never happened," he said, laughing. "It couldn't happen. Maybe her fever simply broke or maybe the doctors thought she was sicker than she was. But she wasn't cured by the Virgin Mary, and her hair probably just turned more red as she got older." Therein lies an important distinction between one who believes in miracles and one who doesn't. A believer accepts the miracle as truth, no questions asked. Although I didn't accept my friend's explanations of our family lore, I also knew I could not dissuade him from believing them.

The Healing Dirt

That was how I came to take my ten-week-old daughter an hour northwest of Santa Fe, New Mexico, up into the Sangre de Cristo Mountains, to the little town of Chimayo and its El Santuario. The area had been a holy ground for the Tewa Indians, a place where they believed fire and water had belched forth and subsided into a sacred pool. Eventually, the water had evaporated, leaving only a puddle of mud. The Tewa went there to eat the mud when they wanted to be cured. Sometime around the year 1810, during Holy Week, a man called Don Bernardo Abeyta is said to have been performing the Stations of the Cross in the hills at Chimayo. Suddenly, he saw light springing up from one of the slopes. As he got close to it, he realized the light was coming from the ground itself. He began to dig with his hands and there he found a crucifix. He ran to the Santa Cruz church, which was in a nearby town, and the priest and parishioners went with him and took the crucifix back to their church. The next morning, the crucifix was missing. Somehow it had returned to the place it was found. The same thing happened two more times, so they decided to build a chapel—El Santuario—at the spot. This chapel contains the hole, called *el pocito* (the well)—with the healing dirt.

Like many sites that claim miracles, Chimayo is difficult to reach. Grace and I flew from Boston to Albuquerque, changing planes en route. There, we met my longtime friend Matt, rented a car, and drove for over an hour to Santa Fe. The next morning we rode into the mountains on what is called the High Road to Taos, along curving roads covered with snow. Signs are few, and even getting to El Santuario requires a certain amount of faith. Along the way, we had to stop more than once so I could breastfeed the baby. Despite all of this, I never once grew discouraged. Before I left, my father had hugged me and said, "Go get that dirt, sweetheart." No matter what, I would get it for him and bring it safely home.

Chimayo is called the Lourdes of America because of all the healings that have been associated with it. When one thinks of miracle healing sites, Lourdes is probably the place that first comes to mind. If I hadn't already taken a serendipitous trip there fifteen years earlier, it is probably where I would have gone. In 1982, when I was working as a flight attendant, I was called to work a trip one day while I was on standby. It wasn't until I hung up that I realized the only destination I had been given was "Europe." This was unusual.

I was twenty-five years old and at a point in my life where I had abandoned many of my childhood ways. I had moved from my small hometown in Rhode Island to live in Manhattan. I was working at a job that was not usually associated with someone who had graduated sixth in her high school class and with high honors from college. Instead of the young lawyers I had been steadily dating, I was now madly in love with an unemployed actor. And, perhaps most important, I had given up not just on the Catholicism with which I was raised, but on religion altogether. Like many people I knew at that time, I liked to say that I believed in God, but not in organized religions. The truth is I didn't really think much about God back then, except in sporadic furtive prayers for my immediate needs: Don't let me be late, Please have him call, Help me decide what to do.

When I arrived at Kennedy Airport and looked at my flight schedule, I was delighted to see that the first part of the trip involved dead-heading—flying as a passenger—to Paris that evening and staying overnight. The next day, at Charles DeGaulle Airport, I spotted several other flight attendants waiting for the same Air France flight. They all looked glum. After introductions, I asked if any of them knew where we were headed. "Didn't they tell you?" one of them moaned. "We're going to Lourdes!"

It was Easter week, when upward of a hundred thousand people go to Lourdes, and the streets were clogged with people with varying degrees of illness and deformity, nurses and nuns in starched white uniforms, tourists with cameras snapping pictures of the dying prone on their stretchers, the cripples atrophied in their wheelchairs, the blind with their white canes. But none of this prepared me for what was to come.

It took us almost four hours to board the flight back because of all the wheelchairs, stretchers, and medical equipment. Already the doctor on board had administered emergency care to a dying man. A mother told me that her daughter, seventeen years old and blind, had a rare disease in which her brain was destroying itself. "There's nothing to be done," she whispered. "This was our last chance." The girl sat beside her, staring blankly from eyes the light blue of faded denim. When I placed a meal tray in front of a sixty-year-old man suffering from multiple sclerosis, he grunted, gathered all his strength, and threw it back at me, his eyes ablaze with anger. "It's not you," his wife apologized, her head bent to hide the tears that streamed down her cheeks. "He's angry at everyone."

I sought out the priest who had led a group of a hundred people from Philadelphia. "Do you believe that any of these people will be cured by a miracle?" I demanded. I was young and jaded and arrogant, a stranger to death or illness.

"A miracle," he said, "is usually instantaneous. But some of these people have things that it will take X rays and tests to see if they are cured."

I looked at the young girl with the brain disease. Certainly then she had not had a miracle.

"The church has physicians," he explained, "who study alleged miracles." He told me about the process, how a miracle case must be proved by a medical history and the records and notes of everyone who has treated the person. Scientific evidence such as X rays and biopsies are examined. "And," he added, with what I interpreted as skepticism, "the cure must be a total cure. No relapses or reoccurrences."

"How many of these instantaneous cures have happened at Lourdes?"

He averted his eyes. "I think three," he said. "But you're missing the point," he said, "This is all they have left to do. Miracles come in unexpected ways."

It seemed to me a sad journey. Especially when out of the approximately forty cases a year investigated by the Consulta Medica, only about fifteen are deemed miracles. (The Consulta Medica is the Catholic Church's official body for investigating miracle claims.) Such a statistic in 1982 would have made me even angrier that these people had gone so far, with such hope, only to be disappointed. But by the time I went to Chimayo, I was a different person, and that statistic actually bolstered my belief that the dirt there might cure my father.

I was no longer the skeptical, arrogant young woman who had left Lourdes in a self-righteous huff. Just three months after my trip there, my brother died unexpectedly, and I found myself wanting to find faith somewhere, to believe in something more solid than my fleeting encounters with Buddhism, the Quakers, Ethical Culture, and the Unitarian Church. Over the years between then and my fa-ther's illness, I'd been married and divorced, suffered a miscarriage, lost jobs, changed careers, remarried, given birth to two children, and moved back to my home state of Rhode Island. And I'd returned to church, though not the Catholic Church of my childhood.

When I arrived at El Santuario, I had the fear of my father's death to motivate me and an open heart, a willingness to believe that a cure—a miracle—was possible. Matt had come with me to bring back dirt for his friend, who was dying from Hodgkin's disease. Not even the signs posted everywhere—NOT RESPONSIBLE FOR THEFT—could deter us. Here was a small adobe church with a dirt parking lot, a religious gift store, and a burrito stand called Leona's, which was written up as the best burrito place in New Mexico in all of my guidebooks.

We proceeded under an archway and through a courtyard where a wooden crucifix stood, then into the church where the altar was adorned with brightly painted pictures by the artist known as the Chili Painter. But we hadn't come to see folk art. We had come for a miracle. So we quickly went into the low-ceilinged room off the church in search of the *pocito*. What we found first was a testimony to all the cures attributed to this place. The walls were lined with crutches and canes, candles and flowers, statues of saints, all offer-ings of thanks for healings. Despite the signs asking people not to leave notes because of the fire danger around the lit candles, and not to write on anything except the guest book, the offerings had let-ters tucked into their corners. One statue had a sonogram picture pinned to the saint's cloak. Another had a letter in Spanish: "Thank you for the recovery of our little Luis. Our baby boy is now well. Mil gracias."

Against one wall of this room sits a shrine to the Santo Niño, who is believed to walk about the country at night healing sick chil-dren and wearing out his shoes in the process. As a result, an offering of shoes is given to him whenever a child is healed. The shrine at Chimayo is full of children's shoes, handmade knit booties, delicate silk christening shoes. Roses and letters of thanks adorn the statue, which is seated and holds a basket of food and a gourd to carry water.

In this small room, I began to tremble. I felt I was in a holy place, a place that held possibility. I had not felt that sense of possibility in the hospital and doctors' waiting rooms that had dominated my life these past few months. Even when a surgeon promised to remove my father's tumor if "the sucker will only shrink some," I didn't get the sense of peace I had as I stood surrounded by these testimonies to faith. One, from Ida P. of Chicago, stated that her husband still had six more radiation treatments to go when, on a Sunday, she brought him the dirt. On Monday the tumor was gone.

Ducking our heads, Matt and I entered the even smaller room that housed the *pocito*. It was just a hole in the dirt floor. The walls here were also covered with offerings, including a note that said: "Within this small room resides the stillness of souls that have discovered peace. Listen to their silence. JK, New York," Matt and I knelt in front of the *pocito* and scooped the dirt with our bare hands into the Ziploc bags we had brought. I cannot say what Matt was thinking as he dug. But I had one prayer that I repeated over and over: Please let my father's tumor go away.

To Trust and Love Again

Unlike other sites attributed to miracle healings, Chimayo is not associated with any particular saint. At Lourdes, people believe that Saint Bernadette intercedes on their behalf. Four years before my visit to Chimayo, I went on a long weekend trip to Montreal, Canada. One of my stops was a visit to Saint Joseph's Basilica, where a priest named Brother André was said to have healed people through prayer and oil from a particular lamp. The cures were frequent and often spontaneous. For the year 1916 alone, 439 cures were recorded. "I do not cure," Brother André said. "Saint Joseph cures."

But I did not visit Saint Joseph's Basilica for a cure. I went because the relic displayed there is a particularly gruesome one: Brother André's heart. I've always attributed my love of the more grotesque aspects of Catholicism to my Italian upbringing. My memories of my first trip to Rome are dominated by the various bones and pieces of cloth that churches display. The notion of viewing a heart was especially appealing. However, once I entered the ornate basilica and viewed the heart in its case, I decided I should also see the place where people go to pray to Brother André for a miracle. The walls of this room, too, were lined with offerings, the canes and braces of those who have been healed.

In many ways, I was even more of a cynic than I had been when I'd visited Lourdes. The death of my brother and the emotional havoc it wreaked on my family had left me in a spiritual vacuum from which I had not yet recovered. More recently, a love affair had gone bad, and I was questioning not just my spiritual beliefs, but also my ability to trust and love again.

That day in Montreal, I was not in need of a physical healing, but I had been in turmoil for several months, a turmoil that it did not seem would have an ending anytime soon. For someone who had entered the basilica on a lark—to view a human heart—I was strangely moved by the place, and by the people around me who knelt and prayed. Their conviction was obvious, and in many ways I envied their ability to believe in the power of prayer, or saints, or miracles. I knelt, too, and thought of all the events that had led me to this dark time I was living. At its core was a betrayal in love, a broken promise, a broken heart. A decision—whether to trust this person again—seemed unreachable. I replayed the past months like someone watching a home movie, and then I asked for resolution.

Resolution came. Not that day, or even that month, but many months later. I would not even now claim that the resolution came from the moments I spent praying in Saint Joseph's Basilica. What I gained there was a peace of mind, a calming of the soul, without which I could not have reached a decision. Perhaps more important is that I also began my journey back to faith through that visit. Although the Catholic Church excludes such healings from consideration for miracles, as they do the cures of any mental disorders or diseases that have a high rate of natural remission, I believe a healing of some sort began there. Three years later, as I stood in El Santuario de Chimayo hoping for a miracle of the physical sort, I remembered that day in Montreal and the feeling that overtook me there. As WK from California wrote after her own visit to Chimayo: "It didn't cure me, but then it's God's will. Peace of mind is sometimes better."

A Graced World

Buoyant from our time spent at El Santuario, Matt and I went off to find one of the weavers that live in and around Chimayo. Carefully following the signs for Ortegas, we ended up at a small store that sold carvings and local folk art, not rugs. "Is this Ortegas?" we asked, confused, when we entered. Matt was as certain as I that we had followed the signs exactly and turned in where they pointed. The pony-tailed man behind the counter, Tobias, smiled at us. "You've been to get the dirt," he said. Later, Matt and I would both comment on how gentle his face was. Perhaps it was this gentleness that led me to tell him why I had come and the particulars of my father's disease. He nodded. "He'll be cured," he said. "I've seen it myself, the healings."

He told us the story of a couple who had arrived at his door—"like you two!" The man was grumpy, angry at his wife for insisting they come all this way from Los Angeles when her doctors had told her a cure was hopeless. Sympathetic toward the wife's plight, Tobias invited them to dinner. Reluctantly, the man agreed. As they sat eating on the patio of a nearby restaurant, a strange light began to emit from the woman's breast. Soft at first, it grew brighter and larger until it seemed to encompass her entire chest, like a cocoon. Then it slowly dissipated. It was the skeptical husband who spoke first. "Did anyone else see that?" Each of them had. "My tumor is gone," the wife said confidently. Although Tobias did not know what kind of cancer the woman was suffering from, he was certain then that it was breast cancer, and that she had been cured. He was right on both accounts. Back in California, baffled doctors pronounced her completely free of breast cancer.

"It works," Tobias said.

Matt asked him how, with thousands of people visiting the *po-cito,* the dirt was never depleted.

"Oh," Tobias said, "the caretaker refills it every day. Then the priest blesses it."

This mundane refilling disappointed me. The story I had heard about the dirt was that it replenished itself in some inexplicable way.

"It's not the dirt," Tobias told us. "It's the energy of all the people who come and pray into that *pocito* that makes miracles happen."

Of course, there is no real explanation for what makes miracles happen. But there are plenty of explanations that attempt to disprove them. Just as my friend gave many reasons why my grandmother lived through her bout of scarlet fever, skeptics use scientific, historical, and geographic data to explain away "miracles." Simply put, people either believe or don't. In my own search to understand miracles, I came across books and articles in support of each side.

Joe Nickell, the senior research fellow for the Committee for the Scientific Investigation of Claims of the Paranormal, has written an entire book debunking everything from stigmatas to the Shroud of Turin. On miracle healings, he believes that some serious illnesses, such as cancer and multiple sclerosis, can undergo spontaneous remission, in which they go away completely or abate for long periods of time. Nickell also cites misdiagnoses, misread CAT scans, and misunderstandings as explanations for miracle healings. He reports that as of 1984, six thousand miracles had been attributed to the water at Lourdes but only sixty-four of those had been authenticated as miraculous. Those sixty-four miracles, he claims, were most likely spontaneous remissions, as in the case of a woman who was "cured" of blindness, only to discover she was suffering from multiple sclerosis and the disease had actually temporarily abated.

In response to such skepticism, Dr. Raffaello Cortesini, a specialist in heart and liver transplants and the president of the Consulta Medica, told Kenneth L. Woodward, the religion editor of *Newsweek* magazine and the author of *Making Saints,* "I myself, if I did not do these consultations, would never believe what I read. You don't understand how fantastic, how incredible—and how well-documented—these cases are. They are more incredible than historical romances. Science fiction is nothing by comparison." Believers in miracles do not even need such substantiation.

Still, advances in medical science have made the number of accredited miracles decrease over the years. Pope John Paul II, in his address to a symposium of members of the Consulta Medica and the Medical Committee of Lourdes in 1988, agreed that medicine has helped to understand some of these miraculous cures, but, he added, "it remains true that numerous healings constitute a fact which has its explanation only in the order of faith. . . . " Because proving miracle cures has become so difficult, the church has lightened its requirements on miracles for canonization. It is true that historically, miracles were much more commonplace. In the thirteenth century, Saint Louis of Anjou was responsible for a well-documented sixty-six miracles, including raising twelve people from the dead. Obviously, today's doctors might easily disprove not only many of Louis of Anjou's miracles but also a good number of those that came before and after him. That still leaves us with the ones that no one—not even Joe Nickell—can explain that have occurred since the advent of modern medicine.

Other skeptics point to geography as a factor in alleged miracles. Since many miracles depend on the intervention of saints, and since most saints are European, a higher number of miracles occur there. Certain countries, such as Italy, boast more miracles than others. Physicians from Italy—southern Italy in particular—believe so strongly in miracles that they are more willing to accept a cure as miraculous. The culture there is such that saints and miracles are a part of everyday life. As I drove through southern Italy recently I was struck by how common statues of saints were. They appeared on roadsides, hanging from cliffs, in backyards, on city street corners, virtually everywhere. Almost always there were offerings at the statue's feet, flowers, bread, letters. This was where my own ancestors came from, and I can attest to our family's openness about letting miracles into our lives.

But other cultures share this openness, this willingness to recognize the miraculous. Rather than disproving miracles, I wonder if it doesn't support their existence. It was Augustine who claimed that all natural things were filled with miracles. He referred to the world itself as "the miracle of miracles." I saw this acceptance of daily, small miracles when I visited Mexico City during the Feast of the Virgin of Guadalupe. It was there, in 1531, that a local man named Juan Diego, while walking outdoors, heard birds singing, saw a bright light on top of a hill, and heard someone calling his name. He climbed the hill and saw a young girl, radiant in a golden mist, who claimed to be the Virgin. She told him she wanted a church built on that spot. When Juan Diego told the bishop what he had seen, the bishop asked him to go back and demand a sign as proof that this was really the Virgin. When he returned, the apparition made roses miraculously bloom, even though it was December. Convinced, the bishop allowed a cathedral to be built there. More than ten million people annually visit the shrine in Mexico City, making it the most popular site, after the Vatican, in the Catholic world.

Although it was an impressive sight to behold when I made the walk to the Basilica of the Virgin of Guadalupe along with people, many on their knees, who had come from all over Mexico, that spectacle of adoration was not what struck me about Mexico and its relationship to the miraculous. Rather, it was the way the culture as a whole viewed miracles that impressed me. Street vendors everywhere sold *milagros,* the small silver charms that mean, literally, "little miracles." The charms take the shape of body parts—arms, legs, hearts—and are pinned to saints in churches, to the inside of people's own jackets, everywhere. When I told a vendor that my mother had recently broken her hand, he gave me a *milagro* in the shape of a hand, at no charge.

Throughout Mexico one can also view *retablos,* paintings made on wood or tin that request favors for everything from curing someone of pneumonia to asking that children not fall out of windows or that a woman have a safe childbirth or that a house not catch on fire. Although many churches have glorious collections of *retablos,* these paintings also adorn the walls of shops and homes, humble requests for miracles large and small. "Oh, yes," a friend of mine who lives in San Miguel d'Allende told me, "here in Mexico it is a miracle if someone's oxen do a good job or if it doesn't rain on a special day. Miracles happen every day here."

As if to prove her point, we encountered one such miracle the night before I left Mexico City. Several of us climbed into a cab to go to a restaurant, but the driver was unfamiliar with the address. Everyone studied the map and planned the route, but still we couldn't find the street. Several times we stopped and asked directions. We still couldn't find it. After forty minutes and yet another set of directions, the cab came to a screeching halt. "We're here!" our driver exclaimed happily. "It's a miracle!"

Perhaps, then, part of understanding what a miracle is comes from one's openness to the possibility that they exist and occur regularly. It could be argued that one has to be Catholic to have this ability, since predominantly Catholic countries and cultures claim to have such an attitude. There are many Catholics who would agree that they believe in miracles simply because of their religion. Since I haven't actively participated in Catholicism since I was a young teenager, I would not have credited Catholicism with my own belief in the miraculous. But in retrospect, the roots of that belief must be in my Catholic and Italian upbringing, a combination that certainly indoctrinated me into believing of a general kind.

In fact, the connection between miracles and healing stems largely from the miracles attributed to Jesus. One could, then, broaden the definition of who more readily accepts miracles to include all Christians. Yet I suppose that someone could believe in miracles without believing in the teachings of Christ, or even without believing in God. Conversely, one can believe in God without believing in miracles. What seems most likely is what Kenneth

Woodward explains: "To believe in miracles one must be able to accept gifts, freely bestowed and altogether unmerited." Once one has the ability to do that, it is a small leap to then accept that these gifts have come because someone has intervened on your behalf. Woodward goes on to say that "in a graced world, such things happen all the time." If one presumes that the world is without grace then one cannot accept any gifts, especially those that come from prayer.

When I made my pilgrimage to Chimayo, I had reached a point in my life where I believed in a graced world. I believed that the birth of my son was miraculous, that the love I shared with my husband was a gift, as was my ability to shape words into meaningful stories. Of course I credited hard work, talent, and character, too. But I had come to believe in Augustine's view of the world as the "miracle of miracles." When I arrived back in Rhode Island with the dirt from El Santuario, I felt that anything could happen.

Twenty-four hours after my father held the dirt, he was in respiratory failure and was rushed to the hospital by ambulance. It was Christmas Eve, three months after his diagnosis. Although it would have been a perfect time to have a crisis of faith, quite the opposite happened. I simply believed that he would survive. What happened next surprised me more than his bad turn of health.

While he was in the hospital, his recovery from what turned out to be pneumonia deemed unlikely, his doctor performed a CAT scan, assuming the tumor had grown. My father had only had two treatments of chemo and he needed five before there was any hope of the tumor shrinking. Visiting him, I asked if he was prepared for a bad CAT scan.

"Oh, no," he said with great confidence, "the tumor is gone." "Gone?" I said. He nodded. "I sat here and watched as cancer left my body. It was black and evil-looking and came out of my chest like sparks, agitated and angry." I was willing to believe the tumor might disappear, but such a physical manifestation was more than I had considered. True, Tobias had told us of a light enveloping a sick woman's chest, and it had seemed miraculous. But here was my father, a practical, no-nonsense midwesterner, telling me a story that hinted of science fiction.

The next day my mother called me from the hospital. "Ann," she said, awed, "the CAT scan shows that the tumor has completely gone. It's disappeared." In the background I heard my father chuckling, and then my mother made the doctor repeat what he had said when he walked into the room with the results: "It's a miracle."

An Answered Prayer

Here is the part where I would like to say that my father came home, tumor-free, cancer-free, miraculously cured. The part where I would like to tell you that, well again, he traveled with me to New Mexico, to El Santuario de Chimayo, to leave his CAT scan results in the little low-ceilinged room beside the baby shoes and notes of thanks and crutches and braces and statues and candles.

Instead, my father went home, had one more dose of Taxol, and the next day was once again rushed by ambulance to the hospital in respiratory failure. He spent almost two weeks in intensive care, diagnosed with double pneumonia. From there, he was moved onto the cardiac ward for a week and then into rehab. Weakened by his near-death illness, he moved around using a walker and had no memory of his days in the ICU. My family remembered it all too well, however: the all-night vigils by his side, sleeping on chairs, waiting for doctors and tests and change. Once he was in rehab, his doctor repeated the CAT scan, suspecting a recurrence of the tumor. But there was none, and a date for his release was set.

Two days before he was to come home, he spiked a fever and acquired a cough that proved to be the onset of yet another bout of pneumonia, this one a fungal pneumonia common in patients undergoing chemotherapy, and usually fatal. The doctors prepared us for the worst. "He will never leave the hospital," his pulmonary specialist told us. His health failing, my father instructed us on how to prepare the Easter breakfast specialties that he had been in charge of for the last twenty-five years—how to turn a frittata so it doesn't break, the secret to making light pizzeles.

The day before Easter he began to die. His oxygen supply was so low that his legs grew blue and mottled. A priest was called and administered the last rites, now known as the sacrament of the sick. But when the priest walked away, I grabbed my father's hand and sought a miracle yet again: "Daddy," I said, "please come back. For me and Sam and Grace." At the sound of my children's names, my father struggled not only to open his eyes, but to breathe, a deep life-sustaining breath. By that evening, he was sitting up. "I thought I was a goner there," he joked. Easter morning he told my mother that her frittata was too dry. I stayed with him all day. We watched a movie that night, and then he went to sleep.

The doctor suspected the cancer was back and had spread to my father's brain. He did CAT scans on his bones, lungs, and head. But my father remained tumor-free and cancer-free. Despite this, he died a week later, from the pneumonia he'd caught because of a compromised immune system. More than once since then I have found myself wondering not *if* I got a miracle or not, but whether I prayed for the wrong thing. Should I have bent over the *pocito* and asked for my father to live rather than for the tumor to go away? What I am certain of is this: I got exactly what I prayed for on that December afternoon at El Santuario de Chimayo.

Around the world, at Lourdes and Fatima, on the Greek island of Tinos and in a municipality called Esquipulas on the far eastern part of Guatemala, in Montreal and Chimayo, people are making pilgrimages, asking for miracles to save their lives or the lives of their loved ones. At least, that is what they believe they want, and they will settle for nothing less. After my father died, I still wanted to find someone whose miracle had happened, who had prayed for God to spare their loved one, and for God to have answered.

In my search I traveled to the remote Italian town of San Giovanni Rotondo on the Monte Gargano, the "spur" of the Italian boot that divides the plains of Apulia from the Adriatic Sea. There, a Capuchin monk known as Padre Pio is said to have performed miraculous cures, even after his death in 1968. No ordinary man, Padre Pio had the stigmata, the gift of transverberation (a wound in his side like the one Jesus had), and the ability to bilocate—to be in two places at the same time.

On our way from Naples to San Giovanni Rotondo, an all-day car ride through mountains and rugged terrain, I read the story of Padre Pio aloud to my husband and our eight- and four-year-olds. My husband kept rolling his eyes. More than once he whispered to me, "The guy was a kook." But when I'd finished, I asked the children if they believed that Padre Pio was capable of everything the book said. Did they believe he could heal people, too? "Oh yes!" they both said without hesitation. He was, they concluded, a very special person.

It was a brutally cold March afternoon when we arrived at the cathedral there. The wind blew at over fifty miles an hour. But still the church was packed. I made my way downstairs to Padre Pio's tomb, where the kneelers around it were full of pilgrims with offerings of roses. A father stood beside his young son, who sat hunched and twisted in a wheelchair. As they prayed, the father lovingly stroked the boy's cheek. Watching them, I was convinced that the boy would not walk out of here, leaving his wheelchair behind. I did not believe that the boy would ever walk. But rather than feeling anger at this, as I had years earlier at Lourdes, I felt a sense of peace, a certainty that the boy and his father would leave here spiritually stronger, that they would somehow have the courage to deal with the disease the boy had been given.

True, Padre Pio has been given credit for many miracles. In one, a young girl was born without pupils in her eyes. Her grandmother prayed to Padre Pio without any results. A nun urged her to make a pilgrimage from her small town to San Giovanni Rotondo. There, the monk touched the girl's eyes, and she could see. On their way home, they stopped to visit a doctor who, upon examining the child, was puzzled. The girl could see, but she still had no pupils. As in all places where miracles are said to happen, the legends of the healings are whispered among those who go. They are written about in the small brochures one can buy for a few dollars at the church. But it is only the hopeful, the desperate, who crowd around the water, the dirt, the heart, the tomb.

As I stood to leave Padre Pio's tomb, a middle-aged man and his mother hurried into the room. The woman held a statue of the Virgin Mary, an offering. But what I saw on their faces was a look that I recognized too well, a look I wish I was not familiar with. They wore the shocked and grief-stricken expressions of those who know they are about to lose someone they love. Perhaps they had just received the news. Or perhaps the person had taken a turn for the worse. They had come here because the doctors had told them there was nothing else that could be done. It was a matter of days or weeks or months. The only thing left to do was ask for a miracle.

Another Miracle

Despite the fact that I am a woman who is firmly rooted in the physical world, practical and realistic and skeptical about many things in life at the end of the twentieth century, I still traveled across the country with my newborn daughter, believing I could bring home a miracle for my dying father. Almost a year to the day that my father died, I went back to El Santuario de Chimayo. Father Roca, who has been the parish priest there for forty years, talked to me in his tiny office inside the church. I had written to him months earlier and told him my story. In person, he is a man who dispenses smiles and stories as easily as holy water; several people came in while I was there and, without missing a beat, he blessed their medals and crucifixes, sprinkling holy water, murmuring prayers.

"I have reread your letter many times," he told me. "I am so happy for your family." Thinking he was confused, I said, "But my father died." Father Roca shrugged. "It was God's will. The tumor went away, yes?" I nodded. "Do you know who came here one month before he died? Cardinal Bernadin. From Chicago. He came here and asked me to take him to where the dirt was. I led him to the *pocito* and then left. Fifteen minutes later he emerged, smiling, at peace. 'I got what I came for,' he said." "He wasn't cured," I said. Father Roca smiled. "I know."

I spent about twenty minutes with Father Roca. He told me about the crucifix that was found here. He told me about the miracles he had personally witnessed: the woman who was so sick that her son had to carry her to the *pocito* but who walked out on her own; the young man who came to pray en route to throwing himself off the mountain in despair, but after praying at the *pocito,* decided to return to his wife and baby. To Father Roca, the miracles of El Santuario de Chimayo are not just physical. Rather, they are miracles of inner transformation. "There is," he told me, "something very special about this place."

Later, I returned to the small room with the offerings, and the smaller room with the *pocito* that the caretaker refilled every day. I prayed there, a prayer of thanks for the miracles that had come my way since I'd last visited Chimayo: good health, the love of my children and my husband, the closeness of my family, and, finally, the courage to accept what had come my way. If someone at the shrine on my first visit had told me the miracle I would receive was peace of mind, I would have been angry. But miracles come in many forms, both physical and spiritual. Before I left El Santuario, I again removed a Ziploc bag from my pocket and filled it with dirt. Back at home, my aunt had recently been diagnosed with lung cancer. She needed a miracle, too.

Bereft

GRIEF

I tell you, hopeless grief is passionless;

    That only men incredulous of despair,

    Half-taught in anguish, through the midnight air

Beat upward to God's throne in loud access

Of shrieking and reproach. Full desertness

    In souls as countries lieth silent-bare

    Under the blanching, vertical eye-glare

Of the absolute Heavens. Deep-hearted man, express

Grief for thy Dead in silence like to Death—

    Most like a monumental statue set

In everlasting watch and moveless woe

Till itself crumble to the dust beneath.

    Touch it; the marble eyelides are not wet:

If it could weep, it could arise and go.

            —ELIZABETH BARRETT BROWNING, 1806–1861

My Brother

My brother died. I had expected him to, sometimes it seemed as if it would be a good thing if he were to just die. And then he did die. When he was still alive I used to try to imagine what it would be like when he was no longer alive, what the world would seem like the moment I knew he was no longer alive. But when that moment came, the moment I knew he was no longer alive, I didn't know what to think, I didn't know what to feel.

He had been dead for a long time. I saw him two months before he was actually dead. He was lying in his bed; his head was big, bigger than it used to be before he got sick, but that was because his body had become so small. The bed in which he lay dying I had bought for him. It was a small bed, a bed for a child. The sheets on the bed I had bought at Ames, a store in the small town in which I now live, a place he would never see. He would never see me in the place I now live, but I could see him in the place in which he was then living. He lived in death. Perhaps everyone is living in death. I actually do believe that, but usually it can't be seen; in his case it was a death I could see. He was alive, he could speak, he still breathed in and out, he still sometimes would demand a particular kind of food and then decide that he liked it or did not like it, but he wasn't alive in a way that I had ever seen anyone before. He was lying in his bed with the thin sheets on top of him, his eyes open, wide-open, as if they had been forced to be that way, his mouth open, as if it had been forced to be that way; he was lying in his bed, and yet he was somewhere else. When I saw him that time, the last time before he died, and he was lying in bed, his hands were invisible; they were beneath the sheets, the sheets were not moving up and down; his eyes were open and his mouth was open and his hands were not visible. And that was exactly the way he looked when the undertaker unzipped the plastic bag in which he lay when I went to see him at the undertaker's. When I saw him, though, lying in bed, two months before I saw him at the undertaker's, he was in his mother's house. She is my mother, too, but I wasn't talking to her then, and when I am not talking to her, she is someone else's mother, not mine. I could see him through the louvered windows while I was standing on the gallery. It was at the end of one of those days, like so many I used to know when I was a child, and that I wanted to run away from: in the east the darkness was already falling down from the sky; in the west, the sun, having exhausted itself from shining with such relentlessness, was hurrying to drop below the horizon. Not a bird sings then; chickens fly into trees to roost for the night, the trees become still; no one quarrels, people's voices are muted. It is not the usual time of day to be born or to die, it is the usual time of day to prepare to be born or to prepare to die; that was the time of day when I first saw him two months before he died. He did not die in the middle of that night.

When I was looking at him through the louvered windows, I was not thinking of myself in the sense of how it came to be that he was lying there dying and I was standing there looking at him. I was thinking of my past and how it frightened me to think that I might have continued to live in a certain way, though, I am convinced, not for very long. I would have died at about his age, thirty-three years, or I would have gone insane. And when I was looking at him through the louvered windows, I began to distance myself from him, I began to feel angry at him, I began to feel I didn't like being so tied up with his life, the waning of it, the suffering in it. I began to feel that it would be so nice if he would just decide to die right away and get buried right away and the whole thing would be done with right away and that would be that. I entered the house and stood in the doorway of the room in which he was lying. The house had a funny smell, as if my mother no longer had time to be the immaculate housekeeper she had always been and so some terrible dirty thing had gone unnoticed and was rotting away quietly. It was only after he was dead and no longer in the house and the smell was no longer there that I knew what the smell really was, and now as I write this, I cannot find a simile for this smell, it was not a smell like any I am familiar with. I stood looking at him for a long time before he realized I was there. And then when he did, he suddenly threw the sheets away from himself, tore his pajama bottoms away from his waist, revealing his penis, and then he grabbed his penis in his hand and held it up, and his penis looked like a bruised flower that had been cut short on the stem; it was covered with sores and on the sores was a white substance, almost creamy, almost floury, a fungus. When he grabbed his penis in his hand, he suddenly pointed it at me, a sort of thrusting gesture, and he said in a voice that was full of deep panic and deep fear, "Jamaica, look at this, just look at this." Everything about this one gesture was disorienting; what to do, what to say; to see my brother's grown-up-man penis, and to see his penis looking like that, to see him no longer able to understand that perhaps he shouldn't just show me—his sister—his penis, without preparing me to see his penis. I did not want to see his penis; at that moment I did not want to see any penis at all.

What I am writing now is not a journal; a journal is a daily account, an immediate account of what occurs during a certain time. For a long time after my brother died I could not write about him, I could not think about him in a purposeful way. It was really a short time between the time that he became sick and the time he died, but that time became a world. To make a world takes an eternity, and eternity is the refuge of the lost, the refuge for all things that will never be or things that have been but have lost their course and hope to recede with some grace, and even I believe this to be true, though I also know that I have no real way of measuring it.

His death was imminent and we were all anticipating it, including him, but we never gave any thought to the fact that this was true for all of us, too: our death was imminent, only we were not anticipating it . . . yet. Death was the thing that was going to happen to him, and yet every time I got on an airplane to go and pay him a visit, I was quite afraid that I would never come back: the plane would crash, or in some way not at all explainable, I would never come back.

There is a photograph of my brother in a book (an album) full of photographs collected by my husband. They are family photographs and they are in this book because my husband wanted to give our daughter a snapshot view of the first five years of her life. The photograph of my brother that is in this album shows a young man, beautiful and perfect in the way of young people, for young people are always perfect and beautiful until they are not, until the moment they just are not. In this photograph his skin is smooth; his skin looks as if it were a piece of precious fabric covering a soft surface (the structure that was his face), and if this fabric were to be forcefully pressed with the ball of a finger, it would eventually return to its smooth and shiny surface, looking untouched by experience of any kind, internal or external. He was beautiful then. He did unspeakable things then; at least he could not speak of them and I could not really speak of them to him. I could name to him the things he did, but he could not name to me the things he did. He stole from his mother (our mother, she was my own mother, too, but

I was only in the process of placing another distance between us, I was not in the process of saying I know nothing of her, as I am doing now), he stole from his brothers; he would have stolen from me, too, but the things he could steal from me were not available to him: my possessions were stored on a continent far away from where he lived. He lied. He stole, he lied, and when I say he did unspeakable things, just what do I mean, for surely I know I have lied and once I stole stationery from an office in which I worked. His unspeakable things were things he was unable to speak openly about. He could never say that anything in front of him was his own, or that anything in front of him came to him in a way that he did not find humiliating. He was a thief, he was not proud to say that most of what he had had come to him through stealing. In the place in which he lived when his skin was smooth and unblemished—he was really young then but beyond adolescence—he had some books on a shelf; they were school textbooks and one was a history of the West Indies, though really it was a history of the British West Indies. This book was a book he took from his school. I understood that, taking a book from school; when I was a little girl, living on that small island, I used to steal books from the library, not my school, but the library; the school that I attended had no books that I wanted to steal. I would not have wanted to steal a book about history; I stole only novels, and all the novels I stole were novels I had read, they were all written in the nineteenth century. I was not interested in history then, only so now; my brother had history books on his shelf. He was obsessed with the great thieves who had inhabited his part of the world, the great hero-thieves of English maritime history: Horatio Nelson, John Hawkins, Francis Drake. He thought that the thing called history was an account of significant triumphs over significant defeats recorded by significant people who had benefited from the significant triumphs; he thought (as do I) that this history of ours was primarily an account of theft and murder ("Dem tief, dem a dam tief"), but presented in such a way as to make the account seem inevitable and even fun: he liked the costumes of it, he liked the endings, the outcomes; he liked the people who won, even though he was among the things that had been won. But his life was real, not yet a part of history; his reality was that he was dead but still alive; his reality was that he had a disease called AIDS. And no matter what anyone says, or for that matter what anyone has discovered so far, it seems to me that to be so intimately acquainted with the organism that is the HIV virus is to be acquainted with death. We are all acquainted with death; each moment, each gesture, holds in it a set of events that can easily slide into realities that are unknown, unexpected, to the point of shock; we do not really expect these moments; they arrive and are resisted, denied, and then finally, inexorably, accepted; to have the HIV virus is to have crossed the line between life and death. On one side, there is life, and the thin shadow of death hovers over it; and on the other, there is death with a small patch of life attached to it. This latter is the life of AIDS; this was how I saw my brother as he lay in his bed dying.

Journey

But something had changed, or was changing. Everything always did, no matter how much he loved what he had. The only redemption would be if all the tumbling and rearrangement were to mean something. But he was aware of no pattern. If there were one great equality, one fine universal balance that he could understand, then he would know that there were others, and that someday the curtain of the world would lift onto a sunny springlike stillness and reveal that nothing—nothing—had been for naught, neither the suffering of all the children, . . . nor love that ends in death: nothing. He doubted that he would have a hint of any greater purpose, and did not ever expect to see the one instant of unambiguous justice that legend said would make the cloud wall gold.

—MARK HELPRIN *Winter's Tale*

MAY 29, 1992

I get up early, drive Emily to school, and try to get back to sleep. But I can't. The pictures in my mind of Lucas dying will give me no rest. How can I erase, or at least soften, these images and remember him as he was in health, his sweet face, happy smile? How could they have put him and us through those changes? I never felt warned about those possibilities in the dry words of the "informed consents." What is the process now other than waiting for time to pass? Should I try to get back to work next week? Would it help to travel far away or will I just miss him in a different place? I need some faith in God, but where was He when we needed him, when so many were praying on our behalf? I feel old, as if I have lived too long, seen too much, suffered beyond any hope of redemption. I am empty, barely capable of loving those who need me. My best hope for immortality lies in a churchyard. And the world goes on as if nothing has happened. I don't want to be a part of it.

I've got to figure out how to redirect these memories. I took Emily to a class party this afternoon at the home of one of her teachers. While the girls swam and the mothers chatted, I found a quiet spot overlooking a pond and woods. Thankfully, everyone left me alone. As usual, my mind filled with memories of Lucas in the hospital, enduring all those horrors—and us with him. Both Clare and Emily appear better able to focus on his happiness and the pleasure he gave us. I've got to learn how to do this if I am to get past this bitter place that in Lamentations is "the wormwood and the gall."

Tonight Clare told me that Amy, the four-year-old in the room next to Lucas who got a bone marrow transplant a week after he did, died yesterday. The entrance to the PICU should have carved over it "Relinquish all hope, ye who enter here."

I closed the door to Lucas's room today only to be confronted by his poster of Bugs Bunny and the legendary "That's All, Folks!"

I can't decide what to do next, particularly about getting back to work. Nothing draws me there or seems important, but maybe I better try it so I don't just brood. I also need to see my therapist from other times, Dr. McClary, and talk about what has and will become of me.

MAY 30, 1992

Lucas was brave, now I must be brave. I'm not quite sure what that means, but facing the loss and finding reasons to live seem the main tasks. The hole in my life left by his death is beyond filling. It is a void stretching into whatever future I have left. I cannot see a child on the street or boys playing soccer or teenagers hanging out at the mall without thinking of what was denied my wholly innocent son. The fact that he had a wonderful life for the six years he was ours is insufficient consolation. He deserved much more.

Emily has been sleeping on cushions at the foot of our bed. About midnight last night she suddenly awoke, walked into Lucas's room, lay down on his bed, and went back to sleep. She has no recollection of this today.

We have decided on a seven-day cruise to Bermuda in June for our grieving getaway. After watching a TV commercial in the hospital, Lucas said that he wanted to go on a cruise when he got better. How will it be without him?

This terrible thing has happened to me. My little boy, whom I loved more than life itself, is dead of a disease that came from my body. I cannot let this become the defining moment of my life. I have people who love and need me and I must somehow absorb this calamity and go on. I have borne burdens before and I can bear this one.

JUNE 1, 1992

Why do I and all these other people live on when my son cannot? I breathe, I eat, I can walk outside, smell the fragrance of spring, feel the warm breeze. All these simple blessings were, one by one, taken from Lucas.

Sometimes, when I feel tired and try to sleep, I suddenly sit upright, panicked at the thought of what he, and we, went through in that hospital. Only time can dim those images, but how can it happen when they keep lurching to the front of my mind?

Today Clare went to the funeral of Amy, the little girl who lived only one week longer than Lucas. What kind of world is this? I went to see Dr. McClary, gave him a copy of my hospital journal. I need help.

It's the middle of the night. No chance at sleep. Both Emily and Clare were crying tonight. I've always been able to forgive myself mistakes before, but this time is different; I don't know if I can and it scares me. My involvement in Lucas's death and the slow, progressive way it occurred makes me frantic when I recall it. It's been only thirteen days and I suppose I may be expecting too much, but I feel used up. What can the future hold but more terrible surprises?

Clare doesn't want me to be angry at Bob Norton, but he's the person I see as recommending the transplant, then leaving us at the end. I'm mad enough at myself; he's entitled to some of it. I sent him a copy of my journal today with the following cover letter:

Dear Bob,

I wanted you to know that we believe that you and the rest of the oncology staff did everything you could to save Lucas. I also think that, for all your collective experience, the ordeal that a family of a dying child goes through is not fully understood, even by those like you who have seen it many times. I hope you will read the enclosed journal that I kept during Lucas's illness. I send it to you unedited; I have not yet been able to read it and perhaps never shall. I think you might find something in it that will help you respond to the plight of other families who place their precious children in your care and then must cope with unimaginable disaster.

While I do not hold you responsible for what has happened to us, I think you will understand why I am sorry I ever met you.

Gordon

JUNE 2, 1992

I am not a tragic figure, nor will I become one. But I do get anxious, frightened really. If this child can be taken from me in such a hideous way, then what am I to believe in, to hold on to? I have lost any purchase on my life. The landmarks are familiar, as in a dream in which I move but to little purpose, not knowing what to expect next. And where is he, where is Lucas? I embraced him, kept him from harm, slept next to him. And then I had to watch him grow sick and die. And I could do nothing to save him. Nothing to protect Emily from the awful sights, nothing to deliver Clare from the collapse of her best hopes. What does it all mean? I pray that God will at least grant me the favor of being the next to die. I cannot mourn anyone else.

JUNE 3, 1992

For something to do I write letters of thanks for condolence messages and include an appeal for Lucas's memorial fund. He deserves more than a gravestone. That suite at the Tremont was a help to us and we would like to create a similar place for other families facing what we did.

My own good health rebukes me. The simple acts of eating and drinking seem unfair when he could do neither for so long.

It still seems inconceivable to me that he's not upstairs sleeping with Clare on this early summer morning. I should be getting ready to wake him up so he can watch a bit of TV before I drive him to school on the scooter. In my memory I take his helmet off, hand him his backpack from the basket. He puts it on, kisses me, and marches confidently toward the kindergarten door. How old will I be before I stop missing that?

Today Clare, Emily, and I went to Lucas's grave and planted some bougainvillea that a friend had given us. The flowers left after the funeral were dying.

I took the child seat off my bike. I thought of the many miles that Lucas and I traveled together. He was almost too big for this; learning to ride a two-wheeler was next. Clare wondered how I could bear removing it. What I couldn't bear was seeing that empty seat every time I walked through the garage. What are we going to do with all his things?

Tomorrow I'm going to try to work for a couple of hours. Two weeks since he died. It seems both an instant and a lifetime. I'm reading *Closer to the Light,* accounts of near-death experiences in children. It's reassuring in the peace they seem to have experienced, but discouraging in the reminder that Lucas did not return. I transferred Lucas's college account balance to Emily.

It becomes clear that I must somehow emerge from this experience a better person or I will not have fulfilled my obligation to Lucas's memory. This grief must give way to some emotion of more lasting meaning. It is a waste of time to grope for rational explanations of what has happened, even worse to flagellate myself for decisions made out of love.

JUNE 5, 1992

Today I went to get my hair cut. The barber said, "Where's your son today, in school?" At the bank the assistant manager came over to ask how Lucas was. Later I went for a bike ride, my first alone without the child seat. I went by Lucas's grave and invited him to join me. Perhaps he did.

JUNE 6, 1992

I worked for three days this week, three to four hours each day. I surprised myself with my ability to focus, though thoughts of Lucas intruded frequently. The worst moment came when a patient, at the end of the session, asked how my son was doing. Doesn't anybody read the paper?

Tonight I went with a friend to my first baseball game in the new Orioles stadium. I noticed as never before all the six- and seven-year-old boys at the ballpark. Lucas is now frozen forever at six-and-a-half in my mind and in my heart. As I grow older, will I try to picture him as he would be then? Will the passage of time give me some relief from the senseless and demeaning jealousy I feel toward all fathers of healthy sons? What I miss most are two things: the unalloyed admiration I received from him and the love that he evoked in me. Being his father was the thing I was best at; I find it paralyzingly hard to go on without it.

JUNE 7, 1992

The mornings are terrible. I awaken early and there is an instant's peace before I remember who I am and what has happened. Then comes the crushing realization that he is not here beside me and never will be again. My mind begins again to review the forks in the road we traveled to the place of his dying.

Clare and I went to church today for the first time since the funeral. It was a baptismal service. We cried through most of it.

JUNE 10, 1992

Clare and Emily went to the elementary school and gave one of Lucas's books to each of his eighteen kindergarten classmates with a picture of him and an inscription: "To _____ from Lucas Livingston, a friend to remember."

When he was alive, Clare often referred to Lucas as an angel. He had this otherworldly goodness and happiness about him. As I think about him now, I think he was and is an angel who has temporarily dematerialized but who is with us still, loving us, watching over us, waiting for us to shed our earthly selves and join him. This is the most comforting belief I can conjure and returns some sense of order, meaning, and, above all, hope to his death.

JUNE 12, 1992

I took the day off from work today to prepare for the Bermuda cruise tomorrow. Inactivity accentuates my feelings of oldness. I trim my beard and remember that Michelle Kupiec, Lucas's teacher, said that his favorite songs were "My Father's Old Gray Whiskers" and "Baby Beluga."

I saw someone in a wheelchair the other day and it hit me that what I am feeling is similar to the experience of an athlete who finds himself suddenly and permanently injured, unable to do what he has spent his life training for. I can't be Lucas's father any longer and this loss is, in a selfish way, as hard to mourn as the knowledge of all that he will miss.

What will it be like on this cruise, my sad heart afloat?

JUNE 13, 1992

We're under way. The departure from New York Harbor was full of memories of our trip up here with Lucas two years ago: passing the Empire State Building and the World Trade Center. Clare was crying quietly and couldn't bear to look at the Statue of Liberty where Emily, Lucas, and I had climbed to the top on that rainy day. It weighs heavily upon us that he asked in the hospital to go on a cruise "after I get better." We promised him we would and now here we are without him. It doesn't help that there is an extra bed in our room.

JUNE 14, 1992

We plow the sea toward Bermuda, lugging our memories with us. I continue to read about angels, which I hope will contribute to the peaceful acceptance that I so long for. With all the metaphysical thought and reading his death has provoked in me, I wonder if Lucas died to save my soul.

It strikes me as ironic that I started this journal when I thought to tell the story of my experience in Vietnam. Now in the course of a year, everything has changed. My oldest and youngest sons are gone and I am left grasping for some meaning in their deaths. Maybe I will find it the way I started, in the writing.

JUNE 15, 1992

Today we went to the Queen's Birthday parade in Hamilton. In the afternoon we rented scooters and traveled to a beach near St. George. While Clare, Emily, and Emily's friend Kathryn sunbathed, I walked through the nearby fort. I felt so alone, thought of the things I could be showing Lucas, wondered what would have been his reaction to the old swords, muskets, and uniforms, the dim, stone-lined passageways, even a "ghost of St. George" on display.

I realized tonight that Clare and Emily are the only ties holding me to the earth. Without them, I think I would try to follow Lucas. There are moments when I think of him that my longing for his touch and his smile is so intense that I wish I could will my heart to stop. I suppose that this feeling will lessen with time, but I'm not sure I want it to. I'm afraid that what will fade is the memory of what it felt like to love him.

JUNE 16, 1992

The realization that my grief, perhaps all grief, is essentially self-pity may allow me to find my way past it. What is needed, of course, is courage. I was everything to him that I could be, the best I have ever been. My task now is to transform those feelings into something that will sustain and nourish those lives still entrusted to me. Surely I am up to that, particularly since Clare and Emily are giving everything of themselves to help me.

As we looked out over the ocean today at Elbow Beach, it was impossible not to be struck with the similarities to the Bahamas: the palm fronds swaying against the sky, the clear, turquoise water. Lucas loved playing in the sand, running from the incoming waves. I never taught him to swim. There seemed plenty of time for that.

He didn't know much about me, either. As with my other children, I anticipated with pleasure gradually telling him what I had done and seen. It's hard to have that bit of immortality snatched away, the idea that he might tell *his* children about me. It was like that with Andrew's death too. One of his college professors wrote a condolence note mentioning how proud Andrew had been, when the class was studying Vietnam, to bring in something I had written about my time at war.

Andrew's birthday. I remember our cruise on the *Rotterdam* seventeen years ago. My father took the kids and me at about this time of year. I recall one photo from that trip, a picture of Andrew at age seven, squatting on a Bermuda beach, looking at a shell, I think. He was so skinny and vulnerable. Another passenger on the ship who saw us in the swimming pool said, "Your kids look really happy." And so they did.

I'm old now, fifty-four in two weeks. I feel so much older since Lucas's death. I had lost my fear of aging, imagining that watching Lucas and Emily grow would pleasure the rest of my life. My other children are well on their ways as adults now and have little need of me. If I convince myself that reunion with Andrew and Lucas awaits, I can have no fear of death.

The loss of my sons has brought me to the edge of an abyss. I stare into it and see only darkness. I would fill it with faith, but whatever belief I had in a just universe has been undone. I, of all people, should have been aware of what a fantasy this notion was. God knows I have seen enough injustice and random death. But I guess I harbored an unconscious belief that the really terrible, life-decimating tragedies were reserved for others. Now I wonder about curses and stigmata.

I've always felt lucky because I've always been lucky. When this happens, at some point you start to feel that you deserve it, that you've somehow earned it. I don't feel lucky anymore.

I told Clare tonight that "I think about him all the time, don't you?" The answer, of course, was yes, and we both began to cry. I said something about being sure he was all right. She said, "I hope so. . . . I just want him back." I start to tell her how sorry I am, but she knows that and I can't even think the words without remembering Emily at his bedside when he died: "I'm so sorry, Luke. I'm so sorry." I don't see how I'm going to get past this.

JUNE 19, 1992

> Sorrow is no longer the islands but the sea.
> —NICHOLAS WOLTERSTORFF *Lament for a Son*

It is the last night of the cruise and we near New York. It has been a good time for Emily, who appears to have lost herself playfully with her friend Kathryn. Clare and I have brought our grief with us; and as we did things, I know she was thinking as I was, "Wouldn't Lucas love this beach? How much fun it would be to show him this parade, all these boats, explore the ship with him, look out at the ocean." How long, I wonder, will everything we do be accompanied by such regret? The familiar things of home remind us of him; the new things we do underline the regret that he will never do them. The sight of a blond-headed little boy brings me near tears.

The ship as a metaphor for life has been much used and the reason is apparent. I feel as though, in my rush toward an unknown port, I have lost overboard two children who were the most compelling reasons and rewards for the journey. Andrew chose to abandon ship, but fate took Lucas in spite of our attempts to rescue him. The life preserver I threw, my bone marrow, sank and took him down with it. The ship sails on, destination as uncertain as ever, but my heart feels buried at sea.

I know I sound morose, but for the most part I'm not. I joke with Emily and Kathryn, read escapist novels, feel an undiminished closeness to Clare. I fear, though, some permanent loss of capacity for joy that I imagine will grow more subtle, less noticeable with time. Lucas died one month ago today.

I've thought a lot about courage lately. In my work I have come to believe it is the quality most important in healing psychic wounds. Much of my life has been devoted to trying to define its meaning and so conform my behavior. With the loss of my sons, I wonder now what is required of me to behave bravely and with dignity. Clare seems to be able to do this as I wish I could, without reflection or self-consciousness. She went through that terrible two months of his dying in an unflinchingly loving and steadfast way that I could only partially emulate. Now I want to pay tribute to their valor, hers and Emily's and Lucas's; I'm afraid I don't have the words.

> What happens when you let go, when your strength leaves you and you sink into darkness, when there's nothing that you or anyone else can do, no matter how desperate you are, no matter how you try? Perhaps it's then, when you have neither pride nor power, that you are saved, brought to an unimaginably great reward.
> —MARK HELPRIN *A Soldier of the Great War*

JUNE 20, 1992

Today, the return. I rode my bike—mindful again of its terrible lightness on the hills—out to visit with Lucas. I told him of our trip and my sadness that he had not been with us to marvel at the scents and colors, to ride behind me on the scooter in Bermuda, to sleep in our cabin on the great ship. I sat for a long time next to his still unmarked grave and wept for all I have lost. Then I took our familiar route home around the lake and past his school. In the tree outside the kindergarten room are hanging many hand-colored decorations, no doubt an end-of-school project. His should be among them.

It is summer now. Tomorrow is Father's Day.

JUNE 21, 1992

Clare and I went to church today and again cried through most of the service. I am undone by the stained-glass image above the altar depicting Christ as a shepherd holding a lamb close to his heart while on his left, pressed against his leg, is a young sheep looking up. Last year I imagined Andrew as the lamb. Now he is the sheep and Lucas rests on Christ's arm. As the music and the words of the liturgy wash over me, I pray for some sign that Lucas is safe and happy and not alone. I doubt I will receive one, owing, I suppose, to lack of faith.

The pain is getting worse, not better. I can hardly contain it. Today I came upon a collection of his work and his report card, which his teacher, Michelle Kupiec, gave Clare. So many report cards have I seen, but this one ends "Your child's placement will be Grade _____." Her final comment: "6/92: Lucas was a joy and touched the lives of everyone."

JUNE 23, 1992

Today I flew Emily in my plane up to New Haven and dropped her off to spend a few days with Nina. It was my first flight in nearly seven months, since our return from the Bahamas. Even then Lucas must have had leukemia, and us so happily unaware.

As I was flying back alone today, searching for something to feel good about, I began to think about the fact that Lucas at no point thought or, I believe, feared that he was going to die. Because we never believed it until he was unconscious near the end. Clare has spoken about how awful it would have been for him to relapse again and again until he got the clear sense that things were hopeless. I think he was spared that terrible foreboding and for that I am thankful.

What I feared most has happened. Lucas is now forever a six-year-old boy who died. We miss him now as he was and still would be were he with us. In a year he would have been so much different from the child we mourn. In five years we would hardly recognize him and will have only the memories of his angelic countenance smiling forever at us from his photographs—as he was and always now will be. So it's not just the grindstone of time that will dull our pain; it's his not keeping up with us or with the world that will finally, sadly, inevitably bring us some peace. That and the hope that we will see him again on the other side.

JUNE 24, 1992

I go through the motions of normal living. I'm working, bicycling, eating, sleeping, being with Clare. Sometimes I will, like any post-trauma sufferer, flash on images of Lucas in the PICU. I fight off panic and wrench myself back to the present. When I am doing something that we did often, like riding the scooter or bike, I can hardly believe that we will never do it together again. Over and over I can hear him saying, "I love you, Dad." I rode by his grave yesterday and told him how much I missed that.

JUNE 26, 1992

Sometimes it seems that the cracked vessel of my spirit can contain no more pain. Often this occurs as I am trying to fall asleep. The welling up of my grief threatens to overwhelm me and I am seized with the need to cry out. So that I do not awaken Clare, I go downstairs where I content myself with the low moans of a wounded animal until I can once more bring myself to return to the bed we shared so long with Lucas.

JUNE 27, 1992

Today, marked on the kitchen calendar for this date, is the circled number *100*. Thankfully, Clare has not asked me about it. In April, we were trying to make plans for the summer and I counted to the one-hundredth day after the transplant, the point when the intensive phase of his outpatient treatment would be complete. How long ago it seems since that flash of optimism. Three days until my birthday. When Clare and Emily ask me what I want, I can think of nothing except my little boy.

JULY 1, 1992

I was thinking this evening that I have always felt a wish that I could have another five minutes with my father to say good-bye. Not so with Lucas. He got everything I had to give from the day of his birth until the hour of his death. There was nothing left unsaid or undone. I treasured every moment with him and felt his unqualified love in return. Only this knowledge will allow me to heal.

JULY 4, 1992

Today Emily and I went for a glider ride; I had arranged it for her as a Christmas present. It was a beautiful day, scattered clouds at five thousand feet, the point at which we disconnected from the tow plane. We were up for about forty-five minutes, circling with only the sound of the wind. The pilot found a thermal updraft and we climbed a few hundred feet before settling gently back to earth. It was an experience to remember, the two of us squeezed tightly together in that small backseat, the Plexiglas canopy filled with clouds and sky.

None of us had much enthusiasm for going to the fireworks at the lake. I couldn't stand the thought of walking my bike up the hill without Lucas on the back. So we stayed home and felt the explosions rock the night.

JULY 9, 1992

Now we are on Cape Cod, at a friend's house. We flew up, with Clare alone in the backseat where Lucas always slept with his head in her lap. We had last been to Provincetown in August 1986, when he was a baby, flying down from New Hampshire for a day of whale watching. I walked a couple of miles on the beach last night, toward Wellfleet. I could almost feel the gentle grasp of Lucas's hand as I walked. I came upon a stone, worn to a smooth oval by the sea and spoke aloud, showing it to him before tossing it futilely into the dunes. It is growing possible now to think of living the rest of my life with this empty place in my heart. We laugh, eat, sleep, and do not speak of our missing child. I know that Clare, like me, thinks of him all the time, even as we make love.

We are in a large, airy house on a bluff overlooking Cape Cod Bay. The tides ebb and flow below us and, amid all this history, I feel acutely the brief flash that is my existence. Yet it seems important to find some meaning beyond the pain and loss that is my portion now.

The summer has a curiously misspent quality about it. We had come to think of it as a summer of healing for Lucas, with our activities organized around his continuing need for care: frequent outpatient visits, a surgical mask in public. Now our obligations to him are over and we are free to go to all these places: Bermuda, Cape Cod, Wyoming. The baggage I bear is my grief and the frustrated desire to share all this with him. I didn't realize how much I had come to see everything through his eyes, enjoying his curiosity and wonder; how it pleasured me to explain new things to him. Emily already knows so much that I often feel I have little to give her. When I talked to her today about the tides, her knowledge was as great as mine.

The sun is setting off Long Point near Provincetown. It creates a highway of light on the quiet waters of the bay. This view is one of countless such pleasures I have had, but Lucas will not see it with living eyes. I think his last earthly image was his father's face smiling desperately, telling him that he was "going to be okay." How can I be here, loving him still but unable to touch him—or to share with him this sunset?

JULY 12, 1992

People talk about having "a personal relationship with God." I don't think that's possible, at least for me. I think I can have relationships with the world God made and the people in it. If indeed "there is that of God in every man," then I suppose as one lives and interacts with others, one is relating to God. I believe that, having created the

world and given humankind some moral direction, God has left us
free to choose how to live and how to react to the things that befall
us, not by the hand of God, but by fate and the natural laws of the
earth. The most we can ask from Him is some help in marshaling
our strength and courage. If the cards we are dealt are favorable—as
they have been for most of my life—we are lucky and the game is a
pleasure. When, instead, we confront tragedy and pain, we can
flinch or be angry, but still we play on as best we can until we die.

JULY 25, 1992

Now we are in Wyoming at a friend's house on the Snake River near
Jackson. The Tetons rise abruptly from the high, flat valley like af-
terthoughts of the Creator. Snow is visible near the tops, a reminder
of how harsh and long the winters must be here.

I've gotten back to *A Soldier of the Great War* by Mark Helprin,
the book I was reading when Lucas died, and have found much of it
speaking to my current feelings, particularly since the main character, Alessandro, loses both his father and his son:

> "Look at the clouds," Alessandro said. "They pass so gently and so
> quietly, but as if with such resolution. Someone once said they were
> rafts for souls."

JULY 29, 1992

Clare was moaning softly in her sleep this morning so I awakened
her. She had been dreaming: We were late picking Lucas up at
school. When we arrived, the fenced-in area in front of the kindergarten was filled with children, but look as we might, we could not
find him. The dream left us both weeping for a long time, holding
on to each other. This place, perhaps because of its beauty, has given
us the chance to freely grieve together.

I rode a bike about three miles south on the dike along the river
this morning. I saw an eagle airborne in the wind and ospreys fishing. I tried to visualize Lucas's soul riding on the passing clouds, but
it's a poor substitute for his soft hand and sweet smile.

This afternoon Clare, Emily, and I are going whitewater rafting. We are in the process of creating new memories—without Lucas— which will inevitably dim the old.

AUGUST 1, 1992

We have returned home, recovered from the time change, and are ready to get on with our lives. This Tuesday we are to meet with the owners of the Tremont Plaza hotel to talk about arrangements to provide a suite there in Lucas's memory for families of children receiving bone marrow transplants. How can we be talking about a memorial? How could he have not seen Wyoming with us? He would have so loved that rodeo.

AUGUST 4, 1992

Though my grieving is undiminished, I seem to have less to say about it these days. Perhaps that's how it is with a permanent loss: you examine it from every angle you can think of and then just carry it like a weight. As with all burdens, I would wish this one to become lighter with time. Perhaps it will. It is the way of grief, I suppose, to create new memories and live in a time never inhabited by the lost loved one. When things—when I—change enough, perhaps the laceration in my heart will heal and calcify until I can bear it without the continual imminence of tears.

I remember asking Clare at times when I was playing with Lucas, "Is it possible to be too close to a child?" I didn't believe it was, of course, but now I wonder. There persists the irrational thought that since my love for Lucas was so great, I was somehow required, like Abraham, to choose between my son and God. Unlike Abraham, and because I would have chosen my son, I received no reprieve.

AUGUST 12, 1992

I can hardly bring myself to go to bed at night, and then only very late, so that I am constantly fighting fatigue during the day. When I close my eyes to sleep, images of Lucas rush in and overwhelm me with sadness and anxiety. The house is still full of him. Pictures at different ages smile at me with the innocent trust that I thought never to betray. In the basement are his playthings and the contents of that hospital room that witnessed the death of our best hopes. His still-made bed seems to await him. Beside it is his "old-fashioned phone," which he received with such delight last Christmas.

Today Emily and I mowed the grass on his grave; later she and Clare planted more flowers. When I used to think about growing old, I feared the prospect of infirmity and a diminished ability to think and act. I never thought to bury pieces of my heart while the rest of me lived on.

AUGUST 14, 1992

I find that pain, like love, can be augmented in the sharing. Clare, Emily, and I carry our grief both separately and together; there is plenty to go around. Sometimes it emerges when we are together, but generally we try to spare each other. We go about our lives, laugh when we can, and wonder when memories of Lucas will cease to occupy our every moment.

> *In our sleep, Pain that cannot forget*
> *Falls drop by drop upon the Heart*
> *And in our Despair, against our Will*
> *Comes Wisdom through the awful grace of God.*
>
> Aeschylus

AUGUST 19, 1992

Tonight Clare and I went to a Compassionate Friends meeting. When my turn came to describe our loss, I just dissolved in tears.

I also find myself getting angry easily these days. Just beneath the anger is my bottomless sadness that the one person who loved me without reservation is gone. I tell myself that he could not indefinitely have believed I was perfect, but I miss that so.

I think often now of my own death, with something akin to anticipation. I worry irrationally that if I live too long he will not recognize me when I come.

If only I could feel his presence still, believe that he was near me in some form. I'm haunted by the fear that his death represented some failure of spirit or faith on my part. And now my inability to reconcile my loss represents a similar lack of belief.

SEPTEMBER 1, 1992

Clare and I have considered the possibility of another child. I suppose it is a natural, though futile, thought. Tonight she gently but decisively made it clear that she could not do this. She's right, of course, but my heart covets one more chance to be a father. I know I just need time to treasure what I have and relinquish the longing for what I have lost. Sometimes it feels to me like he dies again each day. Where is my relief? I feel only obligations and other people's needs for something I pretend to be.

SEPTEMBER 4, 1992

I worked a full week, the first since February. It helps me feel useful and provides some distraction, but in any idle moment I still experience the feeling of hopeless amputation that I expect to carry with me for the rest of my life.

I'm trying to make something out of all this pain that might give it some lasting meaning. But how do I do that? It seems not to be enough just to communicate it. Perhaps it's too soon to be uplifting; I certainly don't feel uplifted. I was thinking tonight that I wish I could feel the presence of God, who I want to believe is somehow with me through all this, but I can't. I don't think I need a burning bush or a voice from the sky, just a sense that I will be able to extract some purpose from my life that will balance the losses I have suffered. I had a little boy who loved Waldo and old-fashioned phones, who thought I had no flaws when it was he who was perfect.

And now I move through my life feeling like an actor in a play I had no part in creating. I say my lines, fulfill my obligations, but what will it take to regain the capacity for joy, which redeems the struggle?

SEPTEMBER 9, 1992

Sleep continues to be a problem. The process of turning off the light and remembering what it felt like to have him there between us makes it impossible to stay in bed unless I'm exhausted, usually not before 1:00 or 2:00 in the morning.

We just received an album created by Michelle Kupiec, Lucas's kindergarten teacher. It contains photos of him in school, some of his writing, and drawings made for him by the other kids. It made me cry, of course, but something else is happening. He looked different to me in the pictures, a little strange, and I realize that I haven't seen him at all in nearly four months; for at least a month before that, he was changed by the drugs and his disease. Time is doing its work and my little boy is receding from me as I continue my journey and he grows smaller in the distance. *I will always love you, Luke, and my last breath will be made easier by the hope of joining you. It's all the breaths I must draw between now and then that worry me.*

Cold Dark Deep and Absolutely Clear

A week and a few days after Wally died, my friend Michael and I stood on the shore at Hatch's Harbor, which is just where Cape Cod Bay and the Atlantic intersect in a roiling line of watery activity called the Race. At Hatch's Harbor the sky always seems enormous, the horizontals of dune and marsh and shoreline particularly vast and dazzling. It is especially pristine because the place isn't easy to reach, accessible as it is only after a long walk through a fire road in the dunes, along a dike built across a huge stretch of marsh, and then round the sandy tideflats skirting a lighthouse whose foghorn tends to sound in all weathers, even the brightest sunlight. The once-manned house is operated by remote control now, the switch apparently off in Connecticut someplace.

In the water that afternoon I saw first one oddly shaped dark form, a sort of mound a few feet from the foaming edge line. It was a seal in the shallow surf, floating on his or her side, eyeing us curiously. My two dogs were with us; I think seals seem to sense them as distant but unlikely cousins, and want to study them. In a moment the watcher submerged, and then rose again a few yards away, a wet black marble bust, the perfectly erect head held with marked dignity and poise. It was joined shortly by another pair of heads. And then another pair, and then another rolling on her side, enjoying the wave of her body and the quick flip of tail. And then there were dozens of watchers, looking toward us with as much curiosity and surprise as we brought to our study of them. The alien world of the water might as well have been, for me, the other world of the spirit; I felt I was looking into the realm of the dead, which I could not enter or know very much about. I thought of Elizabeth Bishop's poem, "At the Fishhouses," in which she describes the seawater of the Nova Scotian coast as

> *Cold dark deep and absolutely clear,*
> *element bearable to no mortal,*
> *to fish and to seals . . .*

Miss Bishop's marine creatures endure what no other mortals can; they seem more like spirits than living things. This other world was both clear and impenetrable, visible and unknowable. Although dozens of likable faces looked back at me, any one of which might almost have been his.

So began a chain of encounters with seals.

Seals are coastal creatures, citizens of two elements. Though most at ease in the water—where gravity's unmoored and their bodies arc and tumble freely, somersaulting and floating on their sides, supported by the movement of just one flipper, the flick of a tail—they bring some of that undulance with them to land, on the rare occasions when one sees them out in the winter sun.

I have always associated seals with Wally, through a chain of private associations with the sort of complexity and irrationality that characterizes the way a poetic image twists together a clutch of meanings, fibers spun into a single, complex yarn, various in texture, glinting with strands of separate and intermingling color. Something in the handsome cast of his head, the depth and clarity of his brown eyes. Something about playfulness and a freedom of spirit—which, however obscured by circumstance or by self-doubt—could also break through unclouded, pure. There's a film called *I've Heard the Mermaids Singing* in which the heroine fantasizes a kind of erotic freedom underwater, an unfettered aquatic *pas de deux* with another woman, which she imagines to the music of Delibes, a ravishing duet from *Lakmé* called "Dôme Epais." This aria is an invitation—one woman inviting another to stroll along an Indian river and pick jasmine—and it is pure fluidity, the unmistakable text of a kind of joy, the pleasure of swimming, of free movement, of floating in an untroubled suspension. Wally loved that music, and I imagine that in part this was because he was not, in his body, a comfortable swimmer, though he longed to be; in his spirit was a latent seal.

Seals bear a noticeable kinship to dogs, which Wally loved, and with which he felt a deep and immediate connection. "You like dogs," a tea-leaf reader in a Boston tearoom once told him, "and dogs like you."

I've just read an Inuit tale, which a friend has sent me, the story of a boy who left his parents behind to live with the seals, and in their camps at the bottom of the sea (where they gather around their fires!) heard their tales of ancient days and times to come.

And I've been thinking of Bishop's seal, who floats, in her poem, in an element like knowledge, and likes to listen to her renditions of Baptist hymns.

And then there's the notion of the seal as merman, of the creature which embodies the two worlds, unlike us, who live firmly in one medium, despite our brief visits to the other. To be of the coast, a mer-being, is to partake of the liminal, that watery zone of possibility where one thing becomes another, where the rules of one world are suspended as we enter into the next. The coast is the shifting zone of change and transformation. A coast is not a line really but a borderland, site of a continual conversation between elements which transforms both.

Movements between the worlds are limited, and often extraordinary. This is Ludovico Guicciardini, writing in *Description of all the Lowlands,* a seventeenth-century guide to Holland:

> They also claim that, around the year 1526, a merman was taken in the Frisian sea, formed in every way like the rest of us; they say that he had a beard, hair on his head and other hairs that we have, but quite setulose (that is, resembling the bristles of a pig), and harsh, and that they accustomed him to eating bread and other ordinary foods; they say that in the beginning the man was very wild, but that later he became gentle, though not totally tame, and he was mute. He lived for several years and finally, having once escaped the same illness, died of the plague in the year 1531.

Travelers between worlds are mute; they cannot tell us what they know. The language of the other element is untranslatable, though here it seems that, accustomed to solid ground, the mer-creature is also susceptible to its epidemics.

The wounded seal is young and startlingly silvery in the February sun. Its injury is a small bloody line along the tip of one side of the graceful little tail, as if perhaps it's been bitten; it doesn't look terribly serious, but of course I don't know how to read their pain, their expressions. He's alone on the shore, a fact which in itself doesn't seem to bode well. Why is he no longer part of the group? When I've seen them in the water or, once, in a sunning herd on the edge of the shore, they seemed happily grouped, like a pack of dogs. Do they abandon the injured or dying, perhaps to divorce themselves from the smell of blood that marks an animal as prey? I've heard that sharks come in, this time of year, to feed on the young ones.

Beached on a low rise of sand, maybe thirty or forty feet from an outgoing tidal river, he is not pleased to see us, particularly the two dogs who are full of curiosity and longing for a game. The seal raises his head and barks and makes a noise like a hiss of warning; my worry for it is mixed with wondering what those teeth are capable of. Though it seems, distinctly, young—the look on its face suggests that we'd say, were it human, this child is lost. I am busy restraining the dogs; their excited noises, and mine, rouse the seal to action. I fear that it's incapable of much movement but it awkwardly flips and starts to scoot down the rise toward the water, picking up speed. At the edge of the tidal stream it looks back to us, then slips into the water. It's no less awkward in three inches of water than it is on sand, but as soon as it reaches a foot-deep stretch of sea it's gloriously fluid, like a heron taking to air; what was compromised and lurching is suddenly capable of splendid and effortless motion.

A body that was wounded sits stranded, incapacitated. Gone into another element, that same being takes gorgeous, ready flight. I am filled, entirely, with the image of my wounded lover leaping from his body, blossoming into some welcoming, other realm. Is it that I am in that porous state of grief, a heated psychic condition in which everything becomes metaphor?

Or does the world consent, in some fashion, to offer me the particular image which imagination requires?

Metaphor is a way of knowing the world, and no less a one than other sorts of ways of gaining knowledge. Years ago, in Boston, I used to go to weekly meetings of the American Spiritualist Church —something like a Quaker meeting for psychics, or potential ones. After some meditation and singing, people would spontaneously give one another the messages they received. Many of these were incredibly detailed, elaborate pieces of perception about other people involving problems, opportunities, advice. Often the messages involved communication from the dead, who would be described to the receiver in exacting detail. I was never much good as a fledgling psychic. Where others saw clear and detailed pictures, I would perceive just a rush of images, seldom organized into anything coherent. But every once in a while I would see a sort of scene, usually a cryptic one, and feel that it related to a particular person in the group. If I told that person my images, I would usually discover that they made sense to her, even if I didn't understand them.

Could metaphoric thinking, the sort of work that artists do to apprehend their reality, be the same function of the mind, applied in a somewhat different way? My way of knowing experience is to formulate a metaphor which describes or encapsulates a particular moment; it is a way of getting at the truth. And a way of paying attention, of reading the world.

My seal said, The wounded one's gone free, gone swimming into what is familiar to no mortal.

The second seal bears no visible wound, but its face is full of distress and exhaustion; the eyes seem enormous, entirely dark, defenseless, world-weary. All of which might be construed as anthropomorphizing, but how could one look into that gaze without empathy? This seal, near the same stretch of beach, was up much higher, a week or two later, where the last stubborn snow held on in the shadow of a dune. Had an especially high tide brought it there? Did it pull itself further from the water, in order to rest on shore? This time the presence of me and my attendant animals wasn't enough to rouse the creature to return to the water; we were simply enough to cause it more pain. The younger and more aggressive of my dogs, the buoyant golden, didn't take long to figure out that the seal was feeble, a fine subject to pester. I got him on the leash, hauling him away, and resolved to call the Center for Coastal Studies as soon as I could get home to see if they couldn't effect some kind of rescue. We rounded the dunes that line the wide marsh, headed back toward the dike and the fire road and home, far enough from the seal for him to be out of the adolescent dog's mind, I thought. I let him off the leash.

But I'd miscalculated, expecting that his usual scattered attention would hold sway. The seal was too thrilling—too vulnerable—for him to forget so easily. He ran back, and I ran after him, to find him yelping madly at the creature, who was barking back and looking at me with a kind of bottomless exasperation. I leashed the dog and hauled him away again, this time keeping him on the lead until we were far away, into the marsh, a half-mile of dunes in between us and his prey.

Which did not turn out to be enough to stop him; when I made the mistake of letting him loose, he took off straight across the tops of the dunes, abandoning the curvy edge of the marsh for the shortest distance to further torment. I ran right across the dune-tops after him, my older and calmer black retriever loping behind me. When I thought I couldn't run anymore—dry-mouthed, heart pounding— I made it to the last crest of dune to find him yelping and leaping perilously close to the seal's head, both of them flashing teeth at one another.

This time the seal's face seemed to convey a kind of helplessness and desolation that cut me to the core. I wanted a way to apologize for bringing this yapping annoyance, this petty grief, into what was already clearly a deeper pain, a silent and solitary occupation. I felt as if the seal were doing some grave work and I not only couldn't help, I couldn't help but harm; I couldn't even keep my brutalizing pet from making things worse.

We left. Beau stayed on the leash at least a mile, till we were well in the middle of the dike that keeps the tide from washing away the modest ambitions of this town's airport runways. Even then, released, he thought of running back, and began to, but I was given from someplace the sudden wise impulse to run in the other direction, toward home; making a game of it convinced Beau to run after me, instead of after his own wildness. It was a moment of choosing between loyalties to different aspects of himself, and he chose domestic partnership.

The woman who answered the phone at the Center for Coastal Studies said they'd had several reports of exhausted seals beaching themselves, resting, then riding out on the next high tide when they recovered. Exhausted from what? I asked. The work of finding food, she said. I didn't know why then, more than any other time, they'd be weary. I described the seal's look of distress and exhaustion, I said I feared it was ill. She said she didn't know if there was anyone who could get out that day and look, but perhaps there was. She took my phone number, but they didn't call.

So my attempts at helping didn't seem to. The fact of the exhausted, incapable body—the fact of illness?—was intractable. I walked or ran on the wide expanse of marsh and dune, under that huge sky, around the single immovable fact.

The wide elemental landscape seemed to heighten and emphasize the lesson. Do what you can, nothing avails; it even seemed, with my panting, excited companion, that I'd made things worse.

The dead seal is an emblem of perfect repose; it lies like a yogi who's left the body for a time, gone completely into himself, the beached body left behind in a state of great quietude, utter silence. The head's turned to the right, so that one cheek rests against the sand. The small flippers lie peacefully at either side, and the perfectly straight spine ends in the symmetrical flourish of the tail. But there is no sense of movement or fluidity in the body, despite the grace and economy of its lines. Could it be one of the same seals I've seen? I think the first one was smaller, the second larger, but who can tell, really, since animation changes the scale of things. Does everything look smaller, in the stasis of death? The seals I'd seen had such purposeful fluidity of movement—beings of water, but of fire, too, the electric liquidity of the body as it turned and flipped, the sleek head raised, the eyes full of fear or defensiveness or exhaustion or—was it?—sorrow.

The eyes. Besides life, they are all that is missing from the body, and it is this absence that finally makes the form before me seem not at rest but dead. Gulls have taken the eyes away with their insistent beaks; their footprints are stamped all around the head like ancient letters on the clay tablets of Babylon. The law which they inscribe is that of hunger; what is soft, what is unguarded, what yields to them is what sustains those white engines, all wings and throat, which carry an appetite so large it obliterates all else. At first when I see that the eyes are gone, I think this is terrible and I imagine I will be unable to keep looking, but it isn't like that. Having been with Wally at the end of his life and then with Wally's body—form in repose—there is something new and unflinching in my looking at flesh. The spaces where the seal's eyes were . . . *sockets* doesn't seem the right word, these are little caverns of bone, reddened with a bit of blood, their depths not entirely visible. They enter deep into the sleek face, beneath the whiskers and the sweet upward curve of the mouth which one wants to read, in the living animal, as a smile. In death the mouth is relaxed, as blank and unreadable as the face of a sleeper.

Wally's body was almost unspeakably beautiful to me. All the last months of his illness, his head had been turning to the left on his pillow in a way that looked uncomfortable or rigid; people were forever straightening him out. This seemed intended to make him comfortable, but perhaps had more to do with the helper's need for a more familiar kind of alignment. In a moment, the muscles in his neck would pull again back to the left, and over time they became so stiff that it was difficult to bring his head back to center. This was something to do with whatever unnamed thing was happening in his brain; as happens after a stroke, the sides of his body behaved in different ways, not quite in concert. After he died, his head lolled to the right freely and loosely, as though the tendons could at last compensate for the time they'd been taut. There was a deep calm to his face; he seemed a kind of unfathomable, still well which opened on and down beneath the suddenly smooth surface of his skin. Which seemed polished, as it cooled, though not stiff; it was as if his body moved toward the condition of marble, but marble that's been palmed and warmed, touched until it picks up something of human heat. The heat in him lasted a long time. I loved that heat. I don't know how long I held his face and his shoulders and stroked him; as he began to cool I kept my hands on his belly, where the last of his warmth seemed to pool and concentrate. Here the fire of the body came to rest, smoldering longest, down to the last embers.

It is strange now to write this—after eight weeks—with the kind of odd detachment that language can lend us. It's as if I am watching myself—not in the plain light of film or the factual journalistic one of videotape, but as if through some kind of antique instrument, one which preserves the luster of the moment, the beauty of its peculiar light. Which seems to me now like the light of Dutch still life: rainy, northern, gentle, interior light that has itself a kind of resonance and presence. The instrument through which I look at that night (curious now that it seems instead like a deep winter afternoon, a snow-locked day at the very heart of winter, far inside the body of time) holds me at enough of a distance that I can describe what I see, that I can bear to look and to render, and yet it preserves the intimacy of those hours. That quality, their intimacy, is perhaps more firmly unassailable than any feeling I've ever known. I have never felt so far inside my life, and Wally's.

A week after he died, a book displayed in a shop window stopped me in my tracks on the sidewalk. It was a volume of reproductions of Michelangelo, and on the cover was a nude man, a figure from the Sistine ceiling, his eyes closed, his fine malleable flesh a kind of ash gray, the gray-white of porcelain clay. Looming behind the surface of his skin, especially in his face, were other colors; a blue like the hinge of a mussel shell, a coppery green. I felt as if I were seeing Wally there, the dead body held up for us to contemplate. The body dead is, in a way, our world's great secret. We see always flesh in motion, animated, disguised beneath its clothing and uniforms, its signals and armatures, its armor of codes and purposes. When do we look at the plain nude fact of the lifeless figure? Pure purposelessness—and thus, in the absence of the spirit, strangely and completely present. Never having a chance to see it, to assimilate our horror of it and go on to actually *look,* how would we know that the lifeless body is beautiful?

And empty. As empty as these spaces where a seal's eyes were, which contain now a little March sunlight, and wind off the surface of the marshy harbor, and the fluid music of shifting bird-cries counterpointing the regular exhalation of the foghorn. Which seems to be warning us, this clear day, for no earthly reason.

Wally's body was the vehicle through which I knew him. All other knowledges proceed through the body, *after* it, as it were. His was a wonderful vehicle, a beloved one, but it was not him. This fact seems so strange to me, so heavily laden, a deep vein of the incomprehensible. I find myself repeating it, trying to formulate it: we are not our bodies. The body is not me. I am my body, but I extend beyond it; just as my attention laps out, as my identity can pour out into the day. I have learned more about this, living beside water; as if the very fluidity of the landscape gets inside us, and encourages our own ability to slip our fixed bounds and feel ourselves as extended, multiple, various. Walking the shore, a warm day in March, toward that huge headland of cloud hung above and ahead, one pure white cliff above the dunelands, I become, momentarily, cloud, running dog, the raddled sonics of gull and wind and breaking wave. The wave seems a separate thing, yet it's a product, an effect, of that which is waving; gone into my elements, I am equally fluid.

The plainness of the poor abandoned body became more plain to me when I encountered Wally's ashes. The week after his death, while I anticipated receiving them, I imagined the relationship I might have to them. It had been terrible, to let the body be taken; had I not been so certain that it was not him I couldn't have done it at all, I could never have allowed it. But even though it was only his body (*only!* as if that were some minor thing) I couldn't allow him to go naked, without something of home, so I sent with him a quilt I'd made for him, years ago, a red and white geometry splashed with starlike red leaves. I am not much of a quilt-maker; my clumsy stitches were done in honor of my quilting grandmother. First I'd thought it would be a November birthday gift, then Christmas—and then eventually the thing spread across my lap and legs kept me warm all winter and into a Vermont spring while I worked on it. The stitches were rough but they were mine, every one of them. His body left wrapped in it. I didn't watch. I took the dogs down to the harbor, beneath a great wheeling starry void, the air so cold and sharp and still it seemed it might crack.

The next day I had to sign papers at the funeral home, and I began to look at different sorts of urns and vessels (everything made for this purpose seemed obscene, or banal, or at least achingly and inappropriately bland). And I began to think what it would be like to receive the ashes, the commingled evidence of body and of fabric. Which did not come and did not come; the day before the service, a week from the night of his death, the funeral director told me the ashes might not arrive, that they were "somewhere between Brockton and the post office." I wasn't very understanding; I told him I wanted him to know how much it meant to me for the ashes to be at the ceremony. I told him I expected that, and after a hesitation he said he'd have them there. "You understand," I said, "how much it means to me." I wasn't sure he did; my statement was an imperative, as though if I ordered him to recognize the magnitude of my need, he would.

In fact, the package arrived at the post office on Saturday morning, and the man from the funeral home arrived in my kitchen at ten-thirty, where a host of friends were getting ready for the day. I went by myself into the bedroom, the room where Wally died, with the plastic box and a kitchen knife to break the sealing tape. I sat with the thing on my lap, cut the binding, and slid the brown polymer coffer—coffin?—open. Sealed there in a plastic bag, strangely cold from its journey through the mails, were the remains of my darling: little pearled bits of gravel, almost like ground clay. There was a moment of piercing, utterly abject grief—*this* is what is left—and I swear it was followed, in less than a minute, by the clearest sense that what I held was inert, only a material, not even alive in the way that clay or soil is. If it was clear that Wally's body wasn't him, then it was even more clear that this sack of—what to call it? stone?—was even less so. The funeral directors have a word for this stuff, one of those deeply debased late twentieth-century words which do disservice to what they name, or rather what they avoid. "Cremains," they call it. It makes me shudder, aesthetically, still, but I admit I understand better the impulse. They may want language to serve to distance us (or them) from the fact of the body's burned residue, but the plain fact is that there is about the material *itself* a kind of distance, a lack of relation to what it was.

In the ancient epic of *Gilgamesh,* the oldest poem in the world, there is a heartbreaking declaration of a beloved's death: "The companion Enkidu is clay." A beautiful and bitter irony, since the poem which preserves the love of Gilgamesh and Enkidu is itself inscribed on tablets of clay. But clay has so much more soul and presence, such a quality of heaviness and sorrow to it, such a definite scent and taste. In that same poem, clay is described as the food of the unmourned dead; its heaviness and moisture perfectly evoke the humor of grief. But ashes have a kind of anonymity, a quality of no-life which feels, at last, vacant, without essence.

So I wrapped the stuff in a silk Japanese kerchief and placed it in the brass box I'd bought. Which I carried, that afternoon, to the service, and which I think only a few people noticed anyway, in the rush and swell of the speaking and the music, the spinning intensity of the day.

I had thought that the ashes would somehow be the service's center of gravity; the place where everything deepened, opening into the darkness of grief. But it wasn't like that; they seemed a sort of afterthought, an extra. When people asked, before that day, what I was going to do with them, I said I'd let them go eventually, scattering them, but in truth I couldn't really imagine it, couldn't think I'd ever really be ready. But once I encountered the lifeless sack of what once carried his life, I could think of dispersing them—thought, in fact, that perhaps then they'd be more alive, mingled again with water, soil, and stone, the rising yeasts of the world. They are going, this spring, out to Hatch's Harbor, where my seal lies, a body resolv-

ing even as I write into thousands of things which are not the body
—entering into gull and tide and the unseeable tiny lives inside
the sand.

I lay my hand on the seal's back. The spring sun has warmed the
fur, which catches the light. I want to caress it; I want to lie down
beside it. I am stopped by some nagging sense of what is clean and
sanitary (voices from elementary school in my head, I guess, about
touching dead animals), and perhaps more by some sense of propri-
ety, of the dignity and unapproachability of the dead. It would not
be right to pretend we could approach their bodies, that we could
hold them. I held Wally's body for a long time, and I could feel as I
did, as I let my hands know him for the last time, that the body was
moving away from me, sinking into itself. Perhaps that is one thing
the soul is: our outward attention, the energy and force in us that
leaps out of the self, almost literally, into the life of the world. The
spirit is that in us which participates. It moves alone, like air or fire,
and it moves with the body, lifting the body's earth and water into
gesture and connection, into love.

Without spirit, the body closes back into itself like an old piece
of furniture, an armoire whose ancient wood is still fragrant, resin-
ous, whose whorled grains and steady sleep refer back to the living
tree. The cabinet is an elegy to the tree from which it arose, the body
a brief unkeepable elegy to the quick and shining self.

Is the body a shell?

A few days ago, on the dogs' morning walk along the harbor—
when I am mostly not awake—I picked up a green crab's shell. Or a
portion of one; the legs were gone. The body contained within the
central carapace had become a sweetmeat for a gull. What was left
was this patinated green husk about the size of a soda cracker, a tiny
breastplate. It resembled, in fact, something retrieved from a sunken
Greek or Roman ship, lost armor pulled from preservative Mediterranean brine.

The reason I put the shell in my pocket was the color of the interior, a startling Giotto blue, a sky from heaven or Arizona rinsed and shining. At home I left the fragment on top of the refrigerator; by afternoon the blue had faded to a kind of milky lacquer, a faintly skyey mother-of-pearl. By the next day it was a pale, iridescent opal. A lovely color, but far in power and register from that initial cerulean. Imagine living surrounded by that blue, bearing in one's own body the most brilliant wash of the summer firmament.

What color is the underside of our skin?

The fragment made me think of Rilke's archaic torso of Apollo, whose head "we cannot know" since it's long since gone; in the power and presence of the fragment a whole sense of spiritual life arises. Broken, the god speaks to us more clearly.

This morning I picked up a second crab. I do not know why this one died; there is no visible sign of damage. It is about the same size as the first. But this one's intact, centered on a white saucer on my desk. Are crabs subject to rigor mortis? If so, this one has only left the world just a little while ago. Move him in any way and the legs shift into a pleasing, vaguely Chinese pattern, the weight of the— torso, is it?—balanced by the two larger claws which reiterate, even in death, their message of menace and power.

It smells of seaweed and ruin.

I will not open this shell; I am less squeamish now about the tumbled mess of the flesh, but I'm no scientist. Yet there is something I love about placing this body next to the fragment of shell whose dry lavender interior reminds me of what was there: even in the smallest chamber, a sky.

JANE BROX

At Sea

Months after everything I was driving headstrong into Boston—as abstracted as everyone else on the road—when out of the corner of my eye I saw an ambulance in silent alarm moving steadily through the rush hour traffic, and all my hasty thoughts stopped. I had to wince back tears as I remembered trying to stay calm when the medic told me not to rush as I followed the ambulance into Lowell.

That late-December day there'd been patchy snow on the ground and the beginnings of a still gray winter dawn as I ran across the orchard to my parents' house. It seemed to take forever before the sirens cut into the morning. Then all at once five husky men—four EMTs and a policeman—tossed aside the chairs in the dining room so the gurney could get through, then stood around the bedposts in my parents' room where my father lay in pain. They'd brought in the cold dawn air. They'd tracked in melting snow.

The policeman turned to me and spoke in awkward apology: "Someone has to come for all the 911's—in case there's anything. But there's nothing like that here. Sorry. Jeez, it's been a bad night." And as he started to tell me about how some old man who lived on Hildreth Street had fallen out of bed, I tried to hear around him so I could discern what the medics were asking my father: "When did it start?" "Can you describe the pain?" "Can you get yourself up?" I was too afraid to enter the bedroom or to ask questions myself, so I stood in the entranceway overhearing what I could. One medic whispered to another: "He's extremely, extremely critical."

What do the dying see? A resolving flare of human love? Does a milky eye clear for the last time? From the little I know now, I think they must see what they always have, are true to their natures at the end—those of earth, tied to the earth. My father, who had always been practical, when given his last choice weakly told the EMTs to take him to the hospital in Lowell rather than Lawrence because, as he later explained, the winter roads were better maintained along that route, and we'd have an easier time getting back and forth if he was in for a long stay.

And it was a straight way there past the house he'd been born in, the orchards he'd planted, and up the hill that had once mired horses in spring in the time when the route was known as the Black North Road, which you can find on maps hundreds of years back, before our family's knowledge of this country, back past the oxen teams and wheel tracks to a footpath crossing the wilderness north of the Merrimack. Now it was a clear gray paved road for a small entourage just under the speed limit: a squad car, an empty rescue truck followed by the ambulance carrying my father—my mother sat up front with the driver—and me following last.

No other traffic that winter Sunday morning, so no siren, and only the merest slowing at intersections. The deliberateness of the ride was a strange foolish comfort as I told myself *it mustn't be too much of an emergency,* even as I knew for sure his kidneys were so weak he could not possibly survive a problem with his heart, and this was the closest he'd have to a last look at where he'd lived his life as we passed the neighbors, the town offices, the Grange hall, passed all the good will and any grudges and misjudgments, the red emergency lights sweeping across everything like a lighthouse beacon falling back across those sleeping in an innocent mist among low coastal hills who, since they are not the ones caught in a fogbound open sea, sleep unawares. Whoever we'd become in those hours, we were different from those on dry land.

Once in Lowell we skirted the river and its bridges and passed the brick mills and Pawtucket Falls where tawny winter water poured over the boards onto icy rocks at the bottom. Then we turned away from the river road, and the ambulance docked at the emergency entrance to The General.

The intensive care unit there is a circle of rooms around the nurses' station. The waiting area is an outer circle embracing the patients' rooms. You can walk around and around through the day and see the same groups of families camped in that outer circle—the ICU has no restrictions on visiting hours: exhausted men and women who'd come from their shifts, smelling of oil or of ink; old women sitting straight-backed, their eyes closed with strain, or maybe prayer; children sleeping at their parents' feet; spent coffee cups and Coke cans and snack wrappers scattered about. The ones who've just arrived hardly leave at all. Those there long enough might start thinking about spotting one another, coaxing one another to go home for some rest: *Come on, you have to keep your strength up. . . .* You never think it could be so plain and small, but there it is: the best hope in that place is a long haul.

For nearly a week we were one family of the eleven waiting there in that circular hall, talking with several surrounding families, comparing progress or the lack of it, reading the slightest movement of a hand or the strength of a sigh for a sign. It seemed we were all on the same journey—odd comfort—and when my father turned quickly, and one afternoon six days after being admitted, his fire drowned in its own ash, we were set adrift on our own small raft again. How strange it was to have lived day and night for a week with those people, and now to hug them one last time and leave them forever to their own fates. I knew that by evening my father's bed would be filled by another.

•

CHERYL STRAYED

Heroin/e

When my mother died, I stripped her naked. Plush round belly and her pale breasts rising above. Her arms were black and blue from all the needles going in. Needles with clear liquid and needles that only the nurses had a hold of and other needles gripping constantly into her, held tight with tape to the translucent skin of her hand or the silk skin of her wrist. And not one of those needles trying to save her. I picked her dead hand up, the arm slack and draping below. It did not want to be held. Her skin was dry and cracked and stabbed. When she died the nurse took the needle out forever. But I wanted it back, and eventually I would get it.

The day they told us my mother had cancer I was wearing green. Green pants, green shirt, green bow in my hair. My mother had sewn this outfit for me. I did not like such a themed look, but I wore it anyway, to the Mayo Clinic, as a penance, an offering, a talisman. We found a vacant wheelchair, and I got into it and raced and spun down the hallway. Cancer, at this point, was something we did not have to take seriously. My mother was forty-five. She looked fine, beautiful, I would later think, *alive.* It was just the two of us, me and my mother. There were others, too, my stepfather working his job, wondering, my grandparents waiting by the phone, wanting to know if it was true, if perhaps the oncologist in Duluth had been mistaken after all. But now, as before, as it would always be, it was only me and my mother. In the elevator she sat in the wheelchair and reached out to tug at my pants. She rubbed the fabric between her fingers proprietarily. "Perfect," she said.

I was twenty-two. I believed that if a doctor told you that you were going to die soon you'd be taken to a room with a gleaming wooden desk. This was not so. My mother sat with her shirt off on top of the table with paper stretched over it. When she moved, the room was on fire with the paper ripping and crinkling beneath her. She wore a pale yellow smock with strings meant to be tied. I could see her soft back, the small shelf of flesh that curved down at her waist. The doctor said she'd be lucky if she lived a year. My mother blinked her wet eyes but did not cry. She sat with her hands folded tightly together and her ankles hooked one to the other. Shackled to herself. She'd asked the doctor if she could continue riding her horse. He then took a pencil in his hand and stood it upright on the edge of the sink and tapped it down on the surface hard. "This is your spine after radiation," he said. "One jolt and your bones will crumble like a dry cracker."

First we went to the women's restroom. Each of us locked in separate stalls, weeping. We didn't say a word. Not because we felt alone in our grief, but because we were so together in it, as if we were one body instead of two. I could feel her weight leaning against the door, her hands slapping slowly against it, causing the entire frame of the bathroom stalls to shake. Later we came out to wash our hands and faces, standing side by side in the ladies' room mirror.

We were sent to the pharmacy to wait. I sat next to my mother in my green pantsuit. There was a big bald boy in an old man's lap. There was a woman who had an arm that swung wildly from the elbow. She held it stiffly with the other hand, trying to calm it. She waited. We waited. There was a beautiful dark-haired woman who sat in a wheelchair. She wore a purple hat and a handful of diamond rings. We could not take our eyes off her. She spoke in Spanish to the people gathered around her, her family and perhaps her husband. "Do you think she has cancer?" my mother whispered loudly to me. There was a song coming quietly over the speakers. A song without words, but my mother knew the words anyway and sang them softly to herself. "Paper roses, paper roses, oh they're only paper roses to me," she sang. She put her hand on mine and said, "I used to listen to that song when I was young. It's funny to think of that. To think about listening to the same song now. I would've never known." My mother's name was called then: her prescriptions were ready. "Go get them for me," she said, "Tell them who you are. Tell them you're my daughter."

My mother said I could have her jewelry box. She said, "When I am done with it." She was lying in the bed my stepfather had made for her, for them, with branches twisting and arching up behind her, leaves and jumping bugs carved discreetly into them. There was a dancing pink girl who lived in the jewelry box. She stood and twirled around to the song that played when you wound it up and opened the box. The song changed as it slowed, became sorrowful and destitute. The girl tottered and then stopped as if it hurt her. She had lips the size of a pinhead painted red and a scratchy pink tutu. When we shut the box she went down into it, stiff as a board, bending at the feet.

"I always wonder what the ballerina is thinking," my mother said dreamily.

When my mother got cancer I'd folded my life down. I was a senior in college in Minneapolis, and I'd convinced my professors to allow me to be in class only two days each week. As soon as those days were over, I drove north to the house in rural Minnesota where I had grown up, racing home, to my mother. I could not bear to be away from her. Plus, I was needed. My stepfather was with my mother when he could be, when he wasn't working as a carpenter in an attempt to pay the bills. I cooked food that my mother tried to eat. She'd say: pork chops and stuffed green peppers, cherry cheesecake and chicken with rice and then holler the recipes out to me from her bed. When I'd finished she'd sit like a prisoner staring down at her steaming plate. "It smells good," she'd say. "I think I'll be able to eat it later." I scrubbed the floors. I took everything from the cupboards and put new paper down. My mother slept and moaned and counted and swallowed her pills, or on good days she sat in a chair and talked to me, she paged through books.

"Put these on for me." My mother sat up and reached for a pair of socks. It had been a few weeks since we'd learned of her cancer, and already she could not reach her own feet without great pain. I bent at my mother's feet. She held the ball of socks in her hand. "Here," she said. I had never put socks onto another person, and it was harder than you might think. They don't slide over the skin. They go on crooked and you have to work to get them right. I became frustrated with my mother, as if she were holding her foot in a manner that made it impossible for me. She sat back with her body leaning on her hands on the bed, her eyes closed. I could hear her breathing deeply, slowly. "Goddammit," I said, "help me." My mother looked down at me, silently.

We didn't know it then, but this would be the last time she was home. Her movements were slow and thick as she put her coat on and she held onto the walls and edges of doors as she made her way out of the house. On the drive to the hospital in Duluth she looked out the window. She said, "Look at the snow there on those pines." She told me to toot my horn when we went past Cindy's house in Moose Lake. She said, "Be careful of the ice. It's black ice." She held an old plastic milk jug with the top cut off so she could vomit into it during the drive. My mother put one hand up to her ribs, where the cancer lived, and pressed gently. "Wouldn't that be something, to get into an accident now?"

Three years after my mother died I fell in love with a man who had electric blue hair. I'd gone to Portland, Oregon, to visit a friend, seeking respite from the shambles my life had become. I had thought that by then I'd have recovered from the loss of my mother and also that the single act of her death would constitute the only loss. It is perhaps the greatest misperception of the death of a loved one: that it will end there, that death itself will be the largest blow. No one told me that in the wake of that grief other griefs would en-sue. I had recently separated from the husband I loved. My stepfa-ther was no longer a father to me. I was alone in the world and acutely aware of that. I went to Portland for a break.

We'll call the man with electric blue hair Joe. I met him on his twenty-fourth birthday and drank sangria with him. In the morn-ing he wanted to know if I'd like some heroin. He lived on a street called Mississippi, in North Portland. There were a whole gathering of people who'd rigged up apartments above what thirty years before had been a thriving Rexall drugstore. Within days I lived there with him. In the beginning, for about a week, we smoked it. We made smooth pipes out of aluminum foil and sucked the smoke of burn-ing black tar heroin up into them. "This is called chasing the dragon!" Joe said and clapped his hands. The first time I smoked heroin it was a hot, sunny day in July. I got down on my knees in front of Joe where he sat on the couch. "More," I said and laughed like a child. "More, more, more," I chanted. I had never cared much for drugs. I'd experimented with each kind once or twice, and drank alcohol with moderation and reserve. Heroin was different. I loved it. It was the first thing that worked. It took away every scrap of hurt that I had inside of me. When I think of heroin now, it is like re-membering a person I met and loved intensely. A person I know I must live without.

The first time they offered my mother morphine, she said no. "Mor-phine is what they give to dying people," she said. "Morphine means there is no hope."

We were at the hospital in Duluth. We could not get the pillows right. My mother cried in pain and frustration when the nurses came into the room. The doctor told her that she shouldn't hold out any longer, that he had to give her morphine. He told her she was *actively dying.* He was young, perhaps thirty. He stood next to my mother, a gentle hairy hand slung into his pocket, looking down at her in the bed.

The nurses came one by one and gave her the morphine with a needle. Within a couple weeks my mother was dead. In those weeks she couldn't get enough of the drug. She wanted more morphine, more often. The nurses liked to give her as little as they could. One of the nurses was a man, and I could see the shape of his penis through his tight, white nurse's trousers. I wanted desperately to pull him into the small bathroom beyond the foot of my mother's bed and offer myself up to him, to do anything at all if he would help us. And also I wanted to take pleasure from him, to feel the weight of his body against me, to feel his mouth in my hair and hear him say my name to me over and over again, to force him to acknowledge me, to make this matter to him, to crush his heart with mercy for us. I held my closed book on my lap and watched him walk softly into the room in his padded white shoes. My mother asked him for more morphine. She asked for it in a way that I have never seen anyone ask for anything. A mad dog. He did not look at my mother when she asked him this, but at his wristwatch. He held the same expression on his face regardless of the answer. Sometimes he gave it to her without a word and sometimes he told her no in a voice as soft as his shoes and his penis curled up in his pants. My mother begged and whimpered then. She cried and her tears fell in the wrong direction; not down over the lush light of her cheeks to the corners of her mouth, but away from the edges of her eyes to her ears and into the nest of her hair on the bed.

I wanted it and I got it, and the more heroin we got, the stingier we became with it. Perhaps if we snorted it, we thought, we'd get higher on less. And then, of course, the needle. The hypodermic needle, I'd read, was the barrier that kept the masses from heroin. The opposite was true with me. I loved the clean smell of it, the tight clench around my arm, the stab of hurt, the dull badge of ache. It made me think of my mother. It made me think of her, and then that thought would go away into the loveliest bliss. A bliss I had not imagined.

There was a man named Santos who we called when we wanted heroin. He would make us wait by the telephone for hours, and then he'd call and instruct us to meet him in the parking lot of a Safeway. I sat in the car while Joe took a short drive with Santos in his yellow Pinto, and then Joe would calmly get back in the car with me and we'd go home. On some occasions we went to Santos's house. Once, he sat in his front window with a shotgun across his lap. Once, he clutched my thigh when Joe left the room and told me that if I came to see him alone he'd give me heroin free. Another time, he held his baby daughter, just a month old. I looked at her and smiled and told Santos how beautiful she was, and inside of me I felt the presence of my real life. The woman who I actually was. The kind of woman who knows the beauty of a baby, who will have a baby, who once was a baby.

The days of my mother's death, the morphine days, and those that followed, the heroin days, lasted only weeks, months—but each day was an eternity, one stacked up on the other, a cold clarity inside of a deep haze. And unoccupied as well. Just me and my mother, or the ghost of her, though others surely came and went.

Some days, flowers came to my mother's hospital room, and I set them on the edges of tables and windowsills. Women came, too. Women who volunteered for the hospital. Old Catholic women, with hair cut close to the scalp or woven into long braids and pinned to their heads. My mother greeted them as she did the flowers: impervious, unmoved, resolute.

The women thought it would be for the best when my mother died. They sat next to me on the vinyl furniture and told me in low tones about the deaths of their own mothers. Mothers who had died standing at kitchen sinks, in the backseats of cars, in beds lit with candles. And also about the ones who made it. The ones with the *will to live*. Of tumors vanishing and clean blood and opaque bones. People who fought it, who refused to die. The ones who went and then came back. The survivors. The heroes. It would be for the best, they whispered, when it was over. Her life, that is. My mother's.

People who I knew came, and I did not recognize them at first. It seemed they all wore strange hats or other disguises during this time, though I am certain that is not true. They were friends of my mother. They couldn't bear to stay in the room, so instead they left chicken potpies and bread. Scalloped potatoes and blocks of cheddar cheese. By then, my mother could not eat half a banana. Couldn't lick a lick of a Popsicle without retching it back up. They said her name to her, and she said their names back to them, hoarse and confused. She said, "How nice you came." And she put a wan smile on her face. Her hair was flattened against her head, and I reached to smooth it into place.

I asked my mother if she would like for me to read to her. I had two books: *The Awakening*, by Kate Chopin, and *The Optimist's Daughter*, by Eudora Welty. These were books we'd read before, books we'd loved. So I started in, but I could not go on. Each word I said erased itself in the air. It was the same when I tried to pray. I prayed fervently, rabidly, to God, any god, to a god I could not identify or find. I prayed to the whole wide universe and thought perhaps God would be in it. I prayed and I faltered. God, I realized, had no intention of making things happen or not, of saving my mother's life. God would come later, perhaps, to help me bear it.

She taught me to knit, my mother, and I did this in the room while she slept and lived the last while. It occurred to me that she had taught me to knit for this particular occasion. So that I would have a place to put my hands and my eyes.

"What are you making?" she asked.

"A scarf."

"For who?" Her hand pinched the sheet that covered her.

"I don't know," I said. "I am simply knitting a scarf."

The best part about knitting is the tapping, tapping, tapping of the needles. A sound so silent that it is like the language of snakes or rabbits or deer.

Eventually the nurses and doctors stopped paying any mind to what my mother said or wanted. They looked to me to decide how much morphine to give her. They said I had a choice: she could be in great pain, but fairly conscious, or she could be comfortable, but higher than a kite, and usually passed out. Ultimately, it was not up to me.

"Promise me one thing," she said. My mother was not dramatic or concise in her dying. She hadn't offered a single directive in the past days, and I was desperate for guidance. "That you won't allow me to be in pain anymore. I've had too much pain."

"Yes," I said, "yes."

There was using heroin and also not using it. In the mornings when I woke, groggy and drained, I'd stand in front of the mirror and talk to myself. I was shocked by my own life. This was not meant to be, I'd think in the mornings. Stop it, I said, No more. And then I would shower and dress in my black pants and white shirt and black bow tie and take a bus downtown to serve people coffee and pancakes. At two in the afternoon I'd take the bus home again with hopefully sixty bucks in my pocket for another score of heroin. This is how it went.

Joe waited for me to get home. He cooked me macaroni and cheese and called Santos. He pulled me into his bed and jumped up when the phone rang. I made him stick the needle into me the first time, and then he taught me how to do it myself. What I loved about Joe is that he didn't love me, or himself. I loved that he would not only let me, but help me destroy myself. I'd never shared that with another person. The dark glory of our united self-destruction had the force of something like love. I get to do this, I thought. I get to waste my life. I felt a terrible power within me. The power of controlling the uncontrollable. I get to be junk, I thought.

But this was not to be. My husband, Mark, called me. He was in town and wanted to see me. The friend I'd come to visit in Portland had told him about Joe and about my using heroin, and in response he drove from Minneapolis to talk to me. I met him within the hour at our friend's house. He sat at a table in the kitchen with the branches of a fig tree tapping on the window nearby. He said, "You look, you look . . . different. You seem so, how can I say this, you seem like you aren't here." First he put his hands on mine, and we held onto one another, locked hand to hand. I couldn't explain it to him, the why. And then we fought. He stood up and screamed at me so loud that I put my hands over my head for cover. His arms gestured madly into the air, at nothing. He clawed at himself and ripped the shirt from his own back and threw it at me. He wanted me to go home with him in an hour. Not for a reunion, but to get away, not from Joe, but from heroin.

I told Mark I needed to think. I drove back to Joe's apartment and sat in the lawn chair on the sidewalk. Heroin made me dumb, or distant, rather. A thought would form and then evaporate. I couldn't get a hold of my mind. I sat in the lawn chair on the sidewalk, and a man walked up to me and said his name was Tim. He took my hand and shook it and told me I could trust him. He asked if I could give him three dollars for diapers, then if he could use my phone, and then if I had change for a five-dollar bill, and on and on in a series of twisting requests and sorry stories that confused and compelled me to stand and pull the last ten dollars I had out of my jeans pocket. He saw the money and pulled a knife out of his shirt. He held it gently up to my chest and said, "Give me that money, sweetheart."

I packed a few things and called Mark. When he pulled up to the corner where I was waiting, I got into his car. By sunset, Portland was long gone. In Montana we checked into a motel to sleep. I held myself in bed, rocking with a headache, a sickness in my gut. Mark brought me water and chocolate and watched television. I sat in the car as we drove across the country, and I felt my real life present but unattainable, like heroin had taken me entirely from myself. Mark and I fought and cried and shook the car with our fighting. We were monstrous in our cruelty. We talked kindly afterward, shocked at ourselves and each other. We decided that we would get divorced. I hated him and I loved him. He had known my mother. I felt trapped, branded, held, and beloved. Like a daughter. "I didn't ask you to come to Portland," I screamed. "You came for your own reasons," I said.

"Maybe," he said.

"You love me that much?" I asked. "You came all this way to get me? Why?"

"Because," he said, "just because."

I wanted my mother to love me, but more. I wanted her to prove it, to live. To go to battle and win. And if she was going to die, I wanted her to tell me, in the end, how I should live, without her. Until that point I had wanted just the opposite. I could not bear for her to tell me what to do or how to live. I had wanted to be unknown by her, opaque to her wondering eyes.

The last days, my mother was not so much high as down under. When she woke, she'd say, "Oh, oh." Or she'd let out a sad gulp of air. She'd look at me, and there would be a flash of love. Other times, she'd roll back into sleep as if I were not there. Sometimes when my mother woke she did not know where she was. She demanded an enchilada and then some applesauce. She'd say, "That horse darn near stepped on me," and look around the room for it, accusingly. During this time I wanted my mother to say to me that I had been the best daughter in the world. I did not want to want this, but I did, inexplicably, as if I had a great fever that could only be cooled by those words. I went so far as to ask her directly. "Have I been the best daughter in the world?" She said, yes, I had, of course. But this was not enough. I wanted those words to knit together in my mother's mind and for them to be delivered, fresh, to me. I was ravenous for love.

One day a woman with a clipboard asked if I'd go with her to the cafeteria. She said that she wanted to talk to me about a donation my mother had made. Her name was Janet and she was dressed in a navy-colored shirt with little white fringes on each shoulder, as if she were the captain of something. Her fingernails were long and red and they clicked together when she moved her hands in certain ways.

When we sat down with two cups of coffee between us, she told me that my mother was an organ donor but that because she had cancer throughout her body they would only take her eyes.

"Her eyes?"

"Well, not the whole eye, of course, but parts of the organ." Janet took her cup up into her hands, one fingernail tapped against it. "We make it a policy to inform people close to the donor. In your mother's case, upon death, we will need to place ice on her eyes in order to preserve them." She thought about this a moment. "This way you will understand what is happening when you see that we must put the bags of ice on her face. The removal is performed within a few hours after death." Her fingernails went up to the sides of her face, hovering in midair. "Small incisions will be made at the side of each eye." Janet showed me this, pointing with her own sharp nails. "The skin will be sutured carefully to disguise signs of this procedure." She swallowed a sip of coffee and looked at me. "It does not preclude an open-casket viewing."

I dreamed of heroin. I woke in the middle of the night with a wanting so deep I was breathless. I had started seeing a therapist to talk about heroin. She told me that this wanting was normal, that indeed when you use heroin the brain responds by activating pleasure neurons that would normally remain dormant. She said it would take months for them to calm. Until then, they go on aching to be fed. Trying to trick your body into it. I could see them, spindly arms with mouths like flowers, blooming or wilting and then blooming again. "What about pain?" I asked her. "Are there neurons in the brain that come alive only with agony? And if so, how long does it take for them to die, to fold back into themselves and float away?"

I saw Joe two more times. I'd kept in touch with him; calling him late at night from Minneapolis, I could hear the heroin in his voice, making it soft and open. Within a month, he was at my door. He looked weak and pale. He sat on my couch and shot up and then lurched into my kitchen and bent to vomit into my sink. He wiped his face and smiled. "It's worth it," he said, "getting sick. Because you feel so good through it all." We spent a week in my apartment using the supply of heroin he'd brought with him. I knew I had to end this and, finally, I did. He left when I asked him to. The second time I saw him, a year had passed and I was moving to Portland for reasons unrelated to him. We went to the beach for the day. He was no longer the smart, sexy, simpering man I'd fallen for, but a junkie. Joe had scabs on his skin from constant scratching, his bony arms were bruised and punctured. He didn't care anymore what color his hair was. I sat on the cool sand watching the Pacific Ocean roar in while Joe locked himself into the public rest room to shoot up. I held myself stiff against the desire to join him. The ocean inched nearer and nearer to me with each passing minute. I was both sickened by Joe and compelled. I felt in the presence of a dying man, a young, dying man, and I knew that I could never see him again if I wanted to live. And I did.

My mother didn't have time to get skinny. Her death was a relentless onward march. The hero's journey is one of return, but my mother's was all forward motion. She was altered, but still fleshy when she died, the body of a woman among the living. She had her hair, too, brown and brittle and frayed from being in bed for weeks.

From the room where she died I could see the Great Lake Superior out her window. The biggest lake in the world, and the coldest. To see it, I had to work. I pressed my face sideways, hard, against the glass, and I'd catch a slice of it going on forever into the horizon. "A room with a view!" my mother exclaimed. "All of my life I've waited for a room with a view."

I arranged the flowers closer in to my mother, to the edges of the tables, so that she could see them without having to turn her head. Bouquets of pink carnations, yellow roses, daisies, and tiger lilies. Flowers that originated on other continents and were brought here to witness my mother's dying.

My mother wanted to die sitting up, so I took all the pillows I could get my hands on and made a backrest for her. I wanted to take my mother and prop her in a field of yarrow to die. I covered her with a quilt that I had brought from home, one she had sewn herself out of pieces of our old clothing. "Get that out of here," she said savagely, and then kicked her legs like a swimmer to make it go away.

I watched my mother. It was March, and outside the sun glinted off the sidewalks and the icy edges of the snow. It was Saint Patrick's Day, and the nurses brought my mother a square block of green jello that sat quivering on the table beside her. It was the last day of her life and my mother did not sleep, she did not wake. She held her eyes still and open. They were the bluest thing in the room, perhaps in all of Duluth. Bluer than the lake. They were the color of the sky on the best day of your life.

My mother died fast but not all of a sudden. A slow burning fire when flames disappear to smoke and then smoke to air. She never once closed her eyes. First they were bitter and then they were bewildered and they changed again to something else, to a state that I have had, finally, to see as heroic. Blue, blue eyes. Daggers of blue wanting and wanting. To stay, to stay.

Legacies

MUSIC, WHEN SOFT VOICES DIE

Music, when soft voices die,

Vibrates in the memory;

Odours, when sweet violets sicken,

Live within the sense they quicken.

Rose leaves, when the rose is dead,

Are heap'd for the beloved's bed;

And so thy thoughts, when thou art gone,

Love itself shall slumber on.

—PERCY BYSSHE SHELLEY, 1792–1822

ANDRE DUBUS

Sacraments

A sacrament is physical, and within it is God's love; as a sandwich is physical, and nutritious and pleasurable, and within it is love, if someone makes it for you and gives it to you with love; even harried or tired or impatient love, but with love's direction and concern, love's again and again wavering and distorted focus on goodness; then God's love too is in the sandwich. A sacrament is an outward sign of God's love, they taught me when I was a boy, and in the Catholic church there are seven. But, no, I say, for the church is catholic, the world is catholic, and there are seven times seventy sacraments, to infinity. Today I sit at my desk in June in Massachusetts; a breeze from the southeast comes through the window behind me, touches me, and goes through the open glass door in front of me. The sky is blue, and cumulus clouds are motionless above green trees lit brightly by the sun shining in dry air. In humid air, the leaves would be darker, but now they are bright, and you can see lighted space between them, so that each leaf is distinct; and each leaf is receiving sacraments of light and air and water and earth. So am I, in the breeze on my skin, the air I breathe, the sky and earth and trees I look at.

Sacraments are myriad. It is good to be baptized, to confess and be reconciled, to receive Communion, to be confirmed, to be ordained a priest, to marry, or to be anointed with the sacrament of healing. But it is limiting to believe that sacraments occur only in churches, or when someone comes to us in a hospital or at home and anoints our brows and eyes and ears, our noses and lips, hearts and hands and feet. I try to receive Communion daily, and I never go to Mass day after day after day, because I cannot sleep when I want to, I take pills, and if the pills allow me to sleep before midnight, I usually can wake up at seven-thirty and do what I must to get to Mass. But I know that when I do not go to Mass, I am still receiving Communion, because I desire it; and because God is in me, as He is in the light, the earth, the leaf. I only have to lie on my bed, waking after Mass has already ended, and I am receiving sacraments with each breath, as I did while I slept; with each movement of my body as I exercise my lower abdomen to ease the pain in my back caused by sitting for fifteen hours: in my wheelchair, my car, and on my couch, before going to bed for the night; receiving sacraments as I perform crunches and leg lifts, then dress and make the bed while sitting on it. Being at Mass and receiving Communion give me joy and strength. Receiving Communion of desire on my bed does not, for I cannot feel joy with my brain alone. I need sacraments I can receive through my senses. I need God manifested as Christ, who ate and drank and shat and suffered, and laughed. So I can dance with Him as the leaf dances in the breeze under the sun.

Not remembering that we are always receiving sacraments is an isolation the leaves do not have to endure: they receive and give, and they are green. Not remembering this is an isolation only the human soul has to endure. But the isolation of a human soul may be the cause of not remembering this. Between isolation and harmony, there is not always a vast distance. Sometimes it is a distance that can be traversed in a moment, by choosing to focus on the essence of what is occurring, rather than on its exterior: its difficulty or beauty, its demands or joy, peace or grief, passion or humor. This is not a matter of courage or discipline or will; it is a receptive condition.

Because I am divorced, on Tuesdays I drive to my daughters' school, where they are in the seventh and second grades. I have them with me on other days, and some nights, but Tuesday is the school day. They do not like the food at their school, and the school does not allow them to bring food, so after classes they are hungry, and I bring them sandwiches, potato chips, Cokes, Reese's peanut butter cups. My kitchen is very small; if one person is standing in it, I cannot make a three-hundred-and-sixty-degree turn. When I roll into the kitchen to make the girls' sandwiches, if I remember to stop at the first set of drawers on my right, just inside the door, and get plastic bags and write *Cadence* on one and *Madeleine* on the other, then stop at the second set of drawers and get three knives for spreading mayonnaise and mustard and cutting the sandwiches in half, then turn sharply left and reach over the sink for the cutting board leaning upright behind the faucet, then put all these things on the counter to my right, beside the refrigerator, and bend forward and reach into the refrigerator for the meat and cheese and mustard and mayonnaise, and reach up into the freezer for bread, I can do all of this with one turn of the chair. This is a First World problem; I ought to be only grateful. Sometimes I remember this, and then I believe that most biped fathers in the world would exchange their legs for my wheelchair and house and food, medical insurance and my daughters' school.

Making sandwiches while sitting in a wheelchair is not physically difficult. But it can be a spiritual trial; the chair always makes me remember my legs, and how I lived with them. I am beginning my ninth year as a cripple, and have learned to try to move slowly, with concentration, with precision, with peace. Forgetting plastic bags in the first set of drawers and having to turn the chair around to get them is nothing. The memory of having legs that held me upright at this counter and the image of simply turning from the counter and stepping to the drawer are the demons I must keep at bay, or I will rage and grieve because of space, and time, and this wheeled thing that has replaced my legs. So I must try to know the spiritual essence of what I am doing.

On Tuesdays when I make lunches for my girls, I focus on this: the sandwiches are sacraments. Not the miracle of transubstantiation, but certainly parallel with it, moving in the same direction. If I could give my children my body to eat, again and again without losing it, my body like the loaves and fishes going endlessly into mouths and stomachs, I would do it. And each motion is a sacrament, this holding of plastic bags, of knives, of bread, of cutting board, this pushing of the chair, this spreading of mustard on bread, this trimming of liverwurst, of ham. All sacraments, as putting the lunches into a zippered book bag is, and going down my six ramps to my car is. I drive on the highway, to the girls' town, to their school, and this is not simply a transition; it is my love moving by car from a place where my girls are not to a place where they are; even if I do not feel or acknowledge it, this is a sacrament. If I remember it, then I feel it too. Feeling it does not always mean that I am a happy man driving in traffic; it simply means that I know what I am doing in the presence of God.

If I were much wiser, and much more patient, and had much greater concentration, I could sit in silence in my chair, look out my windows at a green tree and the blue sky, and know that breathing is a gift; that a breath is sufficient for the moment; and that breathing air is breathing God.

You can receive and give sacraments with a telephone. In a very lonely time, two years after my crippling, I met a woman with dark skin and black hair and wit and verbal grace. We were together for an autumn afternoon, and I liked her, and that evening I sat on my couch with her, and held and kissed her. Then she drove three and a half hours north to her home in Vermont. I had a car then, with hand controls, but I had not learned to drive it; my soul was not ready for the tension and fear. I did not see the woman until five weeks later. I courted her by telephone, daily or nightly or both. She agreed to visit me and my family at Thanksgiving. On Halloween, I had a heart attack, and courted her with the bedside telephone in the hospital. Once after midnight, while I was talking to her, a nurse came into the room, smiled at me, and took the clipboard from the foot of the bed and wrote what she saw. Next morning, in my wheel-chair, I read: *Twelve-fifteen. Patient alert and cheerful, talking on the phone.*

In the five weeks since that sunlit October day when I first saw her, I knew this woman through her voice. Then on Thanksgiving, she drove to a motel in the town where I live, and in early afternoon came to my house for dinner with my family: my first wife and our four grown children, and one daughter's boyfriend and one son's girlfriend, and my two young daughters. That night, when the family left, she stayed and made love to my crippled body, which did not feel crippled with her, save for some pain in my leg. Making love can be a sacrament, if our souls are as naked as our bodies, if our souls are in harmony with our bodies, and through our bodies are embracing each other in love and fear and trembling, knowing that this act could be the beginning of a third human being, if we are a man and a woman; knowing that the roots and trunk of death are within each of us, and that one of its branches may block or rupture an artery as we kiss. Surely this is a sacrament, as it may not be if we are with someone whose arms we would not want holding us as, suddenly, in passion, we died; someone whose death in our arms would pierce us not with grief but regret, fear, shame; someone who would not want to give life to that third person who is always present in lovemaking between fertile men and women. On the day after Thanksgiving, she checked out of the motel and stayed with me until Monday, and I loved her; then she went home.

She came to me on other weekends, four to six weeks apart, and we loved each other daily by telephone. That winter, she moved to New York City. I still did not drive, and her apartment was not a place I could enter and be in with my wheelchair; it was very small, and so was the shared bathroom down the hall. I could not fly to her, because my right knee does not bend, so I have to sit on the first seat of an airplane, and that means a first-class ticket. Trains are inaccessible horrors for someone in a wheelchair: the aisles are too narrow. A weekend in New York, if I flew there and stayed in a hotel, would have cost over a thousand dollars, before we bought a drink or a meal. So she flew to Boston or rode on the train, and a friend drove me to meet her. I was a virtual shut-in who was in love. One day a week, my oldest son drove me to horseback-riding lessons; in the barn, he pushed me up a ramp to a platform level with the horse's back, and I mounted and rode, guarded from falling by my son and volunteer women who walked and jogged beside me. A driver of a wheelchair van came for me two mornings a week and took me to Mass and left, then came back and took me to physical therapy, then came back and took me home, where I lay on my bed and held the telephone and talked to the woman, sometimes more than once a day. With the telephone, she gave me sacraments I needed during that fall and winter when my body seemed to be my enemy. We were lovers for a year, and then we were not, and now our love remains and sharing our flesh is no longer essential.

On Christmas Eve, in that year when we were lovers, I was very sad and I called her. The Christmas tree was in the living room, tall and full, and from the kitchen doorway, where I held the telephone, I could see in the front windows the reflection of the tree and its ornaments and lights. My young daughters' stockings were hanging at the windows, but my girls were at their mother's house, and would wake there Christmas morning, and would come to me in the afternoon. I was a crippled father in an empty house. In my life, I have been too much a father in an empty house; and since the vocation of fatherhood includes living with the mother, this is the deepest shame of my life, and its abiding regret. I sat in my chair and spoke into the phone of the pain in my soul, and she listened, and talked to me, and finally said: "You're supposed to be happy. It's your hero's birthday."

I laughed with my whole heart at the humor of it, at the truth of it, and now my pain was bearable, my sorrow not a well, but drops of water drying in the winter room.

In March, I decided one day that I must stop talking to her on the telephone because, while I did, I was amused, interested, passionate, joyful; then I said good-bye and I was a cripple who had been sitting in his wheelchair or lying on his bed, holding plastic to his ear. I told her that if I were whole, and could hang up the telephone and walk out of the house, I would not stop calling her; but I knew that living this way, receiving her by telephone, was not a good crippled way to live; and I knew there was a better crippled way to live, but I did not know yet what it was. She understood; she always does, whether or not she agrees.

I did not call her for days, and on the first day of April, I woke crying, and on the second; and on the third, I could not stop, and I phoned my doctor's receptionist and, still crying, I told her to tell him to give me a shot or put me away someplace, because I could not bear it anymore. At noon, he brought me spinach pie and chili dogs, and I said: "That's cholesterol."

"Depression will kill you sooner," he said, and I ate with him and still did not understand that the food and his presence at my table were sacraments. He made an appointment for me with a psychologist, and two days later my youngest son drove me to the office of this paternal and compassionate man, who said: "This is not depression; it's sorrow, and it'll always be with you, because you can't replace your legs."

As my son drove me home, I told him that I wanted a swimming pool, but I did not want to be a man who needed a swimming pool to be happy. He said: "You're not asking the world for a swimming pool. You're asking it for motion."

At home, I called a paraplegic friend and asked him to teach me to drive my car, and two days later he did. I phoned a swimming pool contractor, a durably merry and kind man, and his cost for building me a forty-by-fifteen-by-three-foot lap pool was so generous that I attribute it to gimpathy. Sacraments abounded. I paid for some, and the money itself was sacramental: my being alive to receive it and give it for good work. On that first day, after calling the paraplegic and the contractor, I called the woman, and I continued to call her, and to receive that grace.

On the last day of my father's life, he was thirsty and he asked me to crush some ice and feed it to him. I was a Marine captain, stationed at Whidbey Island, Washington, and I had flown home to Lake Charles, Louisiana, to be with my father before he died, and when he died, and to bury him. I did not know then that the night flight from Seattle was more than a movement in air from my wife and four young children to my dying father, that every moment of it, even as I slept, was a sacrament I gave my father; and they were sacraments he gave me, his siring and his love drawing me to him through the night; and sacraments between my mother and two sisters and me, and all the relatives and friends I was flying home to; and my wife and children and me, for their love was with me on the plane and I loved them and I would return to them after burying my father; and from Time itself, God's mystery we often do not clearly see; there was time now to be with my father. Sacraments came from those who flew the plane and worked aboard it and maintained it and controlled its comings and goings; and from the major who gave me emergency leave, and the gunnery sergeant who did my work while I was gone. I did not know any of this. I thought I was a son flying alone.

My father's cancer had begun in his colon, and on the Saturday before the early Sunday morning when he died, it was consuming him, and he was thin and weak on his bed, and he asked for ice. In the kitchen, I emptied a tray of ice cubes onto a dish towel and held its four corners and twisted it, then held it on the counter and with a rolling pin pounded the ice till it was crushed. This is how my father crushed ice, and how my sisters and I, when we were children, crushed it and put it in a glass and spooned sugar on it, to eat on a hot summer day. I put my father's ice into a tall glass and brought it with an iced-tea spoon to the bedroom and fed him the ice, one small piece at a time, until his mouth and throat were no longer dry.

As a boy, I was shy with my father. Perhaps he was shy with me too. When we were alone in a car, we were mostly silent. On some nights, when a championship boxing match was broadcast on the radio, we listened to it in the living room. He took me to wrestling matches because I wanted to go, and he told me they were fake, and I refused to believe it. He took me to minor-league baseball games. While we listened to boxing matches and watched wrestling and baseball, we talked about what we were hearing and seeing. He took me fishing and dove hunting with his friends, before I was old enough to shoot; but I could fish from the bank of a bayou, and he taught me to shoot my air rifle; taught me so well that, years later, my instructors in the Marine Corps simply polished his work. When I was still too young to use a shotgun, he learned to play golf and stopped fishing and hunting, and on Saturdays and Sundays he brought me to the golf course as his caddy. I did not want to caddy, but I had no choice, and I earned a dollar and a quarter; all my adult life, I have been grateful that I watched him and listened to him with his friends, and talked with him about his game. My shyness with him was a burden I did not like carrying, and I could not put down. Then I was twenty-one and a husband and a Marine, and on the morning my pregnant wife and I left home, to drive to the Officers' Basic School in Quantico, Virginia, my father and I tightly embraced, then looked at each other's damp eyes. I wanted to say *I love you,* but I could not.

I wanted to say it to him before he died. On the afternoon of his last day, he wanted bourbon and water. A lot of ice, he told me, and a lot of water. I made drinks for my sister and me too, and brought his in a tall glass I did not hold for him. I do not remember whether he lifted it to his mouth or rested it on his chest and drank from an angled hospital straw. My sister and I sat in chairs at the foot of the bed, my mother talked with relatives and friends in the living room and brought them in to speak to my father, and I told him stories of my year of sea duty on an aircraft carrier, of my work at Whidbey Island. Once he asked me to light him a cigarette. I went to his bedside table, put one of his cigarettes between my lips, lit his Zippo, then looked beyond the cigarette and flame at my father's eyes: they were watching me. All my life at home before I left for the Marine Corps, I had felt him watching me, a glance during a meal or in the living room or on the lawn, had felt he was trying to see my soul, to see if I was strong and honorable, to see if I could go out into the world, and live in it without him. His eyes watching me light his cigarette were tender, and they were saying good-bye.

That night, my father's sisters slept in the beds that had been mine and my sister's, and she and I went to the house of a neighbor across the street. We did not sleep. We sat in the kitchen and drank and cried, and I told her that tomorrow I would tell my father I loved him. Before dawn he died, and for years I regretted not saying the words. But I did not understand love then, and the sacraments that make it tactile. I had not lived enough and lost enough to enable me to know the holiness of working with meat and mustard and bread; of moving on wheels or wings or by foot from one place to another; of holding a telephone and speaking into it and listening to a voice; of pounding ice with wood and spooning the shards onto a dry tongue; of lighting a cigarette and placing it between the fingers of a man trying to enjoy tobacco and bourbon and his family as he dies.

SCOTT RUSSELL SANDERS

The Inheritance of Tools

At just about the hour when my father died, soon after dawn one February morning when ice coated the windows like cataracts, I banged my thumb with a hammer. Naturally I swore at the hammer, the reckless thing, and in the moment of swearing I thought of what my father would say: "If you'd try hitting the nail it would go in a whole lot faster. Don't you know your thumb's not as hard as that hammer?" We both were doing carpentry that day, but far apart. He was building cupboards at my brother's place in Oklahoma; I was at home in Indiana putting up a wall in the basement to make a bedroom for my daughter. By the time my mother called with news of his death—the long-distance wires whittling her voice until it seemed too thin to bear the weight of what she had to say—my thumb was swollen. A week or so later a white scar in the shape of a crescent moon began to show above the cuticle, and month by month it rose across the pink sky of my thumbnail. It took the better part of a year for the scar to disappear, and every time I noticed it I thought of my father.

The hammer had belonged to him, and to his father before him. The three of us have used it to build houses and barns and chicken coops, to upholster chairs and crack walnuts, to make doll furniture and bookshelves and jewelry boxes. The head is scratched and pock-marked, like an old plowshare that has been working rocky fields, and it gives off the sort of dull sheen you see on fast creek water in the shade. It is a finishing hammer, about the weight of a bread loaf, too light really for framing walls, too heavy for cabinetwork, with a curved claw for pulling nails, a rounded head for pounding, a fluted neck for looks, and a hickory handle for strength.

The present handle is my third one, bought from a lumberyard in Tennessee down the road from where my brother and I were help-ing my father build his retirement house. I broke the previous one by trying to pull sixteen-penny nails out of floor joists—a foolish thing to do with a finishing hammer, as my father pointed out. "You never hear of a crowbar?" he said. No telling how many handles he and my grandfather had gone through before me. My grandfather used to cut down hickory trees on his farm, saw them into slabs, cure the planks in his hayloft, and carve handles with a drawknife. The grain in hickory is crooked and knotty, and therefore tough, hard to split, like the grain in the two men who owned this hammer before me.

After proposing marriage to a neighbor girl, my grandfather used this hammer to build a house for his bride on a stretch of river bottom in northern Mississippi. The lumber for the place, like the hickory for the handle, was cut on his own land. By the day of the wedding he had not quite finished the house, and so right after the ceremony he took his wife home and put her to work. My grand-mother had worn her Sunday dress for the wedding, with a fringe of lace tacked on around the hem in honor of the occasion. She re-moved this lace and folded it away before going out to help my grandfather nail siding on the house. "There she was in her good dress," he told me some fifty-odd years after that wedding day, "holding up them long pieces of clapboard while I hammered, and together we got the place covered up before dark." As the family grew to four, six, eight, and eventually thirteen, my grandfather used this hammer to enlarge his house room by room, like a chambered nautilus expanding his shell.

By and by the hammer was passed along to my father. One day he was up on the roof of our pony barn nailing shingles with it, when I stepped out the kitchen door to call him for supper. Before I could yell, something about the sight of him straddling the spine of that roof and swinging the hammer caught my eye and made me hold my tongue. I was five or six years old, and the world's commonplaces were still news to me. He would pull a nail from the pouch at his waist, bring the hammer down, and a moment later the *thunk* of the blow would reach my ears. And that is what had stopped me in my tracks and stilled my tongue, that momentary gap between seeing and hearing the blow. Instead of yelling from the kitchen door, I ran to the barn and climbed two rungs up the ladder—as far as I was allowed to go—and spoke quietly to my father. On our walk to the house he explained that sound takes time to make its way through air. Suddenly the world seemed larger, the air more dense, if sound could be held back like any ordinary traveler.

By the time I started using this hammer, at about the age when I discovered the speed of sound, it already contained houses and mysteries for me. The smooth handle was one my grandfather had made. In those days I needed both hands to swing it. My father would start a nail in a scrap of wood, and I would pound away until I bent it over.

"Looks like you got ahold of some of those rubber nails," he would tell me. "Here, let me see if I can find you some stiff ones." And he would rummage in a drawer until he came up with a fistful of more cooperative nails. "Look at the head," he would tell me. "Don't look at your hands, don't look at the hammer. Just look at the head of that nail and pretty soon you'll learn to hit it square."

Pretty soon I did learn. While he worked in the garage cutting dovetail joints for a drawer or skinning a deer or tuning an engine, I would hammer nails. I made innocent blocks of wood look like porcupines. He did not talk much in the midst of his tools, but he kept up a nearly ceaseless humming, slipping in and out of a dozen tunes in an afternoon, often running back over the same stretch of melody again and again, as if searching for a way out. When the humming did cease, I knew he was faced with a task requiring great delicacy or concentration, and I took care not to distract him.

He kept scraps of wood in a cardboard box—the ends of two-by-fours, slabs of shelving and plywood, odd pieces of molding—and everything in it was fair game. I nailed scraps together to fashion what I called boats or houses, but the results usually bore only faint resemblance to the visions I carried in my head. I would hold up these constructions to show my father, and he would turn them over in his hands admiringly, speculating about what they might be. My cobbled-together guitars might have been alien spaceships, my barns might have been models of Aztec temples, each wooden contraption might have been anything but what I had set out to make.

Now and again I would feel the need to have a chunk of wood shaped or shortened before I riddled it with nails, and I would clamp it in a vice and scrape at it with a handsaw. My father would let me lacerate the board until my arm gave out, and then he would wrap his hand around mine and help me finish the cut, showing me how to use my thumb to guide the blade, how to pull back on the saw to keep it from binding, how to let my shoulder do the work.

"Don't force it," he would say, "just drag it easy and give the teeth a chance to bite."

As the saw teeth bit down the wood released its smell, each kind with its own fragrance, oak or walnut or cherry or pine—usually pine, because it was the softest and the easiest for a child to work. No matter how weathered and gray the board, no matter how warped and cracked, inside there was this smell waiting, as of something freshly baked. I gathered every smidgen of sawdust and stored it away in coffee cans, which I kept in a drawer of the workbench.

When I did not feel like hammering nails I would dump my sawdust on the concrete floor of the garage and landscape it into highways and farms and towns, running miniature cars and trucks along miniature roads. Looming as huge as a colossus, my father worked over and around me, now and again bending down to inspect my work, careful not to trample my creations. It was a landscape that smelled dizzyingly of wood. Even after a bath my skin would carry the smell, and so would my father's hair, when he lifted me for a bedtime hug.

I tell these things not only from memory but also from recent observation, because my own son now turns blocks of wood into nailed porcupines, dumps cans full of sawdust at my feet and sculpts highways on the floor. He learns how to swing a hammer from the elbow instead of the wrist, how to lay his thumb beside the blade to guide a saw, how to tap a chisel with a wooden mallet, how to mark a hole with an awl before starting a drill bit. My daughter did the same before him, and even now, on the brink of teenage aloofness, she will occasionally drag out my box of wood scraps and carpenter something. So I have seen my apprenticeship to wood and tools reenacted in each of my children, as my father saw his own apprenticeship renewed in me.

The saw I use belonged to him, as did my level and both of my squares, and all four tools had belonged to his father. The blade of the saw is the bluish color of gun barrels, and the maple handle, dark from the sweat of hands, is inscribed with curving leaf designs. The level is a shaft of walnut two feet long, edged with brass and pierced by three round windows in which air bubbles float in oil-filled tubes of glass. The middle window serves for testing whether a surface is horizontal, the others for testing whether it is plumb or vertical. My grandfather used to carry this level on the gun rack behind the seat in his pickup, and when I rode with him I would turn around to watch the bubbles dance. The larger of the two squares is called a framing square, a flat steel elbow so beat up and tarnished you can barely make out the rows of numbers that show how to figure the cuts on rafters. The smaller one is called a try square, for marking right angles, with a blued steel blade for the shank and a brass-faced block of cherry for the head.

I was taught early on that a saw is not to be used apart from a square: "If you're going to cut a piece of wood," my father insisted, "you owe it to the tree to cut it straight."

Long before studying geometry, I learned there is a mystical virtue in right angles. There is an unspoken morality in seeking the level and the plumb. A house will stand, a table will bear weight, the sides of a box will hold together only if the joints are square and the members upright. When the bubble is lined up between two marks etched in the glass tube of a level, you have aligned yourself with the forces that hold the universe together. When you miter the corners of a picture frame, each angle must be exactly forty-five degrees, as they are in the perfect triangles of Pythagoras, not a degree more or less. Otherwise the frame will hang crookedly, as if ashamed of itself and of its maker. No matter if the joints you are cutting do not show. Even if you are butting two pieces of wood together inside a cabinet, where no one except a wrecking crew will ever see them, you must take pains to insure that the ends are square and the studs are plumb.

I took pains over the wall I was building on the day my father died. Not long after that wall was finished—paneled with tongue-and-groove boards of yellow pine, the nail holes filled with putty and the wood all stained and sealed—I came close to wrecking it one afternoon when my daughter ran howling up the stairs to announce that her gerbils had escaped from their cage and were hiding in my brand-new wall. She could hear them scratching and squeaking behind her bed. Impossible! I said. How on earth could they get inside my drum-tight wall? Through the heating vent, she answered. I went downstairs, pressed my ear to the honey-colored wood, and heard the scritch scritch of tiny feet.

"What can we do?" my daughter wailed. "They'll starve to death, they'll die of thirst, they'll suffocate."

"Hold on," I soothed. "I'll think of something."

While I thought and she fretted, the radio on her bedside table delivered us the headlines. Several thousand people had died in a city in India from a poisonous cloud that had leaked overnight from a chemical plant. A nuclear-powered submarine had been launched. Rioting continued in South Africa. An airplane had been hijacked in the Mediterranean. Authorities calculated that several thousand homeless people slept on the streets within sight of the Washington Monument. I felt my usual helplessness in face of all these calamities. But here was my daughter weeping because her gerbils were holed up in a wall. This calamity I could handle.

"Don't worry," I told her. "We'll set food and water by the heating vent and lure them out. And if that doesn't do the trick, I'll tear the wall apart until we find them."

She stopped crying and gazed at me. "You'd really tear it apart? Just for my gerbils? The *wall*?" Astonishment slowed her down only for a second, however, before she ran to the workbench and began tugging at drawers, saying, "Let's see, what'll we need? Crowbar. Hammer. Chisels. I hope we don't have to use them—but just in case."

We didn't need the wrecking tools. I never had to assault my handsome wall, because the gerbils eventually came out to nibble at a dish of popcorn. But for several hours I studied the tongue-and-groove skin I had nailed up on the day of my father's death, considering where to begin prying. There were no gaps in that wall, no crooked joints.

I had botched a great many pieces of wood before I mastered the right angle with a saw, botched even more before I learned to miter a joint. The knowledge of these things resides in my hands and eyes and the webwork of muscles, not in the tools. There are machines for sale—powered miter boxes and radial arm saws, for instance— that will enable any casual soul to cut proper angles in boards. The skill is invested in the gadget instead of the person who uses it, and this is what distinguishes a machine from a tool. If I had to earn my keep by making furniture or building houses, I suppose I would buy powered saws and pneumatic nailers; the need for speed would drive me to it. But since I carpenter only for my own pleasure or to help neighbors or to remake the house around the ears of my family, I stick with hand tools. Most of the ones I own were given to me by my father, who also taught me how to wield them. The tools in my workbench are a double inheritance, for each hammer and level and saw is wrapped in a cloud of knowing.

All of these tools are a pleasure to look at and to hold. Merchants would never paste NEW NEW NEW! signs on them in stores. Their designs are old because they work, because they serve their purpose well. Like folksongs and aphorisms and the grainy bits of language, these tools have been pared down to essentials. I look at my claw hammer, the distillation of a hundred generations of carpenters, and consider that it holds up well beside those other classics—Greek vases, Gregorian chants, *Don Quixote,* barbed fishhooks, candles, spoons. Knowledge of hammering stretches back to the earliest humans who squatted beside fires chipping flints. Anthropologists have a lovely name for those unworked rocks that served as the earliest hammers. "Dawn stones" they are called. Their only qualification for the work, aside from hardness, is that they fit the hand. Our ancestors used them for grinding corn, tapping awls, smashing bones. From dawn stones to this claw hammer is a great leap in time, but no great distance in design or imagination.

On that iced-over February morning when I smashed my thumb with the hammer, I was down in the basement framing the wall that my daughter's gerbils would later hide in. I was thinking of my father, as I always did whenever I built anything, thinking how he would have gone about the work, hearing in memory what he would have said about the wisdom of hitting the nail instead of my thumb. I had the studs and plates nailed together all square and trim, and was lifting the wall into place when the phone rang upstairs. My wife answered, and in a moment she came to the basement door and called down softly to me. The stillness in her voice made me drop the framed wall and hurry upstairs. She told me my father was dead. Then I heard the details over the phone from my mother. Building a set of cupboards for my brother in Oklahoma, he had knocked off work early the previous afternoon because of cramps in his stomach. Early this morning, on his way into the kitchen of my brother's trailer, maybe going for a glass of water, so early that no one else was awake, he slumped down on the linoleum and his heart quit.

For several hours I paced around inside my house, upstairs and down, in and out of every room, looking for the right door to open and knowing there was no such door. My wife and children followed me and wrapped me in arms and backed away again, circling and staring as if I were on fire. Where was the door, the door, the door? I kept wondering. My smashed thumb turned purple and throbbed, making me furious. I wanted to cut it off and rush outside and scrape away the snow and hack a hole in the frozen earth and bury the shameful thing.

I went down into the basement, opened a drawer in my workbench, and stared at the ranks of chisels and knives. Oiled and sharp, as my father would have kept them, they gleamed at me like teeth. I took up a clasp knife, pried out the longest blade, and tested the edge on the hair of my forearm. A tuft came away cleanly, and I saw my father testing the sharpness of tools on his own skin, the blades of axes and knives and gouges and hoes, saw the red hair shaved off in patches from his arms and the backs of his hands. "That will cut bear," he would say. He never cut a bear with his blades, now my blades, but he cut deer, dirt, wood. I closed the knife and put it away. Then I took up the hammer and went back to work on my daughter's wall, snugging the bottom plate against a chalkline on the floor, shimming the top plate against the joists overhead, plumbing the studs with my level, making sure before I drove the first nail that every line was square and true.

JAMES ALAN MCPHERSON

Ukiyo

... How one positions oneself in the world will always reflect to some degree the seminal experiences and indoctrinations of class, race and gender, but may also ... float above them, wondrously unanchored in categorical imperatives, mysteriously untraceable in derivation.

—MARTIN DUBERMAN ON PAUL ROBESON,
The Nation, December 28, 1998

In early November of 1998, after sustaining a fever for almost two weeks, I developed a case of viral meningitis. This disease attacks the brain by way of the spine and can be fatal, especially to memory. I have been told that Jim Galvin, a friend and a colleague, was sent to my home to see about me when I did not answer my telephone. I am told that he found me unconscious, that he called my physician, that an ambulance was summoned, and that I was taken to Mercy Hospital. There I went into a coma that lasted eleven days. The doctors at Mercy decided that I should be placed in intensive care.

RACHEL, MY DAUGHTER, TOLD ME THAT WHEN RICHARD, MY
BROTHER, ARRIVED IN MY ROOM, MY EYES OPENED WIDE FOR
THE VERY FIRST TIME

But a friend in Cambridge, Jim Freedman, a former president
of the University of Iowa, made a number of long-distance telephone calls and used his influence to have me transferred to the
much better equipped intensive care unit at University Hospital.
When the doctors there determined that I would probably not live,
a number of friends called Rachel, at her dorm at Tufts University,
and told her that she had better come. Jim Freedman called my sister, Mary, in Stamford, Connecticut, and advised her of my condition. Mary called my brother, Richard, in Atlanta, and advised him
to come. Jorie Graham, Jim Galvin's wife, was then on a reading
tour. She mentioned my condition to people during her reading at
Ann Arbor, and one of them, a former student and friend named Ei-
leen Pollack, quickly made plans to come. I am told that the students
in the Writers' Workshop prayed for me. Connie Brothers, the ad-
ministrative assistant in the Workshop, told me that so many calls
came in, and so many students went to the hospital, that the staff
imposed a quota. Only Rachel and Richard were allowed to spend
any length of time in my room.

I do not remember any of it.

HOWARD, MY NEIGHBOR ACROSS THE STREET, GAVE MARY, MY
SISTER, A LOAF OF BREAD AND A QUART OF FRESH MILK WHEN
SHE ARRIVED AT MY HOME. HOWARD SAYS HE AND LAUREL,
HIS WIFE, HAD WATCHED ME CARRY A SUITCASE AND A VIDEO
CAMERA TO THE WAITING AMBULANCE.

When I did regain consciousness, for the very first time in my life I
had to rely on *others* to disclose to me my own personal details for
nearly two weeks. There was, in my hospital room, a packed suitcase
and a video camera that I had borrowed from Rachel earlier in the
fall. Jim Galvin told me that when he had found me in my home, I
had refused to leave. Perhaps I was so deranged that I could only be

convinced to leave if I fantasized that I was going, once again, to see Rachel. Another friend, Fred Woodard, told me that when he visited me in intensive care, I had pleaded with him to help me get out. I had apparently tried to leave so many times that my hands and feet were tied to the bed. Jim Galvin said that I told him, "If you were a true friend you would cut these straps!" Rachel said I called the nurses and doctors "fascist bastards" (a line I remember from Lenny Bruce's routine "White Collar Drunks") when they refused to let me go out for a smoke. Rachel said that I was unconscious most of the time, that I was literally covered with tubes and needles and lights. Rachel said my eyes were swollen and discolored, and that she recalls my opening them twice. Once was when she and Marian Clark, another friend, were standing outside my room looking at me through a plastic curtain. I opened both my eyes a little and waved both my hands as high as the straps would allow. Rachel said the lights, when I moved, made me look like a Christmas tree. She said I said, "You are so beautiful!" The second time was when Richard was there. Rachel said I opened my swollen eyes as widely as I ever had and stared at Richard. "I guess you opened them so wide because he was standing over you and he is so tall," Rachel told me.

TED WHEELER, A TRACK COACH, COOKED A MEAL AND BROUGHT IT TO ME FOR A SPECIAL LUNCH

DENTIA MACDONALD, A FORMER STUDENT, BAKED AN APPLE PIE FOR ME AND TOOK IT TO THE HOSPITAL JUST AFTER I HAD CHECKED OUT

JEANNETTE MIYAMOTO CALLED ME FROM CALIFORNIA

SUKETU MEHTA CALLED FROM INDIA

INDERA CALLED FROM INDIA

To this day, I have no clear memory of any of it.

For most of December, while recovering, I sat in a rocking chair by my fireplace in the living room of my home, trying to pull together the details of those lost days. The record of the interior persistence of my life existed only in the memories of other people. Their recollections told me that my sense of humor had remained intact, as had my smoking habit, my sense of duty toward Rachel, and most especially my desire to be free. Moreover, I could still recognize and appreciate beauty, and remained capable of opening my eyes wide if the image coming into view was potent enough to touch me at the deepest level of consciousness. As for my *own* memories, I recall from this great encounter with the edge only a kind of metaphorical wandering, or flights of imagination, or of landings, from the open heavens to the shifting sandbeds of the sea. Perhaps it was Richard's image in the outside world floating above me, the shadowy world that the Japanese name *Ukiyo,* that led me to sitting with some of my father's relatives, females mostly, in a living room in a place I know was South Carolina. We were discussing some disputed facts about our family history. I had promised to make something right for them, something that was of great importance.

ONE OF THE NURSES, AFTER AN EMBARRASSMENT, WASHED
DOWN MY BODY AND THEN HUGGED ME

I believe now that the promise that I made to those women had to do with my relationship with Richard. Before my illness we had been estranged for many years. When he called me at my home after my release from University Hospital, he told me, "You have so many friends. I was amazed by all the friends you have out there." And I told Richard, "That's what Daddy always taught us."

I was referring to the way our father, James A. McPherson, Sr., had operated even within the tightly segregated world that Savannah, Georgia, was during the 1940s and 1950s, when we were growing up. Both Richard and I can remember his believing that the entire system of segregation was a joke. He maintained many heartfelt relationships across racial and class lines. He possessed a generous heart, but liked to drink and gamble, and was always in trouble with the law. I have two very painful memories of emotional dislocations between Richard and me, after our father's death in 1961. The first is from the time of the funeral, a few days after our father died. I was seventeen, Mary was eighteen, Richard was sixteen, and Josephine, our youngest sister, was fourteen. We sat as a family with our mother on a bench in the Sidney A. Jones Funeral Parlor while a minister preached our father's funeral. I can still feel the pain his words inflicted on all of us. He said, "We all knew Mac, and we all know he's better off where he is now." The fact that I walked out of the funeral must have hurt my family, but especially Richard. The second memory derives from a time twenty years later. I had been in his home in Atlanta, and we had had an argument. He had told me, "Remember when I visited you in Berkeley in 1971 and you gave me a reading list? Well, you know what I read? Airplane repair manuals!" And I told him, "Richard, you are an ignorant man."

Richard had ordered me out of his home.

THE CODE SUSTAINING THE WORLD THAT FLOATS AT THE FOUNDATIONS OF THE WORLD IS BASED ON PREDATORY VIO-LENCE AND EXQUISITELY GOOD MANNERS

The exterior news in December 1998, while I sat by my fireplace and healed, was about the impeachment of William Jefferson Clinton. Slowly, there began to form in the various media a consensus that the animosity toward Clinton had grown out of the unfinished business of the 1960s. That is, his public persona remained imprisoned within the popular images that linger in consciousness from that period: draft resisting, flirtations with drugs, sexual adventuring. It seems that an entire generation, those born a few years after me, still remained in the public stocks of suspicion. Those who mistrusted them most were older people, but there were also those of that same generation who had followed orders, who had done their duties, and who had remained loyal to convention. They filtered through the media the voice of Shakespeare's Henry IV as he reprimanded Prince Hal for his youthful dalliances with Falstaff, Bardolph, Gadshill, Poins, Peto, and with Mistress Quickly.

My brother might have been of this group.

I have always maintained that there were two 1960s, one for

black people and another for white people. Simply put, the black people were trying to achieve full citizenship, to get into the mainstream. The young white people, having already experienced the loneliness and the uncertainties of middle-class life, were trying to get out. The black people came from tightly structured communities in which interdependence was essentially a matter of life or death. The white people came out of communities in which the myth of individualism had imposed a norm of habitual suspicion. The white side of this divide was explained to me once, out in Santa Cruz, by a very gentle friend named Don Ferrari, who had been an early inhabitant of the Haight-Ashbury district of San Francisco, before it became a commercial legend. He talked about the spirit of generosity and interdependence that the early residents there tried to achieve. I have since read an old book, based on a series of articles published in the *Village Voice* during the early 1960s. The book, *Moving Through Here,* by Don McNeil, details the noble ambitions of this wave of pioneers against the mythical landscape of the West. The black side of this spiritual divide, set during this same period and against the very same landscape, was told to me by Anne Thurman, the daughter of Howard Thurman, who was one of Martin Luther King's mentors at Morehouse. Thurman had moved to San Francisco to start his own "universalist" church. His daughter, Anne, then a teenager, had found employment in a bank. She had been the only black employee in the bank, and she received what she perceived as brutal treatment. She complained to her father, and the very wise Howard Thurman focused on the inevitable paradox in the quest for greater civil rights. He told her, "Annie, what makes *you* think that they would treat *you* better than they treat *each other?*"

Howard Thurman wisely saw that noble rhetoric must lead to steadfast human *action.*

KONOMI ARA SENT A MESSAGE AND THEN A GIFT FROM JAPAN

TAKEO HAMAMOTO CALLED FROM JAPAN

BENJAMIN CALLED FROM LOS ANGELES

My brother and I grew up together in a segregated Savannah, Georgia. We had enjoyed a thin cushion of middle-class stability early on, when our father worked as an electrical contractor, the only black master electrician, at that time, in the state of Georgia. But he lost his status, as well as control over his life, before Richard and I were adolescents, and the two of us had to go to work to help our mother take care of our two sisters. This training to be supportive of others, especially of needy women, I think now, shaped both our inner dramas. Both of us have what health professionals now call a neurotic need to rescue women. But back then we did not understand the nature of the path we were taking. Richard and I worked very, very hard to get our family off public welfare. In 1961, when I completed high school, I was lucky enough to get a National Defense Student Loan, which enabled me to attend Morris Brown College, a black Methodist college in Atlanta. In 1962, when he finished high school, Richard joined the air force, with ambitions to become a pilot. He visited me once at Morris Brown College before he left for Viet Nam. He had been diagnosed as color-blind, so he would not be trained as a pilot. But he later distinguished himself in Viet Nam, was promoted in rank, and was able to sit out the last years of the war at an air force installation in Athens, Greece.

Between 1961 and 1971, a mere ten years, I had experiences on every level of American society. While in Atlanta, I worked part-time as a waiter at the exclusive Dinkler Plaza Hotel, at the post office, and at the extremely exclusive Piedmount Driving Club (of Tom Wolfe fame) in Buckhead. During the summers I worked as a dining car waiter on the Great Northern Railroad and was able to explore Chicago, St. Paul and Minneapolis, the Rocky Mountains, and Seattle. I remember watching King's March on Washington, in August of 1963, on a great wall of television sets in a department store in St. Paul. I spent my junior year in Baltimore, at Morgan State College, learning about history and politics and literature. After graduating from Morris Brown, I entered the Harvard Law School. I worked there as a janitor, as a community aide in an Irish-

Italian Settlement House, and as a research assistant for a professor at the Harvard Business School. In the summers I took writing classes. In the fall of 1968, I moved to Iowa City, enrolled in the Writers' Workshop, and completed all my coursework in one year and a summer. In the fall of 1969, I took a teaching job at the University of California at Santa Cruz. I lived in Santa Cruz for nine months, and then I took an apartment in Berkeley, and then another apartment in Berkeley. I had begun to publish stories in the *Atlantic* in 1968, and I published a book of stories in 1969. While at Iowa, I had spent my weekends in Chicago researching a series of articles about a street gang named, then, the Blackstone Rangers. I had met and interviewed, in New York, Ralph Ellison, and had just completed an essay on him when my brother and his fiancée visited me, in the fall of 1971, in Berkeley. Both Richard and I had experienced very different decades. He had returned to Savannah from Athens. He had then found employment with Delta Airlines as a mechanic. He had moved from Savannah to Atlanta where he had met, ten years or so after graduation, a high school friend named Narvis Freeman, who was then working toward her master's degree. He and this hometown girl dated, recognized that they liked each other, and decided to get married.

But like my eleven days in a coma, neither of us knew the internal details of the other.

I know now that, to Richard, I must have seemed a product of the popular images of the 1960s. By this time I *had* inhaled marijuana, but I had not enjoyed it. This was because a gun had been at the back of my head while I inhaled. A Blackstone Ranger was holding the gun while we raced along Lake Shore Drive in Chicago. This had been a test. If I wanted to observe the gang and write about it, the gang had to have something incriminating on me in case I was a "snitch." The Rangers had their own code. I had also been a draft-dodger. My local board in Savannah had been trying to draft me since my third year in law school. It did not seem to matter to them that Richard was already in Viet Nam and that I was enrolled in school. What seemed, in my own mind, to matter to them was that my name had been listed on the welfare rolls of Chatham County, Georgia, and that I had gotten as far as the Harvard Law School. Given the norms of white supremacy, this must have been considered "wrong." Moreover, on a deeply emotional level, ever since I had walked out on my father's funeral I had kept my vow that no one would ever say over my body that my life had not been worth anything. I had also vowed that I would never allow *any* circumstance to force me into the hands of people who might do me harm, as my father had been done harm. So I remained in school, communicating with my local board from Cambridge, from Iowa City, and from Santa Cruz. Finally, my boss at Santa Cruz, a writer named James B. Hall, wrote a letter on my behalf to my local board. "You don't want this man," he wrote with his usual irony. "I happen to know that he's crazy." This was sometime in 1970, when the Santa Cruz campus, as well as the campuses of Berkeley, Harvard, Columbia, and Iowa, were exploding with antiwar protests.

Beginning in Cambridge, when I was twenty-two or twenty-three, I began to have a sex life. But I was never a fiend. The old pattern of being a caretaker to wounded females had persisted, and so I rejected one woman who wanted to give to me emotionally in order to bond with one who was needy. I repeated this pattern in Iowa City and again when I lived in Berkeley. It took a very bad marriage to help me break this pattern. This experience also helped me to better understand some of the emotional and psychological damage that the caretaker can inflict on the person who is "rescued." It freezes the helpless person at a permanent point of neediness, and it keeps that person confined in this role. Although the act of rescue may seem heroic at its outset, the interplay between one's own neurosis and the human need of the rescued person's desire to grow can become a battle, if not an endless war.

But when Richard and Narvis came to visit me in Berkeley in the fall of 1971, I was very much unconscious of my *self*.

RICHARD FELDMAN CAME BY WITH HIS JUICER AND SEVERAL
PACKETS OF FRESH CARROTS IN HIS BACKPACK AND MADE A
GLASS OF CARROT JUICE FOR ME

STEPHANIE GRIFFIN SENT ME A TIN OF HOMEMADE COOKIES
FROM UPSTATE NEW YORK

MS. MIWA SENT ME A JAPANESE CALENDAR FROM OXFORD,
MISSISSIPPI

I considered myself, at that point in my life, primarily a teacher. At
Santa Cruz I taught writing and literature to mostly young white
people from the upper middle class. I was living, then, in the basement apartment of a Japanese landlady, in Berkeley, and I had a Japanese girlfriend. When Richard and Narvis visited me in that apartment, I know now, the only experiences we had in common were our
mutual memories of childhood and adolescence in Savannah. We
could talk about family matters, about people from back home who
were still close to us, but Richard's experience of Southeast Asia and
of Athens, Greece, contained strands of memory so deeply private
that they could only be shared, over a great number of years, inside
a close relationship like a marriage. My own experiences were just as
private. But, I still want to believe now, I tried to do the best I could
to bridge this gap. I had invited Ishmael Reed to give a talk to my
students at Santa Cruz. I invited Richard and Narvis to drive there
with us. As I recall, we had a wonderful class. Ishmael was full of
gruff humor and street smarts, and the students were receptive.
When we returned to Berkeley in the evening, the four of us went to
a bar and talked some more. Then I invited Richard and his fiancée
back to my apartment.

GREG DOWNS SENT ME BY MAIL A CHOCOLATE ORANGE

OPAL MOORE CALLED FROM RICHMOND

STUART HARRIS FLEW IN FROM RICHMOND AND BROUGHT A

BOOK ON JAPANESE AESTHETICS AND SOME COOKIES BAKED BY
HIS FIANCÉE. STUART HUGGED ME

MITZI CLAWSON SENT A BOX CONTAINING DRIED BEANS AND
THE MAKINGS FOR FISH STEW

CRAIG AWMILLER SENT FROM OREGON SEVERAL CDS AND
THEN, BY AIR EXPRESS, SOME FROZEN FISH CAKES

I have now in this house and in my office and in storage close to five
thousand books. I left home for college with a single suitcase containing clothes and a National Defense Student Loan. But my love
for books had grown the more I read and the more I traveled. When
I lived in Cambridge I used to joke that I was amazed to see so many
people walking pridefully into bookstores or reading books openly
in cafés and restaurants. I noted that where I came from such actions
constituted an open invitation to be beaten up. As a teacher, books,
back then, became my life, an extension of myself. They were a necessity for a very special reason. I had been raised in almost complete
segregation, had attended a second- or third-rate college, and had
been admitted to the Harvard Law School where I had been exposed
to the legal and intellectual institutions that governed the country. I
had left the law school knowing only two levels of the society: the
extreme bottom and, much more abstractly, the extreme top. This
was still segregation of a kind. Only the experience of reading, I determined, could help me integrate the fuzzy middle areas so I could
have a complete picture. Paul Freund, who taught me constitutional
law at Harvard, used to say that his students knew all the answers
without knowing any of the basic questions. I think now that I was
trying to learn the basic questions through reading so that, when
combined with my own experiences, I could develop a national
mind—a sense of how the entire culture, regional, ethnic, class, in-
stitutional, functioned together, as a *whole.* At the basis of this idea,
I concede now, were ideas I had absorbed from conversations with
Ralph Ellison and Albert Murray. I know it was this very issue of

identity that caused the black 1960s and the white 1960s to come together.

At a time when black nationalist rhetoric had become the new political fashion, I began consciously bonding across racial lines. I thought that the real end of the civil rights movement—beyond economic and political empowerment—needed, if it were to succeed, a moral component that transcended race. It was simply a matter of trying to follow the Golden Rule. This was the open but complex and untested area that lay beyond access to once-closed institutions. It was the human problem raised by Howard Thurman in his question to Annie, his daughter. The search for this moral feeling tone was what the white 1960s had been all about. It was what Martin King envisioned would happen, would *have* to happen, after the once-closed institutions became open and allowed free-and-easy access to what was unquestionably of transcendent *human* value. These were some of the intellectual abstractions through which I faced my brother in Berkeley that evening in 1971.

I gave him some of my precious books, as I had given books to students and friends for many years before that evening.

MY NEXT-DOOR NEIGHBORS, TWO WOMEN, PLOWED MY SIDEWALK AND FRONT STEPS DURING THE TERRIBLE LATE-DECEMBER SNOWS AND FREEZE

Almost ten years later, this time inside Richard's home in Atlanta, the long-delayed confrontation took place. I was then going through a crisis, and it seemed that every place I turned toward those people I had known the longest, there came the same refrain, *Remember that time?,* with some inconsequential slight or omission on my part attached to the sound of an old friendship breaking. I managed the crisis as best I could, finally deciding that the only way I could survive, as a whole human being, was to make a break with those people who bore such hidden grudges. This meant, in fact, that I had to make a clear break with an entire region of the country. It meant I had to turn my back on my entire family. I was willing to pay this price. So in 1981 I settled in Iowa City, made a new home for myself, and in 1989 I went to Japan for the first time. I made new friends there, friends who came often to this country to explore its culture. In about 1992, ten years after I had left the South, two of my Japanese friends were planning to visit Atlanta. I called up Richard, and I asked if he or Narvis, his wife, would greet my two Japanese friends when they arrived at Hartsfield Airport. But Richard told me, "No!" He added, "Remember that ten years ago you drew a line in the sand against the whole South? Well, now I'm drawing a line against *you!* Scratch my name, address, and telephone number out of your address book and never call here again!"

A white lawyer, an old classmate at law school, agreed to go to Hartsfield Airport and greet my two Japanese friends.

I know now that Richard had, by this time, good reason for this total dismissal of me. It seems to me now that I had violated the ritual bond that we had shared since childhood. Our mother had been very ill during those ten years, and it had been Richard who had traveled to Savannah each weekend to see about her. It had been Richard who had brought her to Atlanta to see medical specialists. And when she was no longer able to live alone, it had been Richard who closed down her apartment in Savannah and had moved her into his own home in Atlanta. It was Richard who had cooked for her, had given her daily baths and shots of insulin for her diabetes. And it had been Richard, finally, who was by her bedside in the hospital when she died.

I recognize, now, that I had dishonored our mother for the sake of a lonely principle, and since those years I have been struggling with what I thought had been vital in that principle. To make this clear, to myself as well as to Richard, and to earn the forgiveness of our mother, I have had to imagine the shadowy dimensions of the William Jefferson Clinton drama that is now occupying so much of public discourse. At its basis, as I have said, is the lingering animosity toward those who represented the counterculture of the 1960s.

But there was, and is, something much more subtle at work. The moral energy generated by the civil rights movement benefited black people like Richard and Narvis, his wife. Simply put, a black middle class, with some economic stake in the system, was created. The proper ritual stance, for all such beneficiaries, is gratitude and economic self-celebration. But before the largesse flowed, there had been a much larger goal, one articulated by King as the creation of a "beloved community," one that intersected, at certain points, with the communal goals of the white counterculture. Both movements, at their high points, were beginning to formulate an answer to Howard Thurman's question to Annie, his daughter: "What makes you think that they would treat *you* better than they treat *each other?*" Both King and Gandhi, his mentor, would have answered, "Because they have been practicing *swaraj*—self-rule. Because it is only through wishing for the best for others that one can become and remain truly human." Aristotle called this special kind of emotional relationship "perfected friendship." The Japanese term relationships that are grounded in such natural feelings "*shizen na kamoche.*" I believe, in justification of myself, and also of my father, that it is only in locating these emotional resources inside ourselves, as well as inside other people, that one can create meaningful communities, even across racial lines.

The South, as I had experienced it while growing up, and as I had reexperienced it in Charlottesville, Virginia, during the late 1970s and the early 1980s, just did not offer normative opportunities for this kind of human growth. For me, the goal had never been economic success. For me, it had *always* been a matter of personal growth within a communal context unstructured by race. It is a very hard fact of life that there exists no such community in any part of the country. But, at the same time, it *does* exist in every part of the country, among selected individuals from every possible background. But this community is a floating world, a *ukiyo,* sustained, incrementally, by letters, telephone calls, faxes, e-mail, visits from time to time. It is not proximity that keeps it alive, but periodic expenditures of human energy and imagination and grace. This is what I have now, as a substitute for a hometown. I find it more than sufficient.

This is the thing I wanted very badly to explain to Richard, my brother, after I came out of my coma.

THERE IS A VERY PEACEFUL SPIRIT CONTAINED IN A FIRE THAT IS KEPT ALIVE DAY AND NIGHT AND DAY AND NIGHT AND DAY AND NIGHT

After our mother's death, Mary, our older sister, began to grow closer to our father's family, the core of which still survives in a little community named Green Pond, South Carolina. Mary began attending reunions there. Then she became active in helping to organize the reunions. Rachel attended one such reunion in Atlanta in the early 1990s, and several years ago I attended another reunion in Detroit. It was a loving affair. Richard was there, and though we were wary of each other, we got along very well. Also attending was my father's half-brother, Thomas McPherson, and his wife, Vanzetta. She is a federal district court judge in Birmingham, Alabama. Thomas's sister, Eva Clayton, was also there. Eva represents a district of North Carolina in the U.S. Congress. There was no sense of rank or of status among us. We were simply family, simply community. When I began telling jokes, Eva told me that I should never call her up in Washington, as I habitually called up Mary in Stamford, to recite my latest one-liners. She said that they might, if overheard, land her in trouble.

We took a group trip deep into Windsor, Canada, across the river from Detroit, in order to visit a station on the old Underground Railroad. The tour guide detailed the complex history of this station, one grounded in a communal effort that had transcended race. He noted that a great number of wooden carts, piled high with manure used for fertilizer, would stop periodically at the station. And hidden in the false bottoms of those carts, beneath the great piles of manure, would be fugitive slaves. We were all in good spirits, so I decided to try a one-liner on Richard. I said, "Richard, those carts are the ritual basis of our old Negro expression, 'Nigger, you ain't shit!' Only we have forgotten the celebratory tone that used to go with it. Our fugitive slave ancestors really said when they opened those false bottoms, 'Nigger, you *ain't* shit. *You're a free man!*'"

Richard laughed then, and the years of ice began to melt.

Last year Mary attended another reunion, again with members of our father's family, in Patterson, New Jersey. She sent me a news article about one of the young men descended from this line who, Mary says, is our third cousin. His name is Leonard Brisbon. He is a major in the air force and is the co-pilot of Air Force One. He is an honors graduate of the Air Force Academy and has won many awards. In the article he talked lovingly about his parents and their values, and about his family roots in Green Pond, South Carolina. His lifelong ambition, he said, was to go to Mars. I plan to travel to the next reunion of this branch of my family, no matter where it takes place, in order to meet this cousin. I hope that Richard will also be there. I know he would be very proud of how high this cousin in our family has risen in the air force. In the meantime, I am practicing a new one-liner, one that I plan to try on Leonard Brisbon. I plan to say to him, "You crazy Negro. There ain't no collard greens on Mars!" I am hoping that Leonard Brisbon will laugh, along with Richard. I hope both of them will be able to see me as I *am*.

I also hope to have a much better funeral than my father had.

PERHAPS THIS IS WHAT, IN MY COMA, I PROMISED THOSE LA-
DIES WHO SAT IN A ROOM IN SOUTH CAROLINA

Glenalmond

The omens are equivocal. It is not actually raining, but as I choose my clothes at 7 A.M. that morning, Kirsty, still in her nightdress, comes into my room. "Margot," she says, "why aren't you married?" Why indeed, I think, skidding wildly down some long, dark alleyway into the past. Feebly, parodying the well-known cartoon, I say, "I forgot. Should I wear my black jeans?" But Kirsty, a diligent questioner, is not so easily put aside. "Why did you forget?" she asks, her eyes blue as cornflowers.

I am in Edinburgh, visiting Kirsty and her parents for only a few days, alas, and today is set aside to go to Glenalmond, the valley where I grew up, fifty miles north of Edinburgh. As I drive out of the city, grappling with my rented car, I do my best to put aside Kirsty's questions. Instead I ponder this mysterious business of a journey with its implied beginning and ending. But Glenalmond was not a place I ever journeyed to—it was the place I was, most fully and completely—and if I am to journey there now, I need a place to start. Where should I begin: America where nowadays I mostly earn my living? London where I spend the summers? Kirsty's house? I round a bend and suddenly the road unwinds before me in total familiarity. I am in Blackhall, a suburb of Edinburgh, and the answer is obvious.

Just a few yards from the main road is 4 Craigcrook Place, the home of my redoubtable great aunts. The old heavy door has been replaced, but there is nothing newfangled, like a lock or an intercom, to bar my progress. Inside even the dustbins seem unchanged. A tabby cat comes to greet me and follows, flirting shamelessly, as I climb the stone steps that Little Aunt washed once a month. Can I smell mince and tatties? On the second floor the door of the aunts' flat is ajar, clearly now the cat's home. For a moment, peering into the wedge of darkness, I consider stepping inside. Would the toilet still be acidic green? Would the kitchen still have the black iron range? For the sake of the present occupant, I hope not. I fondle the cat and walk away.

The aunts' flat was the outermost star in my childhood cosmography. We visited them twice a year, an immense journey for which my stepmother packed sandwiches and a thermos of tea. Now I whiz freely along the modern roads. Only an hour later I am entering Methven, the drab village where we came to catch the bus, post letters, buy treats. I stop at Lawson's garage where my father brought his cars, each more decrepit than the last, all called Henry. The man who sells me petrol tells me that Mr. Lawson died shortly before Christmas. I tell him that I am going to Glenalmond. "Oh, you'll notice lots of changes," he says. "All the big houses." Briefly I imagine the valley filled with skyscrapers: Manhattan in Arcadia. I pass the Bell Tree Inn, which I never entered, and Fitzgerald's, the butcher's, whose bloody wares I eyed askance. The premises now house a builder with the appealing name of Goodwillie and Hunter.

Opposite the post office I turn off for Glenalmond. The narrow road climbs steadily for four miles and every bend and hummock, even the thistles, are familiar; I slow down to greet them. Fortunately I meet no other cars. When I broach the final rise into the valley, my heart is racing as if I had been running, not driving, and I pull over. Gradually the tink-tink of the motor fades until I can distinguish the sounds we casually call silence: the wind in the fields, the hum of insects, the bird song. Only a distant, occasional hammering indicates another human presence. The main school, down near the river Almond, is still hidden by oaks and beeches, and on the far side of the river a long line of hills fills the horizon. Looking from east to west, I see the slate quarries, the circular wood and the dark, scree-covered slopes of Sma'Glen.

Let me explain. We are approaching a public school, founded in the 1840's by William Gladstone amongst others. My father taught here for many years, mathematics and geography, and until the age of eight I lived in Glenalmond, happily ignorant of the world elsewhere. My life divides along several fault lines—the death of my mother when I was two and a half, going to an English university, falling in love with a Canadian—but leaving this valley which I knew tree by tree, stone by stone, remains in some ways the most irrevocable of these faults, something done to me for mysterious adult reasons that can never be undone or made whole again. I loathed the village in the Borders of Scotland where we went to live; I detested the girls' school I attended. All I wanted was my old life back again. That safe life, without divisions, where I could find the curlew's nest and knew when snow was coming.

Now the car is nothing save an encumbrance. Ruthlessly I pull onto the grass beside Front Avenue—this is my home and I'll park where I please—and set off with my camera and notebook. In my mind I have a clear set of places I want to visit. The first is the Cairnies where my adopted family lived. This too requires explanation. After all, I did have a family of my own, a father and a stepmother, but they were elderly and often unenthusiastic about my projects: hut-making, tree-climbing, bridge-building. A few hundred yards from our house lived a couple with four children. From my earliest memories I ran in and out of their house all day long, ate at their table, played with their toys, learned to read and not to cheat at games. Their generosity shines throughout my life, then and now, a gift beyond thanks.

As I walk up Front Avenue and along the Main Road I notice in the well-kept grounds an unfamiliar presence: a Coke can under a bush, a crisps wrapper caught in the grass. Trivial compared to what I see daily on the streets of London, but still striking. When I was growing up there was no litter—what would cause it? We had no soft drinks, sweets were doled out one by one, there were no leaflets, no junk mail. People unwrapped parcels carefully, smoothing out the paper to use again, coiling the string. We children carried neither keys nor money; I doubt the adults did either. I tut-tut under my breath.

The Cairnies originally belonged to the Mansfields, who sold it to the school for a song, or two. When I was four a new wing was added onto the beautiful old house and sixty boys lived there along with my adopted family. Best of all, the boys took holidays and then we had the whole house to ourselves. Now the building could easily be empty. Virginia creeper blinds many of the windows and the paint work is stained and peeling. Willow herb has seeded in the garden. But when I press my nose to the hall window, I see the familiar wallpaper, the oak panelling, the broad stairs leading to the drawing room. Despite appearances, the old house is still occupied; the boys' wing, though, has indeed been abandoned.

Walking round the house, I find a door open and, without thinking, slip inside. I am in the corridor next to the boys' dining-hall. Beneath my feet is the linoleum that was laid when the wing was built, red squares bordered in liverish brown, across which we roller-skated vigorously during the holidays. I wander round inspecting cubicles and studies. A wooden plaque listing the head boys hangs at the foot of the stairs, and I recognise the dynasties of my time: Barbour, Frame, Hill. The last name "Sicker—1991" has, inevitably, lost the final syllable. I feel a little like a ghost, padding down these corridors, and so it seems no harm that my ghostly self tries the door that led to our part of the house, only to discover it locked. "Out of Bounds," says a notice.

I slip out of another side door and continue up the hill towards my first home: Bell's Cottage. I lived here with my father and a succession of women: my mother, Little Aunt, my stepmother. As I walk the few hundred yards between the two houses, I scrutinise the landscape. The California redwood, which we called the punch tree, is still there, and the large houses predicted by the man at the garage are nowhere to be seen, but to my eyes major changes lie all around: a beloved bush missing here, a crucial tree gone there. The woods are thick with underbrush and I sense that the local children are no longer doing their job of keeping paths clear. The raspberry canes are heavy with fruit; we would never have let that happen. Later, on the golf course, I pick several pounds of mushrooms.

In my memory Bell's Cottage has a grim aura, a grey harled house with a grey door. Today, however, geraniums blossom in the windows and swallows twitter back and forth beneath the eaves. I am gazing longingly at my bedroom window, not quite daring to go and look in, when the front door opens and a woman in shorts appears. How scandalised Little Aunt and my stepmother would have been. "If she could see herself," they would remark to each other at the rare sight of a woman in trousers; shorts were unthinkable. Embarrassed to be caught gaping, I continue on my way towards the golf course.

The last time I came here, a dozen years ago, was to see the bench presented by the old boys in memory of my father. He spent many happy hours hitting a ball round these fairways. The bench, a simple wooden one with a brass plaque giving his dates, overlooked the first fairway. Today the course is almost deserted, only a couple of men at the third hole and a girl of perhaps nine or ten, hitting balls around near the clubhouse. "I'm just starting," she tells me with a shy smile when I ask about her game. A single bench stands not far from where I remember and I head towards it, hopefully. But it belongs to some clerk of works, the plaque announces, who served the school for a meagre decade.

I am irked. It is one thing for me to ignore my father; quite another for the institution where he taught for nearly half a century to do so. I leave the golf course and walk the mile to the main school past Bell's Cottage and the Cairnies, along the Main Road, down Front Avenue past the car and the immaculate cricket pitch. The hammering I heard when I first arrived is still going on and, as I step into the quad, I discover that the roof of the dining-hall is being re-slated. In contrast to the Cairnies, workmen are everywhere, painting windows, landscaping, peering into drains. A new term is approaching.

At the back of the chapel, surrounded by a dense, dark hedge, lies a small graveyard. I find several unexpected inhabitants: my godfather, a flamboyant master whom I last saw at the bar of the Murray Park Hotel in Crieff; the college electrician whose surname, Proudfoot, gave us children considerable satisfaction; the science master who refused to let me come to the school to study science at the age of sixteen and to whom I probably owe my present occupation. My father, once again, is missing.

He died when I was twenty-two and now, staring at the motley stones, I realize that I have absolutely no memory of his funeral; I could not even say if I was present. I shake my head and wish I had been a more dutiful daughter. But I have two dead parents and, as I step back through the hedge, it occurs to me that I have never seen my mother's grave either. Somehow I know that she is buried in Harrietfield, the tiny village across the river from the school. Leaving the workmen to their industry, I set off to the white footbridge.

Harrietfield consists of a mere few dozen cottages. Even so it takes me a while to locate the church, tucked away behind the single large house. The door is locked. Through the dusty window I see rows of dusty pews. No graveyard. In the whole village I encounter only one person, an elderly woman sitting on a sun porch with a sign beside her: "No milk today, please." She ought, given her age, to be a good informant, but her eyes follow me like two black stones and I do not have the nerve to approach her.

Back at the car, I study the map and discover the graveyard, not at Harrietfield, but a mile away near Chapel Hill. It is already late afternoon, checking all our huts and bridges was no quick task, but still I cannot bear to leave without paying my final respects. A Hungarian friend taught me the Russian custom of sitting down for one minute before leaving a place; in a life full of departures, I have come to find this ritual useful. I drive back to Bell's Cottage and, leaving the car there, walk down the hill towards the Cairnies. For the third time that day it begins to rain. I lean against the soft bark of the California redwood, listening to the patter on the leaves, looking at my two homes and the gap in the woods where the azaleas used to be.

Close to Chapel Hill, a rough track leads off to the right and a short distance away, amongst the trees, I glimpse a cross. This must be it, I think, and swerve onto the track. Almost immediately, I realise my mistake, but turning around is out of the question and reversing well-nigh impossible. What am I doing? I think and, even as the thought bubbles up, the car sticks fast. I turn off the engine. Once again I am alone with the intricate silence.

I walk to the graveyard—after all that is why I am here—and push open the black iron gate. Several of the stones have fallen and many are blurred with moss and lichen. Soon it becomes apparent that this graveyard has not been in use for many years; none of the graves is later than 1920. Feeling doubly foolish, I jog to the nearest steading. The house is surrounded by bricks and ladders and outside is a van with a name I learned earlier today: Goodwillie and Hunter. A pleasant-looking man emerges, holding a hammer. "I'm stuck in a ditch," I blurt out. "Do you have a phone or a tractor?"

"There's a phone upstairs," he says calmly. "And a couple of chaps came by with a tractor a minute ago. Let's see if they're still here."

As I follow him across the farmyard his mates start to heckle. "Not fair," they shout. "Give us a shot. Turn and turn alike." Neither of us responds.

In the barn two unlikely angels are seated on a bale of hay, having a fag: an extremely weatherbeaten man with no teeth and eyes as blue as his overalls and a fat man, shirtless, his fly undone. Mr. Goodwillie and Hunter explains my predicament and, with a flourish of his hammer, hands me over. "Och, you'll be stuck in the dip," the fat man remarks, jovially.

"It'll cost you," chuckles the toothless one. "Fifty pounds an hour."

I return to the car. Within a few minutes the fat man shows up with a tractor and a shirt. He mutters about the exhaust, hooks me up, and pulls me back to the road. When we are once more on terra firma he asks, hesitantly, as if it is really none of his business, what I was doing. I tell him. "You want the new graveyard," he says, pointing. "Just down there. Don't take the car." He refuses payment on the grounds that he is already well paid and drives away.

I hurry after his gesture, worried now that I won't have time to find her. I pass a row of ragged cottages, and step through a gate into a small, walled graveyard. It is only a quarter full, the grass so smooth the word "sward" comes to mind. Hastily, dourly, I begin to search the graves. And there she is, the fifth from the gate along the wall. The stone is quite small, no larger than a pillow, with Eva's name and my father's and my own: "Beloved wife of Kenneth Livesey, mother of Margot." I stare at it, consumed. Then I lie down on the grass, pressing myself close, closer, trying to still my beating heart.

This sounds embarrassingly morbid, like something out of *Tess of the D'Urbervilles,* but in fact it was the reverse. Not morbid but vivid—full of life. Driving away in my treacherous chariot, I am greatly cheered. After my decades of neglect, there she was, Eva, my mother, unscathed. As a writer I've spent years wallowing in the past, subscribing to various theories: it's writ in stone, writ in water, can never be known, can never be escaped, must be remembered, et cetera, et cetera. My answer to Kirsty was a desperate lie. My problem is not forgetting but the reverse: a surfeit of memory.

This evening, however, driving back to Edinburgh beneath a full moon, the past sits beside me, easy as an old friend. Forget that late twentieth century infatuation with the Heisenberg Principle, which claims that the observer always alters the thing observed. What I learned today was my own irrelevance. The past exists irrespective of my observation—I can pay attention, or not: who gives a toss?—but the present, the difficult, intractable present, lies all around me, and it's time now to reach towards it, greedily with both hands.

ANATOLE BROYARD

Toward a Literature of Illness

I was reading *The Transit of Venus,* Shirley Hazzard's most recent novel. Though I admired her other books, I'd always resisted this one. It struck me as too pure, somehow; too heroic; larger or finer than life, and therefore unreal. But now I read it with an almost indescribable pleasure. There were sentences that brought tears of gratification to my eyes and raised the hairs on the nape of my neck.

I was in Brigham Hospital in Brookline, Massachusetts, propped up in bed with an intravenous feeding tube in my arm and a catheter in my urethral canal because a cystoscopy had left me unable to pee. It was a double room and my roommate, a kind of thug who growled when he spoke because he had both a broken jaw and a drug habit, was spraying the air for the fourth or fifth time that day with a cloying deodorizer. He had a television set and a radio going at the same time.

The catheter hurt, and the diagnosis of my case was ambiguous.

When I asked the oncologist the usual question—How much time have I got?—he hesitated before answering. "I would say," he said, "that you have in the neighborhood of years."

I burrowed into the book. I was not escaping into it but identifying with it as fervently as I have ever identified with any novel. The life Shirley Hazzard described was the kind I wanted to live for the rest of my life, for my neighborhood of years. Her book was the prescription I needed and that no doctor could give me. I needed a dose of the sublime. From where I sat in my cranked-up bed, the sublime seemed to be all there was left.

I paused in my reading because I was out of shape and the beauty of the book had winded me. In my mind I composed a letter to Shirley Hazzard. After a brief description of my circumstances, I said, "You offered me an alternative. Art is our ace in the hole. I'm eating your book for lunch, and it's making me hungry."

I was afraid of finishing *The Transit of Venus*. It had become my neighborhood. I put it down and went for a walk around the ward, dragging the metal rack with the IV tube and the catheter bag. From the window of an empty room I looked down at the city, which was dotted with trees. How extraordinary the real world was! Shirley Hazzard was right.

When I got out of the hospital my first impulse was to write about my illness. While sick people need books like *The Transit of Venus* to remind them of the life beyond their illness, they also need a literature of their own. Misery loves company—if it's good company. And surprisingly enough, there isn't much good company in this rapidly proliferating field. A critical illness is one of our momentous experiences, yet I haven't seen a single nonfiction book that does it justice. Even in fiction there are only a handful of great books on the subject: Tolstoy's *The Death of Ivan Ilyich,* Thoman Mann's *The Magic Mountain,* most of Kafka, and Malcolm Lowry's *Under the Volcano.*

While Tolstoy was the grandfather, my favorites among these

are Mann and Lowry. Kafka's illnesses are more existential than physical; they are like Kierkegaard's "sickness unto death." In *The Magic Mountain,* Mann wrote the grand definitive romance of illness, a portrait that, I would say, speaking as a connoisseur now, will never be equaled. His description of life itself showed how precarious it was: "a form-preserving instability, a fever of matter . . . the existence of the impossible-to-exist, of a half-sweet, half-painful balancing, or scarcely balancing, in this restricted and feverish process of decay and renewal, upon the point of existence."

Mann's hero Hans Castorp, who has only a little "moist spot" on one lung, has been sublimating his passion for Clavdia Chauchat, who is seriously ill, by reading biology books. When, encouraged by champagne, Castorp woos her, he vacillates between the language of physiology, of the doctor, and the language of the lover or poet. "Let me touch devotedly with my lips," he says, "the femoral artery that throbs in the front of your thigh and divides lower down into the two arteries of the tibia! . . . The body, love, death," he says, speaking to her in French, the only language they have in common, "these three are only one. For the body is sickness and voluptuousness, and it is this that causes death, yes, they are carnal both of them, love and death, and that is their terror and their great magic!" After their first and only night together, Chauchat gives Castorp an X ray of her tubercular lungs as a souvenir.

Like Mann, Malcolm Lowry uses the delirium of illness in *Under the Volcano,* where alcoholism is the consul's disease—one that will kill him indirectly. While I have little patience with drunks, I love the consul, because he makes drunkenness too seem like "a fever of matter," like a slip or glitch in our composition, a hopeless reaching for happiness. He is so inventive, so poetic, so tender about his alcoholism, he wastes himself in such grandiose gestures and experiences such incredible distortions without allowing them to break his heart, that I find the novel almost unbearably moving.

When I turned to nonfiction, to books by people who were or had been ill, I expected to find some echo of Castorp or the consul, but for the most part I was disappointed. Two of the better books were written by reporters: *Stay of Execution,* by Stewart Alsop, who was a political columnist, and *Hanging in There,* by Natalie Spingarn, a medical reporter. Their books remind me of the dispatches of war correspondents. While they describe in considerable detail the way cancer attacks and how the campaign against it works, they don't go much beyond this. They tell the reader a lot about the waking life of the cancer patient, but not much about his daydreams or fantasies, about how illness transfigures you. Their books are objective, businesslike. You wouldn't know from them that inside every seriously ill person there's a Kafka character, a Castorp, or a consul, trying to get out. On the other hand there are books about illness that are too eloquent, that are full of chanting and dying falls, so pious that they sound as if they were written on tiptoe. To be ill is an odd mixture of pathos and bathos, comedy and terror, with intervals of surprise. To treat it too respectfully is to fall into the familiar, florid traps of the Romantic agony.

Peter Noll, a Swiss professor of law, goes even further in avoiding the emotional aspect of illness. All through *In the Face of Death,* his strange book about having cancer, he argues, almost legalistically, that he has the right to refuse treatments that would disfigure him and make him impotent. He says that he prefers death to a sexless life in which he would have to wear a bladder on his abdomen. Yet the tone of his book is stoical and philosophical, and he hardly seems the kind of man to rate his potency and his physical vanity above life itself. The discrepancy is so noticeable that one senses a deep, repressed anger—even a secret tragedy—between the lines.

Max Lerner certainly has Mann and Kafka in bed with him in *Wrestling with the Angel: A Memoir of Triumph over Illness.* Like an old campaigner, he welcomes the opportunity to examine, at point-blank range, the threatened human body and soul. His book is the best of the patient's accounts I've seen. My only reservation about it is that his memoir is perhaps too intellectual, not lyrical enough, too much about ideas and too little about the whatness, the sheer here and now, of illness. His thinking about his illness is a bit too professional. Ill or well, he's the same Max Lerner, better known, almost, than the cancer he writes about. He's so firmly rooted in the human condition that he is not possessed by his condition as a critically ill person. At his age he's hard to awe.

Norman Cousins is both a reporter and a reformer in his books about his own and other people's illnesses. He was one of the first to encourage the patient to develop strategies of his own, to provide for himself all the things the doctor didn't order. While he has been criticized for oversimplifying the issues—his insistence, for example, on the healing power of laughter—he has many shrewd things to say. He advises the patient to regard the diagnosis of critical illness not as a threat or a prophecy but as a challenge. He urges the sick person to take an active part in his treatment, to keep reminding his doctor whose life it is.

In *Head First: The Biology of Hope,* his latest book, Mr. Cousins seems very useful in his job as a sort of patients' advocate in the School of Medicine at the University of California at Los Angeles. But while his book is crammed with information and news of research, he is perhaps too fond of unexplained remissions. I like him because he is an evangelist of sorts—and every hospital ought to have one—yet his sense of humor is corny and his yea-saying may put off sophisticated people. For a former editor of the *Saturday Review,* he has surprisingly little to offer about the imaginative life of the sick.

Bernie Siegel, a doctor who says "call me Bernie," is a sort of Donald Trump of critical illness. He sounds like a proprietor or landlord of mortality. The title of his book, *Love, Medicine and Miracles,* tells a lot about him. He believes in love and miracles as much as in medicine, and he has even more spontaneous remissions to report than Norman Cousins. Although he's a surgeon, he might sometimes be mistaken for a pop psychiatrist. Like Mr. Cousins, he is not a gifted writer, and this may cause his suggestions to sound cruder than they actually are. He, like the Simontons, asks his patients to practice "imaging," to think of their "good" cells attacking and overcoming their "bad" cells. Some of his analyses of patients' drawings strike me as recklessly confident.

Yet, for better or worse, he introduces an element of camaraderie into the medical process. He rallies the patient and offers him hope, even if it is "inspirational." In his presentation of himself he reminds me of a doctor I knew who wore such outlandish-looking suits that I couldn't help wondering about his medical judgment. While his book is a best-seller, Dr. Siegel is like an awkwardly drawn angel announcing a controversial miracle. Yet, with all these caveats, he is a godsend to many people who are too sick to stick at his style.

For me, the trouble with most inspirational books is that you can feel them trying to inspire you. They're more "inspiring" than believable; you don't feel that you can trust them. I don't trust anyone who tells me that he loves me when he doesn't even know me. I think that a healthy critical attitude toward such literature is more "positive" than a half-hearted, rearguard attempt at saintliness or *agape*. Though I don't believe I can love my cancer away, I do think I may be able to shrink it a little by pointing out its limitations, by being critical of the way people bow down to it. I can treat it like an overrated text.

Susan Sontag's *Illness as Metaphor* and *AIDS and Its Metaphors* are elegant analyses of how we think about illness and the stigma we attach to it—the "spoiled identity" of the sick, as Erving Goffman puts it. She chooses to address herself more to the conceptualization of illness than to the daily experience of it. Approaching him panoramically rather than individually, she aims a bit high for the sick man lying flat in his hospital bed. It is not his quiddity but his place in the medical polity that occupies her. She is to illness what William Empson's *Seven Types of Ambiguity* is to literature.

In my opinion she's too hard on metaphor when she says that "the most truthful way of regarding illness—and the healthiest way of being ill—is one most purified of, most resistant to, metaphoric thinking." She seems to throw the baby out with the bath. While she is concerned only with negative metaphors, there are positive metaphors of illness, too, a kind of literary aspirin. In fact, metaphors may be as necessary to illness as they are to literature, as comforting to the patient as his own bathrobe and slippers. At the very least, they are a relief from medical terminology. If laughter has healing power, so, too, may metaphor. Perhaps only metaphor can express the bafflement, the panic combined with beatitude, of the threatened person. Surely Ms. Sontag wouldn't wish to condemn the sick to Hemingway sentences.

Oliver Sacks, a neurologist, has become a kind of poet laureate of contemporary medicine. While I can only hint here at all the extraordinary things he has done to open up our thinking about illness in *Awakenings, Migraine, A Leg to Stand On, The Man Who Mistook His Wife for a Hat,* and *Seeing Voices,* I would describe him as a doctor who has a genius for looking around inside the patient's illness for suggestions about how the sick man can cope, how he can live parallel to, or even through, his disability. He reconciles afflicted people to their environment in such a way that they are not so much submitting to it in an impaired exchange as proposing a novel relation. He turns disadvantages to advantage.

When Dr. Sacks severely injured his leg while climbing alone in Norway, he could hardly move and might easily have died of exposure, but as he says, "There came to my aid now melody, rhythm and music. . . . Now, so to speak, I was *musicked* along. I did not contrive this. It happened to me." An imaginative athlete of medical innovation, he finds more means of healing than are dreamed of in our philosophies.

I'm not a doctor, and even as a patient I'm a mere beginner. Yet I *am* a critic, and being critically ill, I thought I might accept the pun and turn it on my condition. My initial experience of illness was as a series of disconnected shocks, and my first instinct was to try to bring it under control by turning it into a narrative. Always in emergencies we invent narratives. We describe what is happening, as if to confine the catastrophe. When people heard that I was ill, they inundated me with stories of their own illnesses, as well as the cases of friends. Storytelling seems to be a natural reaction to illness. People bleed stories, and I've become a blood bank of them.

The patient has to start by treating his illness not as a disaster, an occasion for depression or panic, but as a narrative, a story. Stories are antibodies against illness and pain. When various doctors shoved scopes up my urethral canal, I found that it helped a lot when they gave me a narrative of what they were doing. Their talking translated or humanized the procedure. It prepared, strengthened, and somehow consoled me. Anything is better than an awful silent suffering.

I sometimes think that silence can kill you, like that terrible scene at the end of Kafka's *The Trial* when Joseph K. dies speechlessly, "like a dog." In "The Metamorphosis," a story that is now lodged in everybody's unconscious, Gregor Samsa dies like an insect. To die is to be no longer human, to be dehumanized—and I think that language, speech, stories, or narratives are the most effective ways to keep our humanity alive. To remain silent is literally to close down the shop of one's humanity.

One of my friends had lung cancer, and during an exploratory operation he suffered a stroke that left him speechless. For a month he lay in his hospital bed trying to talk to me and his other friends with his eyes. He was too depressed or too traumatized to write on a pad. He died not of cancer exactly, but of pneumonia, as if his lungs had filled with trapped speech and he had drowned in it.

Just as a novelist turns his anxiety into a story in order to be able to control it to a degree, so a sick person can make a story, a narrative, out of his illness as a way of trying to detoxify it. In the beginning I invented mininarratives. Metaphor was one of my symptoms. I saw my illness as a visit to a disturbed country, rather like contemporary China. I imagined it as a love affair with a demented woman who demanded things I had never done before. I thought of it as a lecture I was about to give to an immense audience on a subject that had not been specified. Having cancer was like moving from a cozy old Dickensian house crammed with antiques, deep sofas, snug corners, and fireplaces to a brand-new one that was all windows, skylights, and tubular furniture.

Making narratives like this rescues me from the unknown, from what Ernest Becker called "the panic inherent in creation" or "the suction of infinity." If I were to demystify or deconstruct my cancer, I might find that there is no absolute diagnosis, no single agreed-upon text, but only the interpretation each doctor and each patient makes. Thinking about difficult situations is what writers do best. Poetry, for example, might be defined as language writing itself out of a difficult situation.

Like anyone who has had an extraordinary experience, I wanted to describe it. This seems to be a normal reflex, especially for a writer. I felt a bit like Eliot's Prufrock, who says, "I am Lazarus, come from the dead, / Come back to tell you all, I shall tell you all." Like a convert who's had a vision, I wanted to preach it, to tell people what a serious illness is like, the unprecedented ideas and fantasies it puts into your head, the unexpected qualms and quirks it introduces into your body. For a seriously sick person, opening up your consciousness to others is like the bleeding doctors used to recommend to reduce the pressure.

What goes through your mind when you're lying, full of nuclear dye, under a huge machine that scans all your bones for evidence of treason? There's a horror-movie appeal to this machine: Beneath it you become the Frankenstein monster exposed to the electric storm. How do you appear to yourself when you sit with bare shins and no underwear beneath a scanty cotton gown in a hospital waiting room? Nobody, not even a lover, waits as intensely as a critically ill patient. On a more complicated level, it would be like explicating a difficult poem to try to capture the uncanny, painless yet excruciating sensation that comes with having a needle thrust straight into your abdomen, a needle that seems to be writing on your entrails, scratching some message you can't make out.

When my father died, I tried to write a novel about it, but I found that my whole novel was written politely. I was so pious about death that it was intolerable, and I find that people are doing that to me now. They're treating me with such circumspection. They're being so nice to me. I don't know whether they really mean what they say or whether they're accommodating me. It's as though they're talking to a child, and I want them to stop that. I can't find them anymore. I need their help, but not in this form. The therapist Erving Polster defined embarrassment as a radiance that doesn't know what to do with itself. We need a book that will teach the sick man's family and friends, the people who love him, what to do with that radiance. If they knew how to use it, their radiance might do him more good than radiation.

The space between life and death is the parade ground of Romanticism. The threat of illness itself seems to sound a Romantic note— I've been feeling exalted since I heard the diagnosis. A critical illness is like a great permission, an authorization or absolving. It's all right for a threatened man to be romantic, even crazy, if he feels like it. All your life you think you have to hold back your craziness, but when you're sick you can let it out in all its garish colors.

I'm reminded of an experiment described by Joan Halifax and Stanislav Brof in a book called *The Human Encounter with Death*. Working in a hospital with terminally ill people, they noticed that many of them were so depressed, either by their illness or by the thought of dying, that they couldn't, or wouldn't, talk to the friends and relatives who came to see them. Some of them wouldn't even talk to themselves. In an attempt to relieve their depression, these two psychologists gave certain patients controlled doses of hallucinogens. While this didn't work for everyone, in some cases it produced a blaze of revelation that must have been a final or terminal joy for the patient, his family, and his friends. I would like my writing to have some of this blaze if I can fan it.

Writing is a counterpoint to my illness. It forces the cancer to go through my character before it can get to me. In *Intensive Care,* Mary-Lou Weisman tells us that just before her fifteen-year-old son died of muscular dystrophy, he asked his father to arrange him in an "impudent position" in the hospital bed. I'd like my writing to be impudent. While Norman Cousins looks for healing laughter in low comedy, I'd rather try to find it in wit. The threat of dying ought to make people witty, since they are already concentrated. Oddly enough, death fits Freud's economic definition of wit: He says that we set aside a certain amount of energy to hear out a joke that threatens to go on and on like life, and then suddenly the punch line cuts across it, freeing all that energy for a rush of pleasure.

Norman Cousins and Bernie Siegel are correct in saying that a sick person needs other strategies besides medical ones to help him cope with his illness, and I think it might be useful to describe some of the strategies that have occurred to me. After all, a critic is a kind of doctor of strategies. For example, I saw on television an Afro-Cuban band playing in the streets of Spanish Harlem. It was a very good band, and before long a man stepped out of the crowd and began dancing. He was very good, too, even though he had only one leg and was dancing on crutches. He danced on those crutches as other people dance on ice skates, and I think that there's probably a "dance" for every condition. As Kenneth Burke, one of our best literary critics, said, the symbolic act is the dancing of an attitude.

As a preparation for writing, as a first step toward evolving a strategy for my illness, I've begun to take tap-dancing lessons, something I've always wanted to do. One of my favorite examples of a patient's strategy comes from a man I know who also has prostate cancer: Instead of imagining his good cells attacking his bad cells, he goes to Europe from time to time and imposes Continental images on his bad cells. He reminds me that in an earlier, more holistic age, doctors used to advise sick people to go abroad for their health.

The illness genre ought to have a literary critic—in addition to or in reply to Susan Sontag—to talk about the therapeutic value of style, for it seems to me that every seriously ill person needs to develop a style for his illness. I think that only by insisting on your style can you keep from falling out of love with yourself as the illness attempts to diminish or disfigure you. Sometimes your vanity is the only thing that's keeping you alive, and your style is the instrument of your vanity. It may not be dying we fear so much, but the diminished self.

Somebody other than a doctor ought to write about the relation between prostate cancer and sexuality. As I understand it, the prostate gland is like a raging bull in the body, snorting and spreading the disease. All of the various treatments are designed to tame the prostate. There's room for hermeneutics here. Is desire itself carcinogenic?

It's not unnatural for the patient to think that it's sex that is killing him and to go back over his amatory history for clues. And of course this is splendid material for speculation, both lyrical and ironical. My first reaction to having cancer was lyrical—irony comes later. It's part of the treatment. While I don't know whether this is lyrical, ironical, or both, I'm tempted to single out particular women and particular practices that strike me now as more likely to be carcinogenic than others. Coitus interruptus, which was widely practiced before the Pill, seems a likely suspect, and oral sex comes to mind as putting a greater strain on the prostate. But after saying this, I want to make it clear that I certainly don't hold my cancer against these women—whatever I did, it was worth it. I have no complaints in that direction. I wouldn't change a thing, even if I had known what was coming. And though this is only a fantasy, this talk of femmes fatales and pleasure you can die of, it's part of the picture of the cancer patient, and I don't want to edit out anything that belongs to my case.

My urologist, who is quite famous, wanted to cut off my testicles, but I felt that this would be losing the battle right at the beginning. Speaking as a surgeon, he said that it was the surest, quickest, neatest solution. Too neat, I said, picturing myself with no balls. I knew that such a solution would depress me, and I was sure that depression is bad medicine. The treatment I chose—it's important to exercise choice, to feel that you have some say—is called hormonal manipulation. It blocks or neutralizes the prostate. It doesn't cure the cancer, but holds it at bay until a better treatment comes along.

The doctor warned me that, like radiation, hormonal manipulation would "kill my libido." I find this hard to believe, especially in the case of a writer, for whom sexuality is inseparable from consciousness. After three months of treatment this has not yet happened, and I persist in believing that it won't. I've been manipulating my sexual hormones all my life, and I don't see how a drug can deprive me of this privilege. My libido is lodged not only in my prostate, but in my imagination, my memory, my conception of myself, my appreciation of women and of life itself. It belongs as much to my identity and my aesthetics as it does to physiology. When the cancer threatened my sexuality, my mind became immediately erect.

If in the future the treatment should interfere with the mechanics of sex, I can imagine all kinds of alternate approaches. As John Dewey said, "We never know what we might find until we're forced to look." When I think about my childhood, it's clear to me that pre-adolescent children often have wonderful sexual experiences. There were games of Spin the Bottle that I'll never forget. I find now that I have terrific dreams about sex, and I wonder whether this kind of unconscious experience can be made available when I'm awake.

I've never thought that good sex was primarily a question of mechanics. Of course the mechanics help, but who knows what we might invent if we didn't rely on them so much? Couldn't there be another level of sexuality? Can the imagination, for example, have orgasms? Is it possible to discover an alternative mode—as signing is an alternative to speech—a form we haven't thought of yet, an avant-garde, nonobjective, postmodern sexuality? What would Oliver Sacks say? I never understood, in *The Sun Also Rises,* why the castrated Jake Barnes and Lady Brett couldn't think of anything to do, why all that wanting had to go begging. In my own case, after a brush with death, I feel that just to be alive is a permanent orgasm.

Looking back over my history as an adult, I can remember how beautiful it was to think about sex, to anticipate it. Before sleeping with a woman I genuinely desired, I used to feel something like a religious meditation, one that was moving toward a miraculous vision. Yet when I read about sex now, it seems to me that we've surrendered too much of that vision to the pursuit of orgasm. Maybe such a vision is the better part of our sexuality. At least we don't lose the capacity for it with illness or age—if anything, the vision intensifies. On the other hand, we all know, even after "good" sex, that sense of anticlimax, a kind of amnesiac feeling of having lost sight of what we had been looking for.

A friend of mine has made thirty or forty million dollars finding lost or unrecognized masterpieces by great painters. When I asked him how he knew the painting in question was by Goya or Tintoretto, he said, "It's a sensual thing. I can feel it in my balls." If he can feel great paintings in his balls, I ask myself, why shouldn't I feel great sex in my sensibility? Of course I don't mean these speculations of mine to be taken altogether seriously—I'm simply freeassociating to sex and sickness—but neither should cancer be taken with such deadly seriousness. I think there's much to be learned in speculating about it, just as medical researchers speculate and freeassociate about cancer in laboratories. My laboratory is literature, and cures have been found here, too, for all kinds of ills.

There's too much talk about anger among the sick, and in the books about them, and I think they should be cautioned against this. The feeling of being unjustly singled out is a cancerous kind of thinking and you can't get rid of it in Elisabeth Kübler-Ross's screaming room. I'm sixty-nine years old, and I've never been seriously ill in my life—what have I got to be angry about? I think sick people are more frustrated by their illness than angry and that they should think about ways to go on with their lives as much as possible, rather than proclaiming their anger like King Lear on the heath. If you reflect that you probably helped to bring your illness on yourself by self-indulgence or by living intensely, then the illness becomes yours, you own up to it, instead of blaming something vague and unsatisfactory like fate. Anger is too monolithic for such a delicate situation. It's like a catheter inserted in your soul, draining your spirit.

Just before he died, Tolstoy said, "I don't understand what I'm supposed to do." Very sick people feel this kind of confusion, too, but I'd like to point out that there's a lot they can do. I feel very busy now, very usefully occupied. There are many ways a sick person can divert and defend, maybe even transcend, himself.

The British psychoanalyst D. W. Winnicott began an autobiography that he never finished. The first paragraph simply says, "I died." In the fifth paragraph he writes, "Let me see. What was happening when I died? My prayer had been answered. I was alive when I died. That was all I had asked and I had got it." Though he never finished his book, he gave the best reason in the world for writing one, and that's why I want to write mine—to make sure I'll be alive when I die.

JANE BROX's first book, *Here and Nowhere Else,* won the 1996 L. L. Winship/ PEN New England Award. "At Sea" is from her book *Five Thousand Days Like This One,* in which she explores her family's legacy in the aftermath of her father's death. Her work has appeared in numerous journals and magazines and has been reprinted in *Best American Essays.* She lives in the Merrimack Valley of Massachusetts.

ANATOLE BROYARD was a longtime book critic, book review editor, and essayist for the *New York Times.* He died in 1990. Among his books are *Intoxicated by My Illness and Other Writings on Life and Death, Kafka Was the Rage: A Greenwich Village Memoir, Life in Black and White, Aroused by Books,* and *Men, Women and Other Anticlimaxes.*

MARK DOTY is the author of five books of poems and three memoirs, *Firebird, Heaven's Coast,* and, most recently, *Still Life with Oysters and Lemon.* He lives in Provincetown, Massachusetts, and Houston, Texas.

ANDRE DUBUS was the acclaimed author of nine works of fiction, as well as the nonfiction collections *Broken Vessels* and *Meditations from a Moveable Chair.* He died in 1999 and lived in Haverhill, Massachusetts.

TESS GALLAGHER is a poet, essayist, fiction writer, and playwright whose works include *My Black Horse: New and Selected Poems, Portable Kisses, Willingly, At the Owl Woman Saloon,* and *The Lover of Horses.* She lives in Port Angeles, Washington.

WILLIAM GIBSON is the author of *The Miracle Worker* and *Two for the Seesaw,* among other plays. "An Exaltation of Larks" is the concluding chapter of his autobiography, *A Mass for the Dead.* He lives in Stockbridge, Massachusetts.

ANN HOOD is the author of seven novels, most recently *Ruby.* Her work has appeared in many journals, and she lives in Providence, Rhode Island, with her husband, son, and daughter.

JAMAICA KINCAID's books include *At the Bottom of the River, Annie John, Lucy, A Small Place, The Autobiography of My Mother, My Brother,* and most recently, *My Garden Book.* She lives in Vermont.

MARGOT LIVESEY is the author of the novels *The Missing World, Criminals,* and *Homework,* and of *Learning by Heart,* a collection of stories. A native of Scotland, she lives in Cambridge, Massachusetts.

GORDON LIVINGSTON, M.D., is a psychiatrist and writer who contributes frequently to the *Washington Post,* the *San Francisco Examiner,* the *Baltimore Sun,* and *Reader's Digest.* He lives in Columbia, Maryland. His book, *Only Spring* (from which "Journey" is excerpted), charts his ordeal, having first lost an older son to suicide, in losing his six-year-old son, Lucas, to leukemia.

REBECCA McCLANAHAN has published four books of poetry (most recently *Naked As Eve*) and numerous essays in such journals as *The Kenyon Review, The Gettysburg Review, Fourth Genre,* and *The Southern Review.* "The Other Mother" is the title piece in her manuscript of essays focusing on motherhood and childlessness. She lives in New York.

JAMES ALAN McPHERSON is the author of *Hue and Cry, Railroad* (with Miller Williams), *Elbow Room, Crabcakes,* and *A Region Not Home: Reflections from*

Exile. He also coedited an anthology, *Fathering Daughters* (with DeWitt Henry). He lives in Iowa City, Iowa.

SCOTT RUSSELL SANDERS has won the Lannan Literary Award and the Great Lakes Book Award for his personal nonfiction. His books include *Hunting for Hope, The Paradise of Bombs,* and *Staying Put.* He lives in Bloomington, Indiana.

DEBRA SPARK is the author of the novels *Coconuts for the Saints* and *The Ghost of Bridgetown.* She also edited the anthology *20 Under 30.* "Last Things" won a Pushcart Prize and a *Ploughshares* Cohen Award. She lives in Maine with her husband and son, and directs the Program in Creative Writing at Colby College.

CHERYL STRAYED is earning her MFA in creative writing at Syracuse University, where she is at work on her first novel, *Linger.*

ACKNOWLEDGMENTS

Thanks to Robert Atwan, Howard Junker, John Skoyles, and Morgan Baker for their suggestions, and to my editor, Helene Atwan, for her tireless encouragement and guidance.